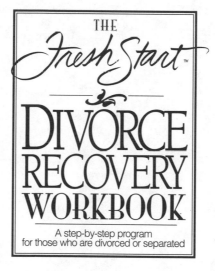

THE

Fresh Start

DIVORCE RECOVERY WORKBOOK

A step-by-step program
for those who are divorced or separated

Also Available from Thomas Nelson Publishers

Men Who Love Too Little, Thomas Whiteman, Ph.D., and Randy Petersen

THE Fresh Start™

DIVORCE RECOVERY WORKBOOK

A step-by-step program
for those who are divorced or separated

BOB BURNS & TOM WHITEMAN

OLIVER NELSON

THOMAS NELSON PUBLISHERS
Nashville

Published in Nashville, Tennessee, by Thomas Nelson, Inc.

Scripture quotations noted NKJV are from THE NEW KING JAMES VERSION. Copyright © 1979, 1980, 1982, Thomas Nelson, Inc., Publishers.

Scripture quotations noted NIV are from the HOLY BIBLE: NEW INTERNATIONAL VERSION. Copyright © 1973, 1978, 1984 by International Bible Society. Used by permission of Zondervan Publishing House. All rights reserved.

Scripture quotations noted NASB are from the NEW AMERICAN STANDARD BIBLE®. © Copyright The Lockman Foundation 1960, 1962, 1963, 1968, 1971, 1972, 1973, 1975, 1977. Used by permission.

ISBN 0-7852-7192-9

Printed in the United States of America.

14 15 16 17 18-03 02 01 00

To

PAUL and PHYLLIS MALONE

whose commitment and labors
in the early years of Fresh Start
helped get us off the ground

and

whose continued efforts
serve as an example to
all who are involved
in the work.

99520

CONTENTS

FOREWORD

Although I've never been through a divorce, I know full well the emotional stages of grieving outlined in this workbook. Several years ago, I went through a devastating breakup of a very close personal and business relationship. I felt the deep pain and rejection you have experienced in going through an actual divorce. I experienced the anger, guilt, bitterness, and even depression you must be feeling, wondering if God is really out there and if he really cares.

I know many of you reading this workbook are in the midst of those emotions. You may even be wondering if life is still worth living. If that's your situation, let me say first that I empathize with you. Second, I'm glad you picked up this workbook. There *is* hope, and there *is* recovery from divorce. But it will be a slow and sometimes painful process.

Through my own recovery, I've learned a very simple truth that I believe you will also discover over the next year or two. Namely, God uses the most difficult circumstances in our lives to teach us the most important lessons. In my own case, I know the difficulties I endured deepened my faith and strengthened my character.

The Fresh Start Divorce Recovery Workbook is not a book you will browse through easily. It deals honestly with the approach to full recovery, not just spiritual Band-Aids to cover up the hurts. It's filled with hard-hitting, interactive material that will allow you to personalize the concepts presented and focus on specific areas you need help with. I believe it's the next-best thing to being at an actual Fresh Start Seminar.

The authors are men who not only hold the appropriate academic degrees (both have earned doctorates), but also know firsthand, through their own experiences, the trauma you face. They have traveled across the country, talking with literally thousands of separated and divorced individuals. They've opened up their lives in this workbook in order to share with you some of the pain that all divorced people face. I believe their experiences will not only be encouraging for you to hear, but also a challenge to you as you seek your own recovery.

If you take the time to read through this workbook and process the material, it will go a long way toward helping you out of your current crisis. May God bless you at this time of transition for you and your family.

Gary Smalley

INTRODUCTION

Dear Diary,
*   Today my husband asked me for a divorce . . .*

Unless that has happened to you, you can't imagine the impact it has on your life. I (Tom) remember well the intense emotion and overwhelming anxiety I felt during my divorce. It took me several years to get over it, and even then I had flashbacks.

Divorce hammered my whole life. I tried to shut everyone out. Not wanting to be hurt in the same way again, I was convinced that the solution was to never love again, never trust again, and never let anyone into my life.

I (Bob) have watched and worked with hundreds of people who have faced the disruption of their marriages. Like Tom, I have known many who have taken longer than necessary to recover, merely because they weren't aware of resources that would help them, or they weren't willing to use them.

The Fresh Start Divorce Recovery Workbook is designed to help you avoid those mistakes. We want to help you work through your present crisis as quickly and productively as possible. We believe there *is* life after divorce. And if you can take this crisis and learn from it, God can actually help you to come out of it better than you were before.

You may be thinking, *Not in my case. That would be impossible.* We've heard many express the same skepticism. Yet later we've heard those same people say, "I wouldn't wish divorce on my worst enemy, but I wouldn't trade anything for what I've learned through it. I know I'm better off today in many ways."

There is hope. God isn't finished with you yet. On the contrary, he may do more in your life over the next year or two than he has accomplished in the past ten. We've seen it happen again and again.

This workbook has grown out of the Fresh Start Seminar, which we're both deeply involved with. More than twenty thousand separated and divorced people have attended these seminars across the U.S. From them, we have thousands of responses that indicate how the Fresh Start program has helped them and what has been most beneficial. This workbook condenses the conclusions of our sixteen years of informal, interactive research. We trust it will guide you through the recovery process.

That doesn't mean you'll be suddenly healed as you flip the last page. Divorce recovery is a long process. But you will gain the tools you need to begin the journey and to stay on track.

HOW TO USE YOUR DIVORCE RECOVERY WORKBOOK

Whether you are going through this workbook alone, as part of a small group, or in a Fresh Start Seminar, we have found that recovery is best achieved when you have someone else to bounce your feelings off—someone who understands you and what you're going through. That is why we have the small groups as part of the seminar program. If you're going through this workbook on your own, you might want to compare notes with someone in your church, neighborhood, or social group who has been through a similar life change. It's best if you can find someone who is a little farther along than you and can encourage you as you sort through your feelings and emotions.

You may have been divorced long ago and gone through recovery already. This workbook will help you review key points, but we also want you to consider something else. Could you reach out to others by starting your own support group? Separated and divorced people live in every town in the United States. And if you can become an instrument of God's healing in the lives of others, we know it will give you a tremendous feeling of purpose and worth.

This workbook has three major parts: Part 1: Coming Unglued; Part 2: Picking Up the Pieces; and Part 3: Other Issues. You may not need to work through the sections that cover phases you have already been through, but you should at least read over them. You may also find the four articles at the end of the book of special interest.

If you'd like to go through the book in a systematic way, you can read a chapter a day and finish in less than two weeks. A study group (or an individual) could cover a chapter a week in three months. But don't hurry through this. There are some sections you may need to take a lot of time with, and others you can fly through.

A few comments on our writing style are in order. Throughout the text we have used the pronoun *I* instead of *we* because we think it seems more personal that way. We also try to alternate feminine and masculine pronouns and references, and we hope we have done so fairly. We want recovering people of both sexes to identify with what we're saying.

This book includes numerous stories, all based on actual individuals we've known or counseled. To protect their privacy, we've changed names and some of the details. In a few cases, we've combined stories to hide individual identities. To all of the Fresh Start alumni we have known, we say thank you for sharing your lives, your stories, and your inspiration.

If you'd like to know more about Fresh Start Seminars, contact us at 2971 Flowers Road South, Suite 220, Atlanta, GA 30341. Or phone 1-888-373-7478. Perhaps your church or organization would like to sponsor a seminar in your area. We also have many other helpful books available for separated and divorced persons.

A special word of thanks to our friend and partner, Tom Jones. The author of Chapter 8 on sexuality, Tom has helped with every aspect of Fresh Start.

We also thank Randy Petersen for his helpful work in rewriting the book and preparing the interactive material. Thanks also to the Fresh Start regional directors, Mike Sanford in the Southeast Region, Tom Jones in the Midwest Region, Nancy Ballein in the Mid-Atlantic Region, and Jay Graham in the South-Central Region. We also acknowledge our special friend, Victor Oliver, at Thomas Nelson Publishers, who helped us get our publishing start and continues to be one of our greatest supporters.

Finally, special gratitude goes to our wives (Janet and Lori) and our children (Rob, Chris, Elizabeth, Michelle, and Kurt). They generously gave up vacation and family time to help us complete this project.

Part 1

COMING UNGLUED

Chapter 1

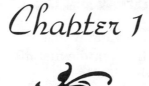

HITTING THE SLOPE
THE STAGES OF
DIVORCE RECOVERY

What's the worst experience you've ever gone through? Many people would say the death of a loved one or a serious illness. But if you've gone through a separation or divorce, your mind probably jumped to that experience.

That only makes sense. We're talking about the death of a relationship, the most intimate relationship there is. Naturally, that will cause a jolt to your way of life. And it will take some time to get over it.

When a loved one dies, we observe a grieving process. It is natural for friends and family to be in mourning. Some cultures have traditions to mark this period, such as a widow's wearing of black. But a divorce requires a grieving process as well, and we must not overlook this fact. Researchers indicate that the process typically takes at least two years.

> **Divorce recovery typically takes at least two years. So don't expect your emotions to stabilize right away. Take it step-by-step, day-by-day.**

Yet we keep rushing things. We want a quick cure—all for our intense pain, and we worry when the pain drags on month after month. But healing takes time.

➤ How long ago did the shock of divorce or separation hit you? (We're not talking about the final legalities, but the first moment when you realized that the marriage probably wouldn't last.)_____

_____

➤ In most divorces, there is a period of limbo. The shock has hit. The marriage seems doomed. But you can't begin recovering yet because nothing is final. There is still a glimmer of hope, however faint. This limbo can last for months, even years. How would you describe your situation? Are you still in limbo?_____

_____

_____

_____

➤ Can you pinpoint a date when the door was finally closed on this marriage? When would it be? _____

_____

➤ Two years is an average figure for divorce recovery. Some recover faster, some slower. But let's pick a date about two years from the door-closing date you just listed. That's a target date for your emotional recovery. List that date here. _____

➤ If that target date is already past or coming up too soon, feel free to adjust it. Choose a date a year or two from now.

Adjusted Date:_____

The purpose here is not to rush you by giving you a deadline you must meet. Instead, this should free you. You don't need to be kicking up your heels tomorrow or next week. You can take the time you need to get over this. And yet, it can be helpful to know where you are and where you're going.

THE SLIPPERY SLOPE

The recovery process typically goes down and then up. You feel awful at first, but then you turn a corner and things start to improve. There may be temporary setbacks along the uphill road to recovery, but you're moving in the right direction.

Looking at the "Crisis Time Line" (also known as "The Slippery Slope"), where would you say you are right now?

A. Beginning to go downhill
B. Near bottom
C. Turning the corner
D. Going up
E. Temporary setback
F. Nearly there

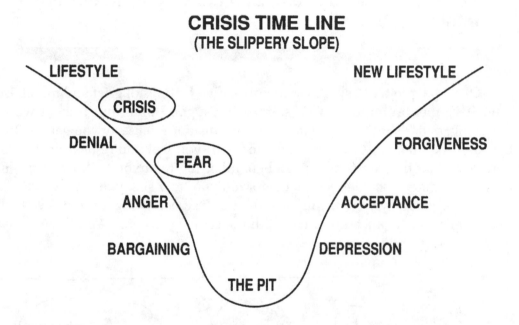

CRISIS TIME LINE
(THE SLIPPERY SLOPE)

LIFESTYLE

CRISIS

DENIAL

FEAR

ANGER

BARGAINING

THE PIT

NEW LIFESTYLE

FORGIVENESS

ACCEPTANCE

DEPRESSION

Remember that divorce recovery, like grief recovery, is a *process*. It is not "wrong" to be at any particular point on that graph. We all go through these stages.

Let's take a closer look at the grieving process. That may help you understand what you're going through right now, as well as the stages that lie ahead.

The Grieving Process

Elisabeth Kübler-Ross first popularized the stages of grief in her landmark book *On Death and Dying*. She identified five emotional levels that people pass through as they deal with the death of a loved one—denial, anger, bargaining, depression, and finally acceptance. Yet this theory applies not only to bereavement but also to other tragedies, including divorce.

As we said before, a divorce is like a death. When a couple are torn apart, for whatever reason, that relationship dies. They will grieve in much the same way they would mourn the passing of a loved one. Even if bitterness and anger keep you from missing your ex personally, you will still miss the intimate relationship and perhaps the way of life you once had. Don't downplay the extent of this grief.

> **A divorce is like a death. Don't downplay the extent of this grief.**

Often people try to skip over their negative feelings of grief and maintain a positive mental outlook. That sounds like a good plan, but it can't work very long, and it's ultimately dangerous. For instance, let's say you get the flu. If you're like me, you won't see a doctor until you feel you're near death. So you lie in bed moaning, aching, and complaining to anyone who will listen until you finally decide to let the doctor tell you how sick you are.

The doctor says, "Yes, you have the flu. It's been going around. I've had five people in my office this week with the same symptoms. You'll feel achy in your head and back, and you'll probably run a fever for a day or two. But if you get plenty of rest and drink lots of fluids, it will run its course in about forty-eight hours."

You drive home, feeling a bit better about your situation. But why? What did the doctor do for you?

Well, first, you found out that what you are going through is normal. In fact, many others have the same illness. That's reassuring. Second, you learned the normal symptoms of your illness—what you can expect to feel. Finally, and perhaps most important, you learned how long you can expect the pain to last. This information, combined with the practical advice about rest and fluids, helps you persevere through your illness.

So it is with our knowledge of the stages of grief, this emotional roller coaster that follows a divorce. First, we learn that what we are going through is normal. You are not alone—others are facing similar problems. This fact in itself offers immense encouragement.

Second, we learn to recognize our symptoms—not physical in our case, but emotional. As we label our emotional stages, we develop a road map that tells us where we've come from and how far we still have to go. If your emotions are confusing or worrying you, this awareness can help a great deal.

Third, our knowledge of the grieving process helps us gain some idea of how long our pain will last—in our case it's a few years, not days. This doesn't mean that you'll be miserable all that time, just that it may take that long to restore a sense of emotional equilibrium, to "get back to normal." Nor does this mean that after a few years, you will be completely free from any sorrow or pain about your divorce. Especially if you have kids, the implications of the breakup will last and last. But after this recovery period, you should be strong enough to deal with painful memories and difficult moments.

Don't be discouraged by this. You're facing a crisis. You have had a nuclear bomb dropped into your life. It will take a while for the fallout to settle, but you can survive if you take the proper steps. And you may even come out of all this a little smarter and stronger.

MAKE IT YOUR OWN

Does the prospect of being emotionally stable in about two or three years make you feel . . .

. . . good because there's light at the end of the tunnel?

. . . bad because it will take so long?

. . . or something in between?

Explain. _____

_____

_____

_____

 Which of the following is the most helpful for you to hear? Why?

    a. "You'll be okay. Everything will be fine."

    b. "Your present feelings are normal and understandable. You're not going crazy."

    c. "Quit moping and start living."

_____

 Is there a close friend you can tell about the kind of things you need to hear? Will it help to have this friend coach you through the recovery process?

_____

 Who will this friend be?

_____

 Have you been aware of the grieving process in your life? Do you think you are handling your grief better than average, average, or worse than average? Why? _____

_____

_____

_____

 How would your closest friends answer that question? Would they say you were handling your grief better than average, average, or worse than average? (You might try asking them.) _____

_____

_____

 What feedback have you received on how normal or unusual your feelings have been? _____

_____

_____

THE SHOCK—"IT WILL NEVER HAPPEN TO ME"

When the wedding bells ring, no one is expecting a divorce. People are supposed to stay together forever, happily ever after. When divorce comes, it's a shock. Even if it comes slowly, as a creeping realization, and drags on for years, the entire divorce event is a jolt to our hopes, dreams, expectations, and beliefs. In the aftermath, many newly divorced people are quite literally in shock.

Before we examine the various stages of coping with this crisis, we must look at the shock itself. What emotional damage is done? The best way to approach this issue is for me (Tom) to tell my story. Your story may be quite different, but you will probably see some similarities, especially in the emotions involved.

MY STORY

I was brought up in a loving and committed Christian family. We even had our own pew at the church: the third row back on the left side. You could count on us being there for every service.

From my earliest memory, I believed in Jesus Christ as my personal Savior. My parents faithfully taught me this truth. In junior high, I began to question this belief system—suddenly, I wasn't content to take my parents' word for it. My period of questioning and rebellion lasted until high school, but at that point I concluded that what my parents had taught me was true. Recommitting my life to God, I decided to go into Christian ministry.

I went on to Bible college and, in my senior year, married my high school sweetheart. We had dated for about four years, and she also wanted to go into Christian work. We both planned to spend our lives together forever, serving God. Even though we were young, we knew we would never get a divorce because God would bless our lives together as long as we honored him.

MAKE IT YOUR OWN

➤ So far in this story, what similarities do you find to your own experience?_____

_____

_____

➤ What differences? _____

_____

_____

_____

➤ As a newlywed, I believed that God would protect our marriage from divorce because we were serving him. To carry the idea a little farther, I felt that divorce happened only to bad people; since we were good people, we were safe.

➤ When you first got married, did you believe you would be spared from the divorce trauma? On what basis did you believe that? Your love? Your maturity? Your family background? _____

_____

_____

➤ What were your beliefs about God and divorce? _____

_____

_____

➤ Did you assume that God would keep such bad things from happening to you? On what basis? _____

_____

_____

THE FORMULA

I had a formula all worked out. It went something like this: as long as I committed my life to God and put him first, then he would bless me. I knew I'd have problems from time to time, but I'd be able to work through them. God would surely protect me from anything serious. That was very reassuring. In a way, it let me believe that I could control my life. I just had to do my part, and God would do his.

This formula was reinforced in my thinking because it worked—at least it seemed to. I had a fairly easy life. I had loving parents, good friends, and now a fine Christian wife, with whom I would share my life.

The formula also worked in reverse. I'd see other couples who were having problems in their marriages. Little by little, I'd notice that they weren't in church as much as they used to be. Soon, I wouldn't see them there at all. Then I'd hear through the grapevine: "Did you get the news about the So-and-So's? They're getting a divorce!"

"Well, that figures," I'd say. "That's what happens when you fall away from God." Or, "That's what happens when you don't have the right priorities." As long as I could explain why tragedy struck that family, I could go on believing it would never happen to me. I was determined to do things right in my marriage and my life.

MAKE IT YOUR OWN

➤ Take the following true-false test. But instead of putting *T* or *F*, rank your responses on a scale of 1 to 10: 1 is something you thoroughly disagree with; 10 is something you thoroughly agree with.

1. Good people usually don't get divorced. _____

2. God generally gives us what we deserve. _____

3. If your spouse walks out on you, it means you've done something wrong. _____

4. If you pray hard enough, God will bring you and your ex back together. _____

5. Before my divorce, I was generally a good spouse. _____

6. I think my divorce was God's way of punishing me for something. _____

7. My divorce has made me question God's goodness. _____

8. In the first year of my marriage, I was sure divorce would never happen to me. _____

9. As I was growing up, my family (or church) taught me that divorce was very wrong. _____

10. Since my divorce, I feel closer to God than ever before. _____

DEBRIEFING

Divorce can shatter your belief system. No matter what brand of faith you have, you hold certain basic beliefs about God and morality. A divorce cuts so close to the core of our being that it can sever our lines of faith. We no longer know how to find our way in the universe.

On the true-false quiz, number 9 is foundational. As children, we pick up many values that we hold for the rest of our lives. Our childhood truths are usually simplistic, true in the generalities but ignoring the exceptions. "Be good and good things will happen to you." That may *usually* work, but what about the biblical story of Job?

Numbers 1 and 2 fall into this category of simplistic truth. They are sort of true, but there are many exceptions. If you cling to those simplistic truths, it is natural to jump to the assumptions of numbers 3, 4, and 6. That is, "Something must be wrong with me, and if I'm good enough, maybe God will put it all back together." But that isn't the way life works. Many fine people have their spouses walk out on them through no apparent fault of their own.

> **It's not a bad thing to reexamine your belief system. The jolt caused by your divorce may help you come to a more mature way of thinking. If you take the proper steps, you may come out of all this a little smarter and stronger.**

Many of us develop a healthy belief in ourselves as basically good, moral people. But a divorce can shake that belief. We begin to assume that we must be bad because we're divorced.

If we manage to hang on to a belief in our own morality, we can begin to doubt God. How could God let this happen to me? What did I do to deserve this?

Chances are, you answered numbers 5 and 7 similarly. If you are convinced that you behaved well, you probably feel that God betrayed you.

Some people find special comfort from God in times of hardship, echoing the sentiment of number 10. That makes sense because God, too, is a sufferer. Both testaments of the Bible portray him as one who sympathizes with those in trouble. But you may feel far from God, guilty or victimized. Those are not unusual feelings.

It's not a bad thing to reexamine your beliefs. Much of the Bible contains such questioning. This period of reexamination can be a good time of growth for you as you adjust your simplistic notions to allow for some of the complexities of real life.

➤ To what extent have your beliefs been challenged by your divorce? Greatly, some, or not very much? _____

_____

_____

_____

➤ In a few words, describe what you believe about God right now. God is . . .

_____

_____

_____.

➤ In a few words, describe what you believe about yourself right now. I am . . .

_____

_____

_____.

STAGE 1—DENIAL

As you've already figured out, sooner or later all those simplistic assumptions break down. The easy formula of "It will never happen to me because I'm good" falls apart.

It happened to me while I was working in a church, seeking to honor God with my life. My wife came to me and said, "I'm not happy anymore, and I don't believe that I love you." Later she said, "I found someone else, and I'm going to be leaving." I was entering the worst crisis of my life.

The news hit me like a locomotive. No one can fully prepare for an announcement like that. I had been happily married, or so I thought. If you had asked me just ten minutes before my wife broke the news, I would have told you everything was fine at home. Sure, we had our problems from time to time, but we could always work them out. After all, we were good Christians. That was all part of the formula.

It was like a bad dream, listening to my wife's explanations and reasoning. I kept thinking, *This can't be happening. She must have had a bad day.*

Then my thoughts turned into *How's God going to fix this mess?* Finally, I was able to accept that it was happening and it was a mess, but I was sure God would make it all better before I got into anything as bad as divorce. All of those reactions indicated that I was entering the first stage of grieving—*denial!*

MAKE IT YOUR OWN

➤ Think back to the first moment you realized your marriage was in trouble. Was it like being hit with a club, was it a slow, steady burn, or would you describe it differently? _____

_____

_____

_____

➤ To what extent was denial a part of your reaction?

a. I denied there was a problem.

b. I denied the problem was serious.

c. I denied that it was serious enough to lead to divorce.

d. Denial was not part of my response.

e. Other: _____

_____

➤ Was denial helpful or harmful (or both) as you dealt with your crisis? How so? _____

_____

_____

_____

(*Note:* There is no "right" answer here. As we'll see, denial can be a helpful defense mechanism, numbing us to sudden pain. But it can also, if prolonged, keep us from dealing with a situation that needs attention.)

Active or Passive

In my story, I was the passive agent. The divorce happened to me; I didn't instigate it. But there are always two sides to such a story. Let's try to see it from the active agent's point of view.

My wife was aware of a problem in our marriage long before I knew anything was wrong. I'm not sure what was going on in her mind, but I can imagine she faced some sort of denial too. When she first realized she wasn't happy in the marriage, she may have said to herself, *But I'm a Christian. I really shouldn't feel this way. I don't want to deal with this.*

Yet her problem just got worse. Denial only made her feel more isolated.

VINNIE INCORRECTLY ATTEMPTS TO EXPLAIN THE LENGTH OF DENIAL.

MAKE IT YOUR OWN

➤ What was the main problem in your marriage that led to the divorce? Alcohol or drugs? Physical or emotional abuse? Another woman or man? Emotional neglect? If possible, write down in a few words the major factor that caused your divorce. _____

➤ When did you first suspect this was a problem? In the last year or two? On the honeymoon? Maybe even while you were dating? As much as possible, pin down a specific time. _____

➤ How long, then, did you deny this problem? _____

➤ When did you finally admit and confront it?

Date of confronting: _____

Length of denial: _____

Look at the time line on page 17. Note that the active agent—the one who instigates the divorce—begins the grieving process well before the passive agent. In some cases, the active agent goes through the entire grieving process and reaches a point of acceptance before announcing to the passive agent that the marriage is over. I have talked to some reluctant active agents who grieved through twenty years of marriage before finally confronting their spouses with "I can no longer live with . . . the abuse, . . . the drugs, . . . the affairs, . . . the unhappiness."

At that point the passive agent begins the grieving process. Often I find that passive agents are confused and bothered by the attitudes of their spouses. The passive one is in turmoil, while the active one seems carefree. The fact is, the active agent has probably gone through that turmoil already and has finally come to the point of acceptance and action.

MAKE IT YOUR OWN

➤ Would you consider yourself the active agent or passive agent in your divorce? _____

➤ Perhaps your roles have flip-flopped as you moved through the grieving process. Did you find yourself changing your mind about what you wanted, vacillating between reconciliation and divorce? _____

➤ What finally prompted you to confront the problems in your marriage?

_____

_____

➤ What did you do about them? _____

_____

TIME LINE OF THE DIVORCE EXPERIENCE

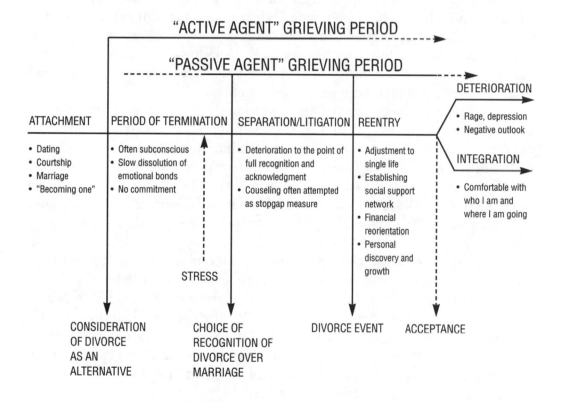

Moving Through Denial

Is denial wrong? No. It's a natural and necessary first step in the grieving process. It provides us with the time we need to prepare for what comes next. But we mustn't stay in denial. We must move *through* it toward a healthy acceptance of what has happened.

Denial is a lot like the shock response your body goes through when you're injured physically. There's usually a numbness in the injured area. You are protected from the full pain of your injury as your body begins to prepare for healing. In the following hours and days, feeling returns to the injured area bit by bit. This is the normal healing process. But if the numbness remains, then you have a more serious problem. It's the same way with emotional denial.

So what keeps us in denial when we should be dealing with the crisis? Primarily fear. We fear what will happen to us.

Will I have to go back to work? What will happen to my kids? What will people think of me? These and hundreds of other fears flood us with more than we can handle. So we are tempted to stay in "la-la land," believing that somehow we'll never have to face the truth.

In my case, my religious formula fed my denial. I didn't tell anyone what was going on with me because I feared what others would think. I wanted to protect my image as "a good Christian," not only with others, but also with myself. I was sure that God would work a miracle to save my marriage. I fantasized about how wonderful it would be when my wife repented and returned home, realizing how wrong she had been.

Some people use their religious faith to prolong denial far longer than is healthy. I met one woman at a Fresh Start Seminar who had been divorced for about fifteen years. Her attendance at the seminar was a first step in trying to deal with the divorce. Her husband had left her for another woman and married that woman as soon as the divorce was final. The jilted wife told me she had prayed for her husband's return for fifteen years, confident that God would bring him back. The saddest thing was that she had also taught her two young children to pray every day that God would bring their daddy home. Now her kids were teenagers, and she was at the seminar, realizing for the first time that her marriage was over and she had to move on with her life.

At a similar seminar on the West Coast, as the speaker was talking about denial, a wedding ring flew past his nose, hit the back wall, and rolled out onto the floor. He reached down and picked it up, saying, "Does this belong to someone here?" A woman in the back row raised her hand and said, "It used to belong to me. I've been divorced for eight years, and I just now took it off."

That's denial extended to an unhealthy degree.

MAKE IT YOUR OWN

➤ For one woman, denial meant praying every day for the return of her remarried ex. For another, it was hanging on to that wedding ring. What symptoms of denial appeared in your life?_____

_____

➤ Are those symptoms now past, or are you still doing those things?

_____

_____

➤ What fears are or were keeping you from moving on? (List up to three.)

a. _____

b. _____

c. _____

➤ Go back to those three things and grade them on a scale of 1 to 10 (with 1 being least fearful and 10 being most fearful). *How valid are (were) those fears? Did you have good reason to be afraid?*

a. _____

b. _____

c. _____

➤ Do you think God can work a miracle to undo the events that have caused you such pain? _____

_____

Depending on your current attitude, you may have answered yes or no. Either is fine, because God can work all sorts of miracles whether we expect them or not; the question is whether he will choose to do so in your life. He has not promised to protect us from all painful experiences—despite what my "formula" said. He has promised to give us the strength to get through them.

> **It's not a lack of faith to accept reality. God can work a miracle, but it's foolish to plan your life on the slim chance that he will. The greatest show of faith is to deal with your new reality in the confidence that God will give you strength to do so.**

Action Point: What action can you take that will indicate you have moved out of denial and are accepting what has happened?

    Suggestions:
- Removing wedding band
- Discarding (or shelving) other mementos
- Socializing again
- Improving your appearance
- Getting a job
- Getting involved in a church or community activity
- Throwing a party
- Talking with your children about the situation

Action Point: Choose some specific action, and write it here and on page 282 (Appendix A).

_____

_____

➤   When will you be ready to do this? List a target date here and on page 282. _____

_____

STAGE 2—ANGER

Once I realized, *Hey, she's really gone,* I was gripped with fear. *What am I going to do?* I wondered. *How am I going to tell people? I'm in Christian ministry. What am I going to tell the kids in my youth group? What am I going to tell my parents?*

My belief in "the formula," as I described earlier, fed this fear. I was convinced that people would assume I had done something to deserve the problems I was facing. In fact, when I confided in one Christian leader, his response confirmed that belief.

"What have you been doing wrong?" he challenged. "What secret sins do you have in your life?" Those words were devastating. I was bleeding emotionally, but it seemed that everyone was trying to figure out what I had done wrong.

I had to resign from my leadership position in my conservative church. As word of my divorce spread, many of the things I feared came true: people were responding negatively to me. That finally helped me break through my denial and into the next stage of the grieving process—anger.

Some people say they waited months or years for their errant spouses to return. I'm not that patient. After two weeks of trusting God to bring my wife back to me, I was enraged. At whom? Certainly at my wife. At those Christians who were trying to place blame. And at God. That's right. Sometimes I think I was more angry with God than with people. After all, I trusted him. We had a deal. I was going to put him first in my life, and he was going to take care of me. He didn't keep his end of the bargain, and I was fuming!

So now, not only had I lost my wife, but I'd also lost my job, my ministry. My ambitions were dashed. With a Bible college education, there wasn't a lot I was trained for besides Christian ministry. I had no future. I was convinced God could no longer use me.

To pay the bills, I found a job slicing lunch meat in a delicatessen. (I had paid my way through school by doing that type of work.) As you can imagine, that wasn't part of my life plan. There was nothing wrong with the work itself, but I still resented having to do it. Each day as I went to work, I was reminded of how far I was from where I wanted to be. On many occasions, I shook my fist at God and yelled, "Leave me alone!"

That anger was often transferred to other Christians. I felt they were rejecting me—and if that's what Christianity was all about, I didn't want any part of it. As time passed, I became angrier and angrier.

MAKE IT YOUR OWN

➤ How angry are you? On a scale of 1 to 10 (10 being extremely angry), rate your level of anger over the last month. _____

➤ With whom are you angry? (Check all that apply.)

- ❑ Spouse/ex-spouse
- ❑ Friends/ex-friends
- ❑ Family
- ❑ Church
- ❑ God
- ❑ Yourself

❏ Add others if you wish:

_____

_____

➤ Using that same 1 to 10 scale, go back and rate how angry you are at each of the ones you checked. How many of those did you check? Three? Four? Relax. You're normal. It's fairly common for people who have been through what you've been through to be mad at everyone.

➤ Is it wrong to be angry? The Bible offers some interesting insight: "In your anger do not sin" (Eph. 4:26 NIV; Ps. 4:4 NIV). How would you put that in your own words?_____

_____

_____

What about anger at God? Surely that's wrong! How can we get mad at the all-righteous Ruler of the universe?

Yet the Bible shows many instances of people spouting off at God—and many of them are portrayed as heroes of the faith. Abraham, Moses, David, Jeremiah, and others let God know what they were really feeling—even if they were steaming.

Many of the psalms—the hymns of ancient Israel!—express anger and disappointment with God. In light of that, use the space provided to write a letter to one of the objects of anger you checked. It could even be a letter to God. This letter should honestly express your feelings of anger (or whatever). *Do not send it, however.* This exercise will help you get some of your feelings out on paper. You don't need to confront others with them yet. (If you have a hard time with pen and paper, get a cassette recorder and tape your letter.)

Dear _____,

_____

_____

_____

_____

_____

Anger isn't necessarily wrong. It is a God-given emotion. It's *how we deal with our anger* that gets us in trouble. I believe in my heart that God understood that I was angry with him.

As I cried out to him, "Why did you do this to me?" he knew what was in my heart, and he forgave whatever needed forgiving. God understood my feelings because his own Son, Jesus Christ, yelled out as he hung on the cross, "My God, my God, why have you forsaken me?" (Mark 15:34 NIV). Jesus understood the pain and rejection I was feeling.

There are four basic ways for us to deal with our anger. The first two are negative, the others positive.

1. Rage. We all know the devastating effects of rage. Most studies have shown that it leads only to more anger. It is certainly one way of venting your emotions, but it can just make you angrier until you've lost control. (Interestingly, while women's anger may be just as intense, men tend to express it more often in rage.)

I remember times when I vented my anger on a door, a wall, or my knuckles. In one case, I really thought I had lost it. My ex-wife was gradually removing the furniture from the house we had shared—with my approval, since I was planning to move out soon. Still, each night as I saw the rooms grow barer and barer, the reality of my situation was eating away at me. One night I came home to a house completely empty except for the bedroom. My emotions erupted. I tore apart the only furnished room I had left, overturning the mattress, knocking pictures off the walls, and generally dismantling the room. Then I lay there, totally exhausted. I looked around and thought, *Who's gonna clean up this mess?*

Anger, in itself, is not wrong. God understands how we feel.

That's the problem with rage. It usually just creates more of a mess. That goes for relationships as well as objects. And it's easier to patch up a wall than a friendship.

THE INSIDE STORY

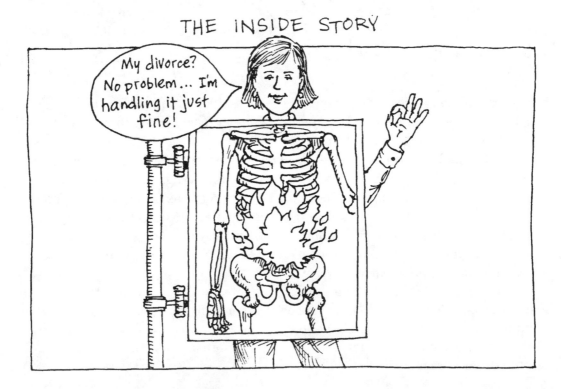

➤ On what occasions have you used violent rage to express your anger?

_____

_____

➤ How did you feel when it happened? _____

_____

_____

➤ What were the consequences?_____

_____

_____

_____

➤ If you could go back to those moments of rage, would you act differently? If so, how? _____

_____

_____

2. Repression. Repression seems to be a nicer option, but it can also be harmful. Instead of venting our anger, we hold it inside. When people ask how we're doing, we smile and say, "Just fine." But inside we feel as if our guts have been ripped out. I repressed my anger for a lot longer than I should have. For at least six months, maybe a year, I felt as if somebody were wringing a dishrag in the pit of my stomach. The feeling was there when I got up in the morning and still there when I went to bed at night. I felt it for so long that I didn't remember what life was like without it. I went to work, slicing lunch meat, and mumbled to myself, "Why do I have to wait on these stupid people?"

> **Repression may seem like a better option than rage, but in the long run it can be just as destructive.**

They would say, "Could you cut that bologna a little thinner?"

I'd give them a big smile and answer, "I'd love to." But inside I wanted to take the bologna and hit them over the head.

Isn't repression better than rage? Not necessarily. It's certainly not healthier. Studies have shown that repression reduces your body's ability to defend itself from disease, stress, and fatigue. You may be knocking years off your life. As I went through my divorce, particularly in the early stages, I had more colds, flu, headaches, and backaches than usual. All that repression was taking a toll on my body. Today I would guess that all of that holding back probably shortened my life span by about three years. I'll let you know when I'm seventy-five.

MAKE IT YOUR OWN

➤ How has your physical health been since the divorce crisis began? Normal? Better than normal? Worse than normal?_____

_____

➤ Have you been repressing your feelings of anger? If so, how can you tell?

_____

_____

_____

3. Redirection. When you take all your angry energy and invest it in something positive—that's redirection. Ultimately, in most cases of anger, the most positive thing you can do is to go to the person with whom you are angry and resolve the problem. But let's face it—when you're going through a divorce, it's nearly impossible to resolve your anger with your ex.

Your anger may be so intense that you can't even imagine having a civilized conversation, let alone resolving your disputes. Give yourself some time. Eventually, you should reach a point of acceptance and forgiveness. In the meantime, you can redirect your feelings into productive activities.

Step 1: Start small. Some might join a health club to improve their physiques. Others might sink their energies into night school, their job, or a hobby. It can be extremely satisfying to do something positive with your life when everything else seems so bleak.

In my case, I knew I had to find something to take my mind off my troubles. I'd come home from work, eat a bowl of cereal, and watch TV. I couldn't sleep at night, so I'd toss and turn or watch more TV. Then I thought, *I've got to do something. Well, I've always wanted to finish the basement. Why don't I make it into a recreation room?*

So after work I'd come home and pound nails into the concrete walls. I'd work until 2:00 A.M. and then sleep like a baby. The next day I'd come home, pound more nails, and sleep some more. After about six months of work, I could look at something worthwhile I had accomplished. I had turned my angry energy into something positive. I had redirected.

Step 2: Invest in people. There's a limit to the satisfaction that a good physique or a finished basement can bring you. Eventually, you need to get involved in the lives of other people.

Take, for example, the Fresh Start program. This program was founded by a group of people who were angry about the way churches dealt with divorce. Instead of railing against insensitive churches, they started seminars to help church people cope with divorce's trauma. Now, most of the people who volunteer their services to Fresh Start are divorced people who are redirecting their anger. Some lead support groups; others provide food. But they all tell me they get a tremendous feeling of fulfillment helping others who are facing the same trauma they went through.

MAKE IT YOUR OWN

➤ In what small way (step 1) can you begin to redirect your anger? Is there a project you could take on, a new hobby or activity? _____

_____

_____

_____

➤ How can you redirect your energy to help other people who are hurting? (Suggestions: church involvement, inviting other divorced people to dinner, being aware of hurting people at work, Prison Fellowship, Habitat for Humanity, the Red Cross, other volunteer organizations) _____

_____

_____

➤ Do you feel ready to do this now? If not, when do you think you will be ready? _____

_____

Caution: You don't want to rush into "people" ministry too soon. That may burn you out and not help anyone. Start your redirection in small, personal ways.

4. Resolution. Ultimately, we should try to resolve the situations that have made us angry—but that may take some time. If you try too soon, you may just end up screaming at your ex or soaking yourself in guilt. But eventually, you may be able to resolve your anger.

You'll find yourself saying something like, "I did a lot of things wrong, and I'd like you to forgive me. I've also felt angry about a lot of things. Can we talk about these things and clear the air? I want to get rid of my bad feelings about you."

That sounds like Mission Impossible, right? But if you keep growing, past rage and repression, and through your redirection, you can ultimately reach a point of resolution.

MAKE IT YOUR OWN

➤   As you evaluate your angry feelings, which of the "4 R's" have you used most: rage, repression, redirection, or resolution? Why?_____

_____

_____

➤   How has your anger (as well as the ways you've chosen to deal with it) affected:

Your relationships with friends?_____

_____

_____

Your family life? _____

_____

_____

Your daily work? _____

_____

_____

Your health?_____

_____

_____

Your attitude in general?_____

_____

_____

Your relationship with God? _____

_____

_____

_____

➤ Can you reverse any of these effects through redirection or resolution? How? _____

_____

_____

_____

➤ List by name some of the people you're angry with (besides your ex-spouse). _____

_____

_____

➤ Can you resolve your anger with any of these people? If so, how?

_____

_____

_____

_____

➤ With whom will you start?_____

_____

Example

Resolution might be as simple as this: "Marilyn, we used to do a lot of things together as couples. But since my divorce, it seems that you and Don have avoided me. I understand you probably feel uncomfortable about the breakup, but I've really needed your friendship. These have been rough times. I must admit I've felt pretty angry with you for shutting me out like that, and I may have said some unkind things in passing. But I'd like to patch things up and be friends again. How can we do that?"

STAGE 3—BARGAINING

Before we discuss the third stage of grief, let me make something clear. These five stages do not necessarily occur in the order presented here. There is usually a *general progression* from denial through anger, bargaining, and depression to acceptance, but each person moves through the process in a unique way. You might jump from denial to depression, and then slip back to anger. It wouldn't even be unusual for you to go through all five stages in the same day.

The third stage, bargaining, can best be explained as trying to find a simple solution to a complex problem. It's like using a microwave for a Crock-Pot recipe. We want to settle it all *right now.*

In my case, I found that denial wasn't helping, and my anger only made things worse. I was desperate for answers. I hurt so much that I would try almost anything to make the pain go away. Such desperation makes many people turn to drugs or alcohol or shallow relationships.

How can I make this pain go away? I asked myself as I worked at the deli. I was smiling to the customers but dying inside. I concluded that the solution was to get my wife to come back home. Everything would then be wonderful. My marriage would be saved. I could go back to church, and everyone would praise God for the miracle he had done in my life. And of course, everyone would like me again. So I began to bargain.

> **True reconciliation requires changes in attitudes and behavior. It is not merely a matter of moving back in together.**

I called my wife and made her an offer she couldn't refuse. "Just come back home and I promise I'll never ask you about *him* again. In fact, we can go on from here as if the past year or so never happened."

You're probably thinking I was a fool to say that. And maybe I was. But many, many people find themselves in similar straits, desperate for a solution, grabbing at a fantasy. My fantasy was that we would live happily ever after, our church would welcome us back, and I would be the best husband ever, winning her eternal love.

Reality, however, usually paints a different picture.

My wife accepted my offer. She moved back in, and the first night was great. Candlelight dinner, flowers—all the things I knew she liked. We were well on the way to making this work. Until day two, when she came home late from work.

"Where were you?"

"What do you mean, 'Where was I?' You told me you weren't going to ask."

"Well, I'm asking now. Where were you?"

"I'm not going to stand here and be interrogated about my day. It's none of your business where I was."

"None of my business? Well, if you think . . ."

You could write the rest of that script. That trial reconciliation lasted about a week. In fact, we had *three* trial reconciliations, and they all ended in disaster.

But shouldn't we work for reconciliation at any cost? That's a hard question. At Fresh Start, we believe that reconciliation is God's desire for our lives, but we also recognize that it's a very difficult process. Both partners have to take a hard look at all of their issues and then begin working on them one at a time with a counselor or other neutral party. The problems take years to develop; they will not be solved in a few days.

And what *is* reconciliation? It's more than a plea to "just move back home." Many times this can be a very negative, sometimes dangerous, option. When there has been abuse, drug use, alcohol, or even an affair, you shouldn't let your spouse move back in and pretend nothing has happened. Look beyond his or her words; watch for changes in behavior, along with a willingness to work on the issue. (The question of reconciliation is important and complex. We'll deal with it more fully in the next chapter.)

MAKE IT YOUR OWN

➤ In what ways have you bargained with your spouse (or ex-spouse)? Go through the following list, and put an M (for "me") next to any lines you've tried yourself. Then go through again, putting H (for "her" or "him") next to those your spouse tried with you.

_____ "I promise it will never happen again if you just love me."

_____ "I'll never take another drink (or do drugs again) if you come home."

_____ "This time I'll put you first in my life if you just trust me."

_____ "I never realized how good I had it. I'll never take you for granted again."

_____ "I've really changed. My temper is under control now. Let me come home, and I'll prove it to you."

_____ "If you just go to two counseling sessions with me, I'll give you whatever you want."

_____ "Just let me have the kids. I'll sign any agreement as long as I can keep them."

➤ What other lines could you add? _____

_____

_____

_____

➤ In general, how did this bargaining turn out?

❑ We both kept the bargain, and things turned out great.

❑ We both kept the bargain, but things fell apart anyway.

❑ I tried to keep my end of the bargain, but I was trading away important aspects of my identity. I couldn't do it.

❑ I just botched my end of the bargain.

❑ The other person reneged on his/her end of the bargain.

❑ It was a bad bargain to begin with. It fell apart.

❑ Other: _____

_____

Bargaining with God

We don't bargain only with our spouses—we also bargain with God. "God, if you just help me through this, if you just solve this problem, I'll dedicate my life and my marriage to you." This reasoning reminds me of the movie *The End,* starring Burt Reynolds. It's a comedy in which everything is going wrong for Burt's character. He decides to kill himself, but he even fails at that. Finally, alone at the beach, he decides to swim out to sea. He gets out rather far, takes a deep breath, and puts his head under water. But as he is waiting there, facing the reality of his death, he realizes, *Hey, I don't want to die. I want to live!*

He starts swimming frantically to shore, but the current is against him. He looks toward the distant shoreline and cries, "Oh, God, please help me! Help me get back. I gotta get back to shore." But the current keeps taking him out to sea.

In desperation, he pleads, "God, if you get me out of this one, I'll give 50 percent of everything I make to you, God. No, I'll give 80 percent of everything, and I'll . . ."

While he's still bargaining with God, the tide begins to shift directions, and he realizes he's being washed toward shore. When he is close enough to make it back on his own, he says, "Never mind, God. I've got it now."

The Indigo Girls have a song called "Hey Jesus" that describes some of the feelings following a breakup. Most of us can identify with it: "If you make my baby stay, I'll make it up to you. And that's a promise I will keep." The succeeding verses of the song show that God didn't work the desired miracle, and the songwriter is pretty upset about it.

The anger turns to depression as the songwriter realizes she is out of her league, arguing with God. Surely, he has "a million things to do" and can't be bothered with minor problems like ours.

This is the problem we have when we bargain with God. He doesn't play by our rules. We want that "microwave" solution. "I'll do this for you, God, and you'll make everything better." But God may be stewing something even better for us in his Crock-Pot.

So is it wrong to bargain? Not necessarily. It is a natural way to deal with a crisis. We are attempting to seize some control of an out-of-control situation. It can be a healthy step toward wholeness. But we should be careful not to make stupid mistakes at this stage. It's possible to trade away your fortune, your dignity, your self-esteem, even your faith, when you are in the desperate stage of bargaining. These would be stupid mistakes. Such transactions seldom save a relationship. They merely impoverish the traders.

MAKE IT YOUR OWN

➤ Have you bargained with God about your marital troubles? If so, what have you offered him? _____

_____

➤ What have you asked from him? Has this bargaining process improved your relationship with God or hurt it? _____

_____

➤ How do you feel about God right now?

❑ Angry ❑ Confused ❑ Cynical ❑ Trusting

❑ Humble ❑ Doubting ❑ Sympathetic ❑ Hopeful

❑ Other:

_____

➤ What stupid mistakes do you need to watch out for in this bargaining stage? Or what stupid mistakes have you already made?

_____

_____

_____

➤ How would you describe your present situation?

❑ I've been in denial, and I've been angry, and now I need to take control of things through bargaining.

❑ I feel pretty sure that we both can make some changes and get back together.

❑ Bargaining probably won't work, but I'm desperate.

- ❑ What does he/she want? I keep searching for the right thing to make him/her love me again.

- ❑ At this point, I'm not worth loving. He/she has used me and discarded me.

- ❑ Does "getting run over by a Mack truck" mean anything to you?

STAGE 4—DEPRESSION

What happens when we finally realize we can't bargain our way back to the blissful marriage we once had? Some go back to denial or anger, but many move on to depression. They hit bottom.

Has that happened to you yet? You realize all your efforts are futile. You are totally helpless to change the other person or your situation. That's depressing!

In my case, I could no longer deny the reality of my impending divorce, and my anger only made me feel worse. Bargaining proved to me that I couldn't maneuver my way out of my problems, so I was left with the conclusion that nothing I could do made any difference. I wanted to give up on everything, including life.

I was convinced I would never be loved again. I would never be happy again. And I would never be used by God again. Basically, my life was over. So I resigned myself to mere existence. For the rest of my life, I wouldn't live; I would just *be*.

If you have ever dealt with alcoholism or other addictions, you've probably heard this statement: "You've got to hit bottom before you can look up." That's the way it is when you go through the grieving process. You must come to a point where you bottom out, where you just give up and say, "There's nothing more I can do."

The timing of this depression varies from person to person, and its length depends on your personality. For me, it hit about six months after my wife left. As I've mentioned, we had a few trial reconciliations, getting back together for a week, then splitting up again. That drew out the healing process; each time, I had a roller-coaster ride of hope and despair.

Through it all, I learned I was helpless. I couldn't change my wife, my friends, my work situation, the mortgage payment on my house. It all added up to more than I could handle by myself, and yet I couldn't bring myself to trust other people or God. Instead of reaching out to anyone, I withdrew all the more.

I stayed in my depression a lot longer than necessary. The lifestyle I chose was not helping any—go to work, come home, eat a bowl of cereal, go to bed. I didn't go out, use the phone, or make new friends. This formula kept me anchored in depression for at least a year. At times I thought I'd be better off dead, and yet a part of me was determined to go on.

I also had an underlying feeling that it was wrong for me to be so depressed. My Christian background had taught me the importance of joy. The gospel, I had learned, is "good news" for people in need. But during that year, the news was not good. Joy was far away. And I felt a bit guilty about that, which only added to my depression. I had slipped through the cracks of God's will. I was emotionally in a place where I did not belong.

You may disagree with this next statement, but stay with me. *It is not wrong to be depressed.* Depression, too, is a natural stage in the grieving process. It is a necessary "hitting bottom." It can be a time of rigorous self-examination, a reordering of priorities. In depression, we learn that we can't trust false promises or shallow friends. All the tricks we've tried to win approval, to get by in this world—they now seem useless because they *are* useless. How do we get out of this mess? We need to get down to basics. We need to grow. As the narrator says in the play *The Fantasticks:* "We all must die a bit / before we grow again."

I don't want to minimize depression or imply that it's no big deal. It can be a very big deal, especially if there is a history of depression in your family, if you've had an extended period of depression, or if you've had serious suicidal thoughts. If any of these descriptions apply to your situation, you need to talk with a professional counselor as soon as possible. If you don't know of a good counselor in your area, ask your physician or pastor for a referral. Or look in your phone book for a local mental health center.

If you're a Christian, you may be asking, "What about joy and good news and all that? Aren't we commanded to 'rejoice in the Lord'? Isn't it morally wrong to be in depression?" No. The Bible portrays a range of emotions. Jacob, Moses, David, "the Preacher" of Ecclesiastes, Nehemiah, Hosea, Jonah, Paul, and others showed signs of depression at times. The Psalms teach us to be honest about our feelings. We all have ups and downs. God is with us through all of it, even when he seems far away.

MAKE IT YOUR OWN

➤ In what ways might depression be good for you?_____

_____

_____

➤ Some people are word people; others are more visual. Here is a chance to play with your artistic side. Below is a figure of a person. That is the beginning of a drawing you'll do entitled "My Depression." Don't worry about artistic excellence—no one is grading this. It may be as abstract or realistic as you like. Draw how you feel.

Moving Through Depression

There are several very positive aspects of depression. That might sound strange, especially if you're in the midst of it, in which case it's hard to think of anything good in *any* area of your life. But let's put things in perspective.

In my case, depression was exactly what I needed. I had been striving for too long, convinced that I was "going to do something about this." I needed a break from the stress and turmoil. Depression gave me that temporary pause, some much-needed rest, and some peace of mind.

In addition, it was the first stage in which I was dealing with my situation as it really was. I was no longer denying. I was no longer blaming everyone else for my problem. I was no longer trying to bargain my way out. I was finally facing the truth. My marriage was over, and I needed to come to terms with that reality. It was a depressing thought, but it was the truth.

This is the point when many people seek help, when they have finally exhausted their efforts. Some lean on God in a special way in this time. Some choose to see a counselor or merely to open up to friends. I've talked to many who decided to attend a Fresh Start Seminar only when they reached this stage.

Another positive aspect of depression is the self-examination that often occurs. Up to this stage, the focus is on everyone else.

- "If only she hadn't . . ."
- "If God would just answer my prayer . . ."
- "Those hypocritical Christians, they . . ."
- "My in-laws started this whole mess."

I reached a point where I realized, *Hey, my wife was involved with someone else* for six months *before I even knew there was a problem. What kind of communicator was I? How much was I in touch with her needs and feelings? Maybe I wasn't the wonderful husband I thought I was.*

I'm not saying we should bathe ourselves in guilt. That happens to people in depression when it goes too far. But we should get a realistic picture of what happened. We need to stop blaming other people and begin to look at ourselves. That can be a very positive step. After all, the only person you can really change is yourself. I finally got to the point where I said, *Maybe there's something about me that I need to work on.* And that was my first step out of depression. I was learning to accept my breakup and move on.

MAKE IT YOUR OWN

➤ Since your marital troubles began, how much time have you spent in depression? _____

➤ Which of the following symptoms have you experienced? (Put a 3 if it's a severe problem, 2 if moderate, 1 for a slight problem.)

_____ Trouble sleeping

_____ Lethargy/boredom

_____ Working too hard

_____ Inability to concentrate on work

_____ Loneliness

_____ Inability to talk with other people

_____ Need to be with others all the time

_____ Susceptibility to colds, flu

_____ Ulcer, digestion problems

_____ Addictive/compulsive behavior

_____ Spiritual apathy

_____ Sudden weight gain

_____ Sudden weight loss

➤ Add up your score. If it's ten or more, you probably need to seek professional help from a doctor or a counselor. Six to nine, keep an eye on it.

➤ As you look back at your marital troubles now, what percentage would you say was your fault, what percentage was your spouse's fault, and what percentage was due to other factors?

You: _____   Your Spouse: _____   Other Factors: _____

➤ Explain what other factors were involved._____

_____

_____

_____

➤ Cross out the numbers you listed for your spouse and other factors. There's nothing you can do about those. The percentage of the problem that was your fault—what did that involve? What did you do wrong? (List no more than three things you "did wrong.")

1. _____

_____

2. _____

_____

3. _____

_____

➤ What can you do to improve in each of these areas? How can you make it less likely that you would do these things wrong again? Find one action step that you can do in the next month to improve in each area. (Note that this step will probably not get rid of the problem totally. But it should make things somewhat better.)

Action Points:

1. _____

_____

2. _____

_____

3. _____

_____

➤ Name one friend who might encourage you to follow through on these steps. When can you ask that person for help? _____

_____

_____

STAGE 5—ACCEPTANCE

Acceptance. Easier said than done. Most people claim to be in the acceptance stage long before they actually are. We usually think we've arrived, or nearly arrived, when something comes along and throws us down the slippery slope again.

I finally moved out of depression by forcing myself to get out of bed and develop some new relationships. Most of my previous friends were married, and many were unsympathetic about my condition. I suppose there were several community activities I could have attended to meet new people, but I felt most comfortable in church. So I went to a church that had a strong singles program—and a specific ministry to divorced people.

The truth is, I had no desire to attend any programs for divorced people. In my mind, I was beyond all that. It had been more than two years since my wife had left. I was certainly over that by now! (Or so I thought.) Besides, I didn't want to be associated with those who were down and out and probably hurting. So my attitude toward the group was ambivalent at first. But at least, I figured, they would have a heart for a divorced person like me.

You might think it was a hunger for spiritual growth that drove me to find a church. No, nothing so noble. I just wanted to meet people again. I was coming out of hiding. I was going to take some risks again. This was a good sign that my depression was nearly ended.

Another good sign was that I was finally taking responsibility for my healing. My attitude had changed from "Look what she did to me" to "Come on, . . . stop lying around and do *something*!"

I was also gaining some objectivity about my wife and the divorce—even apathy. Some people think that they are "over" their ex-spouses because they hate them. But the hate is a way of holding on. As long as your ex can ruin your day or still push your buttons, you're still working through the matter. Freedom is found in a kind of indifference.

> **The key to recovery is in making wise decisions now about how you're going to live and what you are going to believe about yourself.**

That may sound harsh, but it is necessary for divorced people to free themselves from the emotional ties to their ex-spouses. I remember when I first sensed my freedom in this regard. At first, I avoided going to the local mall, fearing that I'd run into my ex-wife. Then one day, about two years after the breakup, I found myself shopping there. It suddenly occurred to me, *Hey, what if I see her here?* It was a brief moment of panic, but very brief—because I realized it didn't really matter. *If I see her here,* I told myself calmly, *I'll just say hi.* It was no big deal anymore. She no longer had the ability to upset my life.

It may be especially difficult to reach this point if you and your ex are sharing custody of children. The kids often become weapons, or battlegrounds, in the continuing struggle between former spouses. There is a tendency to fight the same old battles over and over again.

For instance, the ex-husband brings the kids home late. The ex-wife thinks, *That's just like him, always late. Totally irresponsible. Just like when he left us for that other woman.* And the ex-husband thinks, *That's just like her. Totally inflexible. Always nagging. I'm sure glad I got out of there.*

But if you've reached the point of full acceptance, you don't need to rerun those scenes. The relationship is redefined. Your ex's personality flaws are not your problem anymore. You may need to deal with some issues of how the children are cared for, but you must carefully separate those issues from the original marital conflict.

Acceptance can probably best be summarized in the words of the apostle Paul: "I have learned in whatever state I am, to be content" (Phil. 4:11 NKJV). That's a great survival strategy. If you're now divorced, you need to learn to be content. When you reach that point of acceptance, you will no longer be waiting for the damage of your divorce to be magically undone; you will no longer be raging at your ex; you will no longer be desperately bargaining to turn back the clock; you will no longer be down in the dumps, waiting for some far-off day when you'll finally be happy.

No. You will carve a contentment out of your present situation. You'll say, *I never would have chosen to be in this state, but now I accept it and move on. I will try to make the most of my life as a divorced person.*

Remember, this will take time. I'm not trying to jolt you into acceptance if you haven't fully dealt with your denial or anger yet. But acceptance is where you're headed. It may take two years. I've talked with people who took five to ten years to get there. The key to recovery is in making wise decisions now about how you're going to live and what you are going to believe about yourself. We'll deal with those questions in future chapters.

MAKE IT YOUR OWN

➤ I just talked about finding freedom in indifference. How indifferent are you now about your ex-spouse? Rate yourself on a scale of 0 (totally indifferent) to 100 (he/she still affects my emotions greatly). _____

➤ When you do reach that point of acceptance (which may be another year or two down the road), what do you think your life will be like? In five to ten sentences, describe yourself at that future point. What will be different between then and now? _____

_____

_____

_____

_____

_____

➤ Look back at the diagram of the slippery slope on page 5. Based on what you've read in this chapter, where would you put yourself *right now* on that chart? Mark that with an X.

If you like, try to rate your progress through the past year (or since your troubles began). Where were you *a year ago*? Mark that with an A.

Where were you *six months ago*? Mark that with a B.

Where were you *three months ago*? Mark that with a C.

Where were you *one month ago*? Mark that with a D.

Note that many people do not progress through denial-anger-bargaining-depression in an orderly manner. There's a lot of bouncing around. Sometimes this bouncing is caused by specific events that set you back or propel you forward. Mark any influential events of the past year that have affected your progress.

Despite these events and the bouncing they may have caused, you may still detect a general pattern in your life over the past year. What can you learn from the chart you've just made? Are you moving forward or backward? Are you moving quickly or slowly? _____

_____

➤ Based on that chart, where would you guess you'd be three months from now? _____

_____

POSTLUDE

To conclude my story, I gradually began to take chances and develop new relationships. I had to start trusting people again. And as my trust grew, I also began to think that maybe God was still working in my life. Maybe God wasn't finished with me. I began to notice divorced people who were in Christian ministry. Their lives weren't over! In fact, because of what they had been through, they were doing even more to help people.

Their examples inspired me to keep moving forward, to let God use me once again for his purposes. God continued to work on me—healing me, preparing me—and eventually, he gave me a ministry beyond my wildest dreams. Through my painful experiences, he is helping many other hurting people. I can honestly say that I have gotten back much more than I lost. As I speak to various groups, I often say, "I wouldn't wish divorce on my worst enemy, but I wouldn't trade anything for what I've learned going through it." I pray that someday you'll be able to say that along with me.

Action Point: Fill out the "Adjective Checklist," and see how you score. We'll have you fill out the same checklist once again at the end of the workbook (Appendix B) so that you can chart your progress.

Check all the adjectives that describe how you feel right now. Read through the list by reading across the columns from left to right.

ADJECTIVE CHECKLIST

❏ angry	❏ annoyed	❏ ambivalent	❏ amused	❏ attractive
❏ anxious	❏ bored	❏ apathetic	❏ brave	❏ bright
❏ ashamed	❏ cheated	❏ collected	❏ calm	❏ confident
❏ bitter	❏ confused	❏ hesitant	❏ contented	❏ delighted
❏ defeated	❏ dejected	❏ disinterested	❏ engaged	❏ excited
❏ depressed	❏ detached	❏ different	❏ funny	❏ fulfilled
❏ disgusted	❏ discouraged	❏ glib	❏ grateful	❏ glad
❏ foolish	❏ empty	❏ interested	❏ helpful	❏ happy
❏ guilty	❏ exhausted	❏ hopeful	❏ interested	❏ inspired
❏ hateful	❏ helpless	❏ impatient	❏ involved	❏ independent
❏ inferior	❏ hurt	❏ indifferent	❏ joyful	❏ jubilant
❏ insecure	❏ irritated	❏ judged	❏ loyal	❏ loved
❏ lonely	❏ jealous	❏ at peace	❏ optimistic	❏ overjoyed
❏ miserable	❏ misunderstood	❏ misguided	❏ neglected	❏ needy
❏ overwhelmed	❏ nervous	❏ neutral	❏ pleased	❏ powerful
❏ pessimistic	❏ phony	❏ preoccupied	❏ relieved	❏ resilient
❏ rejected	❏ puzzled	❏ quiet	❏ respectful	❏ satisfied
❏ resentful	❏ restless	❏ reluctant	❏ romantic	❏ secure
❏ sadistic	❏ sad	❏ sexual	❏ sexy	❏ smart
❏ stupid	❏ sorry	❏ shy	❏ supported	❏ strong
❏ suicidal	❏ selfish	❏ silly	❏ thankful	❏ touched
❏ terrible	❏ tense	❏ surprised	❏ tough	❏ trusting
❏ ugly	❏ unappreciated	❏ unsure	❏ useful	❏ whole
❏ unhappy	❏ upset	❏ weary	❏ welcome	❏ well
❏ violent	❏ worried	❏ questioning	❏ willing	❏ wise

➤ To score:

1. Add all of the checks in column 1, and then multiply that number by (−4).

      ____ x −4 = (−____).

2. Add all of the checks in column 2, and then multiply that number by (−2).

      ____ x −2 = (−____).

3. Add all of the checks in column 3, and then multiply that number by zero (getting zero).

      ____ x 0 = 0.

4. Add all of the checks in column 4, and then multiply by 2.
      ____ x 2 = ____ .

5. Add all of the checks in column 5, and then multiply by 4.
      ____ x 4 = ____ .

6. Add the five subtotals to get your total score.

Enter your total score here: _____

This isn't scientifically objective, only a reflection of how you were feeling when you took the test. If your score is in negative numbers, you're feeling bad. Positive numbers mean you're feeling good. There's nothing right or wrong about your score, and nothing you should work at changing. But when you take the test again at the end of the book, you'll be able to compare your feelings from then and now. You'll probably see some major differences.

Chapter 2

CAN THIS MARRIAGE BE SAVED?

THE SEPARATION/RECONCILIATION STRUGGLE

"I can't believe it," said Brian, a pastor I've known for many years. "My wife got a restraining order to kick me out of my own house." I knew Brian's marriage was having some trouble, but I had no idea it had come to the point of separation.

We see this more and more in our society—and even in the church. How do couples reach this point of separation, and ultimately divorce? There is no simple answer. Every separation has its unique reasons.

If you are currently separated, you know the pain and confusion involved. This section of the workbook will help you confront some crucial issues.

If separation is now behind you and your divorce is final, you may still want to read this section, working through issues from your separation that linger. Sometimes divorced people carry a residue of guilt for not "trying harder" during that time of separation, for "giving up hope too soon." If that's true of you, this chapter will help you deal with your second-guessing.

If these issues are long past for you, feel free to skip to Chapter 3.

LIVING IN NEVER-NEVER LAND

My pastor friend Brian quickly learned that separation is one of the most difficult and stressful experiences in life. On the slippery slope of divorce recovery, separation wraps up all the confusion of denial, anger, bargaining, and depression.

"Sometimes I feel like I'm having an out-of-body experience," Brian said. "I really can't believe this is happening to me."

Perhaps you're like Brian, emotionally strung out by your separation. You need to marshal your resources to cope with these circumstances, but your strength is sapped by the uncertainties of your situation. Where are you headed? Will you get back together, or is your spouse gone for good? You bounce between hope and despair, not knowing what to prepare for.

"To make matters worse," Brian added, "other people don't know how to deal with me." Brian's experience is not unusual. When you're separated, your friends don't know whether to comfort you on your impending divorce or cheer you toward a reconciliation. Often, they'll avoid you entirely.

It's a never-never land, with many pitfalls and deep caverns. And it often seems that you're traveling this land all alone.

Making the Most of the Process

Most of us aren't ready for the time and hard work required to get through the separation process. When you split up, you climb onto an emotional roller coaster—just when you think you're going to make it to the top, you slide even more rapidly back down into that emotional pit of despair.

As I said in the last chapter, I was distraught when my wife left me—emotionally, physically, and spiritually drained. And I was defensive, often unwilling to receive any help. I well remember feeling that I could get through the next few days, but when I thought about a year or two down the road, I couldn't imagine how I could make it that far.

> **Even if the other person has instigated the separation or divorce, we're still responsible for our own attitudes and actions.**

The easy thing to do when separated is to give in to our feelings and let them dictate how we act. But that doesn't help. It's better to use this time to get a handle on our feelings and recognize that our future well-being is not determined by the present circumstances.

So take one day at a time, making the most of your present situation. Assume personal responsibility for your future. Don't be a victim of circumstances (or of your spouse's decisions). Make decisions about your future.

When I shared this with Brian, he didn't know how to take it. "Wait a minute! I didn't want this separation. It's her decision. How can you say that I am responsible for my future?"

I understood what Brian was feeling. In most separations, one partner initiates the break, while the other would prefer to stay together. Since marriage requires two willing parties, the separating spouse is essentially forcing his or her decision on the other. But I explained to Brian that although his wife made the decision to separate, he is still responsible for his attitude and actions. By kicking him out, she had dictated the state of the marriage, but she could not control or manipulate him in those areas.

MAKE IT YOUR OWN

➤ I describe the state of separation as a "never-never land." In what other ways would you describe it? _____

_____

_____

➤ If you are now divorced, how long did your separation last? If you are still separated, how long has it been so far? (*Note:* I'm not so concerned about legalities here. I want you to write down how long it was from the point that you first felt separated to the moment that you realized your marriage would not recover or to the present moment if there's still hope.) _____

_____

_____

➤ Of course, many aspects of your present situation are due to the decisions of your spouse (or ex-spouse). But still it's important to *take responsibility for your own attitudes and actions.* Do you understand what I mean by this? What attitudes and actions am I talking about?

ATTITUDES

1. To let go of past hurts.

2. _____

   _____

3. _____

   _____

4. _____

   _____

ACTIONS

1. Do not bring up the old issues whenever I see him/her.

2. _____

   _____

3. _____

   _____

4. _____

   _____

➤ How can you be responsible for these? _____

_____

_____

UNDERSTANDING YOURSELF

As we've seen, the time of separation can produce a great deal of confusion. Therefore, as you move through this transition, it's important to understand and accept what you're going through. For example, I recently took a plane trip to a distant city. After I landed, I *intellectually* understood the change of my location. However, I still *felt* disoriented. It took a good night's sleep to orient my body's equilibrium to my new location.

In a similar way, it's possible for you to understand the factual reality of separation while not gaining equilibrium between the facts and your feelings.

Facing the Facts

Therefore, the first step in understanding is to "own" where we are in the process of separation and be honest with ourselves about it. As a wise person once said: "No one can ever work on a solution until he is aware of the problem."

That means facing all of the possible losses: losing your mate, your marriage, your way of life, and all of the things you have claimed as your own. And it means facing the decisions that inevitably arise during separation. Some of these decisions include:

- Will I have to get a job (or a new job)?
- Should I retain a lawyer?
- Should I move out or stay in the house?
- Are my children going to stay in the same school(s) or transfer to a new school (or school district)?
- Can I talk to my estranged spouse's parents?

These are only a few of the questions you might ask. However, until you face the truth of your situation with honesty, you can't handle the challenges of separation.

Facing the Feelings

The second step in understanding is to get in touch with your feelings. Separation is a time of great swings on the emotional pendulum. I remember talking to Cindy, who had initiated separation after her husband had a third affair. "One day I walked around the house and tore down every picture of Jack from the walls," she told me. "The next morning I woke up and immediately saw the stack of pictures in the corner of my bedroom. I broke into tears. Then I found myself slowly rehanging all of the pictures!"

There are good reasons for emotional mood swings like that. One reason is the harsh reality of rejection. The separation struggle is often the rejection struggle.

Another reason for changing emotions is a breakdown in marital bonds. Characteristics of love begin to be replaced by characteristics of indifference.

There are at least three characteristics of love. The first is *trust.* Trust is when you believe in your partner, in his or her character. You have no need to question the truthfulness of your spouse. Trust says, "I believe in this person even when the circumstances seem to dictate the opposite." The Bible says, "[Love] always trusts" (1 Cor. 13:7 NIV).

During separation, trust begins to be replaced by mistrust. This is particularly true in cases of infidelity or unanticipated separation. Since these situations usually include lying and betrayal, the sense of commitment and loyalty is shattered. You can no longer believe anything your partner says.

The second characteristic of love is *idealization.* Before getting married, the engaged person thinks, *He is just the right one for me. He understands me.* Or, *I have only known her for a short time, but I have been able to share more with her than I have ever been able to share with anybody in the world. She understands me!*

Such idealization is superficial, and it doesn't take too long after the wedding before this romantic fallacy evaporates! However, in a healthy marriage idealization turns to something else—the ability to desire and expect the best from a spouse. Partners begin to view the circumstances of their life together from the best possible point of view.

The opposite of idealization is disillusionment. You begin to question everything your partner does or says, pointing out all his or her problems. What would never bother you about others will drive you bonkers when you see it in your spouse.

I remember talking to one couple in which each partner was absolutely furious over the way the other handled a tube of toothpaste. One squeezed it from the middle; the other rolled it up from the bottom. Disillusionment had set in!

The third characteristic of love is *respect.* Respect involves admiration, a genuine appreciation of your spouse, even with all your differences.

The opposite of respect is disdain. You don't like to be around your spouse anymore. You may even question his or her worth as a human being. One separated spouse confided in me, "I believe my husband is an evil person! I believe he is the most selfish individual in the whole world. I can't even stand being in the same room with him."

During separation you feel a tremendous amount of emotional ambivalence because you flip-flop between love and indifference. At times it seems as though you're chanting, "I love him. I love him not."

A divorce lawyer told me about an interesting pattern he has noticed. He usually spends the first session collecting information on the case. He sits with a pad of paper and asks, "Tell me your story. How has your marriage come to this point?" Then he takes notes on his client's response. "Usually, the client describes the spouse as the worst person in the world," he observes, "a real clone of Adolf Hitler!"

With about ten minutes left in the session, the lawyer reviews his notes, reading back to the client what he or she has said. "As I restate all of the problems, the client begins to defend the spouse! 'Oh, he's not that bad,' 'Did I really say that?' or 'I don't appreciate you saying that about my spouse!'

"When I first started doing divorce cases, this response floored me," the lawyer says. "But now I recognize it as part of the ambivalence of separation."

MAKE IT YOUR OWN

➤ Let's face facts. As you honestly appraise your situation, what are the chances that your separation will end in divorce? _____

_____

➤ If that happens, what specific changes will occur in your life?

❑ Lose custody of kids

❑ Have to move

❑ Financial loss/simplify lifestyle

❑ Lose friends

❑ Lose job

❑ Keep the kids but face major upheaval in their lives

Other: _____

_____

➤ What decisions will you have to make if you do end up divorced? (You don't need to make those decisions now; just list them.) _____

_____

_____

➤ I talk about mood swings. It's common to feel paradoxical emotions in a time like this—feelings that just don't match, happy and sad at the same time, or proud and humble. What pairs of conflicting emotions have you been experiencing? _____

_____

_____

➤ It is natural to move from love to indifference in your feelings toward your spouse. On each of the following lines, put an X where you find yourself right now.

Trust ————————————————————— Mistrust

Idealizing ———————————————————— Disillusioned

Respect ————————————————————— Disdain

GETTING IN TOUCH

Earlier I said you must assume personal responsibility for your future. But how do you do that?

As you face the facts and feelings of your situation, you can do a number of things. A little later we'll discuss making responsible decisions based on the *facts,* but now you need to consider how to get in touch with your *feelings.*

As you move back and forth between feelings of love and disillusionment, your primary task is to get in touch with your feelings so that they will not dominate or dictate your actions. Facing your feelings allows you to concentrate on truth and reality rather than on fantasy and fear. As you get in touch with your feelings, you will be able to evaluate their validity and choose responsible action.

Getting in touch with your feelings is like trying to grab Jell-O. It squirts and oozes around in your hand. There is nothing solid to hold! Feelings can be that way. They tend to be undiagnosed, yet they hold a great influence over you.

I recently had a conversation in which someone made comments about me that I felt were unjust and irresponsible. Unfortunately, the conversation ended before I had a chance to answer. For the rest of the afternoon I carried unresolved feelings from that conversation. In my frustration, I even found myself kicking doors and lashing out at people. After a few hours of this behavior, I sat down and said, *Why am I acting like this?* I traced it back to the undiagnosed feelings that resulted from that conversation.

You need to pinpoint and understand your feelings so they won't control you. How? The best method I know is to begin writing a daily personal journal. Journaling is an opportunity to

- *record* the facts.
- *reflect* on the issues you are going through.
- *examine* the feelings that you have had in the midst of these circumstances.
- *consider* the decisions and actions you have taken (or should take) as a result.

It helps to find a consistent time in your schedule when you can sit down with your journal and record your thoughts. Some people set aside a time early in the morning. Others prefer late in the evening. Still others set aside two or three times during the day to make their entries. Whenever you choose to do it, the benefits of journaling are best when you do it on a daily basis.

And what are the benefits?

First, journaling provides *a list of what you have been going through.* Your journal becomes a daily record of the experiences you have faced and the circumstances that occur during your separation. Most lawyers ask you to provide a thorough rendering of what has taken place in your marriage. The journal can provide this accurate data.

Second, journaling *lets you reflect on your circumstances with some clarity.* As you write your experiences down, you begin to work through them and think about them from a more objective point of view. It allows you the chance to pull back from the whirlwind of circumstances and review how you have responded to them. You can critique the ways you have been thinking and acting. And you can consider alternate behavior.

Third, as you reflect on these things, *you can begin to anticipate how you might feel during similar circumstances in the future.* Based on this anticipation of feeling patterns, you can develop a plan on how to manage your feelings.

For example, Frank tends to cope with negative feelings by pushing them down and suppressing them—acting as if he doesn't have those feelings. As he begins writing in his journal, he expresses his feelings on paper. Then, realizing his tendency to suppress his emotions, he acknowledges that he is not being honest with himself. So he decides to begin managing his feelings by facing their reality.

Janice's boss comes into the office every morning and acts as though she is not even there. Every day Janice tries to give a friendly greeting, but he just walks right by without comment. Of course, his actions cause her to feel rejection and perhaps anger.

As she writes these facts down in her journal, she recognizes that her boss's actions have been getting to her for a long time. But she has denied these feelings, hoping that things would get better. Realizing that she has come upon an important issue, she begins asking herself: *How do I feel when the boss walks by and doesn't acknowledge me? Have I ever done anything to make him act like this? How should I respond to him? How would God want me to respond to him? Didn't Jesus teach that we should treat others as we would want them to treat us?*

As she reflects on these thoughts, she realizes that she feels angry at her boss. Yet she doesn't want her angry feelings to make her treat him in a way that *she* wouldn't want to be treated. So, on the basis of these reflections, she develops a strategy:

- Lowering her expectations of her boss.
- Praying for him.
- Asking him for a five-minute conference to discuss her concerns and to see if she has done anything to merit this response.
- Turning in her resignation, telling him she doesn't want to work for an insensitive jerk—but would he give her a good recommendation? (We have the freedom to say anything we want in a journal!)

You can see how a journal helps you anticipate your attitude and actions in the midst of separation. You could consider how you'll handle things when your estranged spouse comes by to pick up the children. Or how you'll deal with his or her refusal to pay certain expenses. (And in the meantime, you're also keeping a record of the circumstances.)

Finally, you must understand that the emotional swings of ambivalence will eventually be resolved. Separation will end in reconciliation or in divorce. Either resolution will leave one set of feelings unsatisfied. If you reconcile, you'll have to work through the feelings of disillusionment that have developed. If you divorce, you'll have to face the sorrow of the loss of a bonded partner. If you recognize this in advance, you can prepare to face these feelings.

NOTES ON JOURNAL KEEPING

- Find a regular time each day.
- Try to find a place relatively free from distractions.

- Be completely honest. Don't judge yourself before you write. Let it all out.
- Don't worry about spelling, grammar, or style. Just pour the words from your heart to the page.
- Keep your journal private. You will be more honest if you know you're the only one seeing these words.
- From time to time, go back to previous pages and evaluate where you've been and where you're going.

MAKE IT YOUR OWN

➤ What is the best time for you to write in your journal each day?

_____

➤ What factors might keep you from doing this? _____

_____

_____

➤ Write here or in your journal how you've been feeling today.

_____

_____

_____

_____

Note: This workbook may be a helpful journal starter for you. That is, you may get into the habit of journaling by working through this book a step a day. Then, when you've finished, you can keep the same schedule but be writing your journal instead.

Yet I recommend that you begin the journaling process now. Keep the journal *alongside* this workbook. Maybe you could devote your journal time two or three days a week to this workbook, but keep recording your honest feelings on a regular basis.

BALANCED STEPS TOWARD RECONCILIATION

What can we do in the midst of the separation struggle to seek reconciliation in a responsible way? And how can we develop balanced expectations as to whether reconciliation is a possibility? We can take specific steps that will either lead us back toward reconciliation or show us that reconciliation won't happen.

But at this point you may be asking some moral questions. Is divorce *ever* the best option? Isn't reconciliation *always* the "righteous" choice, whatever the circumstances? I'll talk about this more later, but I want to be up front about this. *God always asserts the priority of reconciliation over divorce.* However, as we review the balanced steps toward reconciliation, we need to know that *the rebuilding of a marriage is the choice of two people.* God will not hold a person responsible for what others do or fail to do. He holds each person responsible for what she does with her own life (Ezek. 18).

Many who are separated assume that divorce is the only possible outcome of their circumstances. They are negative pragmatists who only await the completion of the legal process. On the other hand, some assume that reconciliation will inevitably occur. Regardless of the present problems, they maintain a "pie in the sky" optimism.

Pessimism _____ Hope

▲

Try to find a place of balance, somewhere between the extremes of blind hope and utter pessimism. While affirming that God can work in miraculous ways, you must face the reality of your present marital condition and the potential for marital loss.

Even if you didn't initiate the separation, even if you feel that you're a victim of circumstances beyond your control, you are not merely a passive participant in the process. You can take action.

Rebuilding Self-Esteem

The first step toward developing balanced expectations is working on your self-esteem. In most marital breakdowns there is a serious problem of respect between the spouses. James Dobson has done an outstanding job of explaining this problem in his book *Love Must Be Tough*. If you're separated and have not read this book, do so immediately![1] In the meantime, here's a synopsis of that book's theme, appearing in an earlier Dobson work:

> It is of the highest priority to maintain a distinct element of dignity and self-respect throughout the husband-wife relationship. This takes us into a related area that requires the greatest emphasis. I

have observed that many (if not most) marriages suffer from a failure to recognize a universal characteristic of human nature. We value that which we are fortunate to get; we discredit that with which we are stuck! We lust for the very thing which is beyond our grasp; we disdain that same item when it becomes permanent possession. No toy is ever as much fun to play with as it appeared to a wide-eyed child in a store. Seldom does an expensive automobile provide the satisfaction anticipated by the man who dreamed of its ownership. . . .

I must restate the principle: we crave that which we can't attain, but we disrespect that which we can't escape. This axiom is particularly relevant in romantic matters, and has probably influenced your love life. Now the forgotten part of this characteristic is that marriage does not erase or change it. Whenever one marriage partner grovels in his own disrespect . . . when he reveals his fear of rejection by the mate . . . when he begs and pleads for a handout . . . he often faces a bewildering attitude of disdain from the one he needs and loves. Just as in the premarital relationship, nothing douses more water on a romantic flame than for one partner to fling himself emotionally on the other, accepting disrespect in stride. He says in effect, "No matter how badly you treat me, I'll still be here at your feet, because I can't survive without you." That is the best way I know to kill a beautiful friendship.

So what am I recommending . . . that husbands and wives scratch and claw each other to show their independence? No! That they play sneaky cat and mouse games to create a "challenge"? Not at all! I am merely suggesting that self-respect and dignity be maintained in the relationship. . . .

In short, personal dignity in a marriage is maintained the same way it was produced in dating days. The attitude should be, "I love you and am totally committed to you, but I only control my half of the relationship. I can't demand your love in return. You came to me of your own free will when we decided to marry. No one forced us together. That same free will is necessary to keep our love alive. If you choose to walk away from me, I will be crushed and hurt beyond description, because I have withheld nothing of myself. Nevertheless, I will let you go and ultimately I will survive. I couldn't demand your affection in the beginning, and I can only request it now."[2]

Five Criteria for Reconciliation

As you begin to anticipate all that's involved in reconciliation, remember that any plan should include the following points of reference.

1. Reconciliation Requires Two People

Some writers say that one person can bring a marriage back together. Well, maybe one can start the process, but in the final analysis it takes two to tango, and it takes two to make a marriage. As a matter of fact, most counselors report that when only one person comes for marital counseling, the result can be worse than if neither came. For any meaningful reestablishment of a marriage, both partners must express an equal commitment to that end. Mutual commitment brings mutual trust. One-way commitment brings uncertainty, fear, and constant questions about whether things will ever truly work out.

2. Reconciliation Demands an Honest Evaluation of Past Problems and Personal Mistakes

Reconciliation requires that both partners evaluate personal mistakes. Each person must recognize how he or she has contributed to the present tension. As hard as it is to admit, you both contributed to the breakup. You must face what you have done and make plans to correct any destructive attitudes and behaviors.

3. Reconciliation Requires Mutual Repentance and Forgiveness

A later chapter will cover this issue in depth, but it's also a major requirement for reconciliation. Both spouses must demonstrate a sincere repentance and offer mutual forgiveness for the problems acknowledged under point 2. Owning up to our mistakes is hard, but it must happen if we are serious about reconciliation. At the same time, offering forgiveness to our spouses can be just as hard. But repentance and forgiveness form a critical step in moving responsibly toward reconciliation.

By the way, this step cannot be one-sided. When only one partner expresses repentance and forgiveness, there's no mutual sense of accountability for the problems. And there's no closure to the issues that created separation in the first place. To put it simply, there's no mutual honesty in the relationship, making it impossible to take the next step, rebuilding trust.

4. Reconciliation Takes Rebuilding Trust

Even after sincere repentance and forgiveness, when we have experienced a great deal of pain in a relationship, we can't expect to jump back into it as though nothing ever happened. Questions remain in our hearts: *Can I really trust this person after what we have experienced?*

These concerns are an understandable part of the emotional adjustment of moving back into married life. It is somewhat like taking a vacation to Great Britain. Once off the plane, you rent a car and are off on your holiday. However, you immediately feel disoriented because you find yourself driving down the wrong side of the street! It takes a number of days to get accustomed to this difference in traffic flow. After a few days, you get used to it and feel rather comfortable driving on the left.

This emotional adjustment is called *limbic lag.* It is the time between what you *know* is right (like driving on the left side of England's streets) and what you *feel* is right. It takes a while for emotions to catch up to experience.

Whenever you have a problem with someone else—as small as a disagreement with your child or as major as a marital separation—the resolution of the problem will always involve limbic lag. Even when you know you're doing the right thing, it will take time for your feelings to catch up to your experience.

At the same time, this step of rebuilding trust implies more than just feeling better about your estranged partner. You also need to reestablish a foundation of mutual respect and trust in the relationship. As we noticed before, separation disintegrates the love that forms the foundation of marital commitment. When this foundation has been torn down, it must be rebuilt before healthy reconciliation can occur. Reconciliation must be viewed as more than just getting back together. It must be understood as the rebuilding of a committed, trustworthy relationship.

This process requires time and accountability. Just as people need to develop a credit history before taking out a major loan, so reconciling couples need to reestablish a trust history, as each spouse begins to see the other backing up words with actions.

It is easy for a partner to say he or she will change. "If you let me come home, I'll definitely get a job." "If you move back home, I'll stop drinking." "If we get back together, I'll listen to you." It's easy to verbalize promises, but harder to keep them. The only way you'll know if your partner is serious about a renewed marital commitment is to see him or her *acting on it.* Lifestyle speaks louder than words. And lifestyle must be observed over an extended period of time.

5. Reconciliation Takes Time and Effort

It is not unusual for reconciling couples to find themselves falling into the same old ruts and patterns that led to separation in the first place. That's because reconciliation is usually viewed simplistically as "getting back together again." That is what I found in my several attempts at trial reconciliation. Our living arrangements changed, but our lifestyles didn't.

Reconciliation is a decision to work for something far more meaningful than what you had before the separation. What you are looking for is not the resuscitation of a dead marriage, but the resurrection of a new, vibrant, committed relationship.

Reconciliation requires time, energy, and a commitment to break out of old patterns and establish new ones. I'm reminded of Larry and Joan Monroe, a couple who separated after seventeen years of marriage. For a long time Larry couldn't understand Joan's dissatisfaction with their marriage. He was comfortable with things the way they were. After they separated, it took months for him to realize that a healthy marriage would require him and his wife to change their life patterns. After a few weeks of accountability to some new commitments, Larry said, "Hey, this stuff takes work! But I am already seeing the difference it can make. It's hard, but I like it."

MAKE IT YOUR OWN

➤ How has your separation affected your self-esteem?

_____ Improved it. I feel more confident now.

_____ Hasn't affected it.

_____ Worsened it a bit. I am doubting myself more.

_____ Worsened it a lot. I'm a worm.

_____ Other: _____

_____

➤ Do you think that your chances for reconciliation would improve if you had better self-esteem? Why? _____

_____

_____

➤ Which of the following is true for you?

_____ My spouse has better self-esteem than I do.

_____ I think my spouse prefers it when I have a low self-image.

_____ I think my spouse would find me more attractive if I had a better self-image.

_____ My spouse takes every opportunity to tear me down.

_____ I generally try to enhance my spouse's self-esteem.

_____ Lately I've been trying to make my spouse think less of himself/herself.

➤ Finish this sentence: I would feel a lot better about myself if it weren't for _____

_____ .

➤ What can you do to improve your self-esteem? _____

_____

_____

_____

➤ Now might be a good time to stop and read Article 1: "Developing a Positive Self-Image" in the back of the book. How many of your ideas listed in the preceding question did you find in the article? _____

_____

_____

_____

➤ Which of the following criteria for reconciliation are present in your case? (Mark Y for "yes" if it is present. Mark L for "likely" if it's not there yet, but it's likely that it will be. Mark P for "possible" if it's not likely but still possible. Mark I for "impossible" if you feel this will never be true.)

_____ Both partners want reconciliation.

_____ There is an honest evaluation of past problems and personal mistakes.

_____ There are mutual repentance and forgiveness.

_____ Trust between the partners is beginning to rebuild.

_____ Both partners are willing to invest time and effort in the reconciliation process.

CRITERIA FOR RECONCILIATION

1. It takes two.
2. Honest evaluation of past problems and personal mistakes.
3. Mutual repentance and forgiveness.
4. Trust rebuilding.
5. Time and effort.

PAM'S STORY

What steps could you take to work toward reconciliation? Let me suggest a strategy some have found helpful, including my friend Pam. But before I share Pam's story, I want to stress that anyone considering reconciliation needs the objective perspective of a third party. The process of reconciliation is demanding, and it's easy to get caught up in emotional mood swings. As you discuss and evaluate your plan, an objective third person (such as a counselor or pastor) can help you maintain balance and realism in the midst of these changes.

For two years, Pam's husband had been living at his girlfriend's apartment during the week and at the family home over the weekend. At home, he would do all of his household chores and pay the bills. Then on Monday he'd go back to work and to his girlfriend.

Over and over Pam heard her husband say, "I want to be married to you and be the father of our children. But I am working through this stage in my life. You've got to give me space and time to get through this."

Pam honestly believed her husband was sincere and wanted to stay in the marriage. But after two years she'd had just about all she could take! So she asked me, "What can I do?"

1. List your expectations.

We began by having Pam write out a list of her expectations. I encouraged her to make the list as long and as detailed as she liked, including anything she believed would make the relationship healthy. "Don't restrict yourself only to things you believe could happen," I said. "Include everything you feel should be taking place in your marriage."

2. Evaluate your expectations.

Pam came up with quite a list! At that point we spent a great deal of time evaluating the list. We tried to discern between expectations that were realistic and those that were simply dreams. We also worked at understanding which expectations were fair and which ones stemmed from anger or frustration. Finally, we sought to focus on the issues that were vital to an honest, growing relationship. At the end of this evaluation we really had two lists. One was a bare-bones list of critical issues for the health of the marriage. The other was a "dream sheet" of things Pam wanted, but could do without.

3. Prioritize your expectations.

For the moment, we decided to work only on the bare-bones list of critical issues. I asked Pam to do two things with this list. First, she was to grade them according to their importance: A to those of highest priority, B to ones less critical, and so on. Next, I asked her to consider which expectations had to take place before the others could occur.

With the lists Pam was able to develop some realistic expectations. She didn't have to mortgage her future on a hope that somehow, someday her husband might "snap out of it." Instead, she was beginning to build an understanding of what was truly important to her and what must reasonably take place for the marriage to be rebuilt.

4. Develop a game plan.

Armed with the lists, Pam and I worked out a reasonable time line of what needed to take place for a reconciliation. We decided that Pam would take one expectation at a time and determine a realistic time frame. Then she would present her concern to her husband for interaction and negotiation.

The first thing Pam felt needed to happen was for her husband to move out of his girlfriend's apartment. He didn't need to move home, but he needed to demonstrate his seriousness in rebuilding the marriage by terminating the relationship with the other woman.

How long could she give her husband to think about her request and move out of the apartment? "Up to two months," she decided.

5. Negotiate.

Later in the week Pam went out to lunch with her husband. (We decided that negotiation would best take place in a public facility where feelings would need to be controlled!) After talking for a while about mutual interests, Pam presented her first concern for discussion. Note that she didn't dump the whole list of expectations on her husband. That would have been too much for him to take.

Pam said to her husband, "I know that you love me, that you want to be my husband and the father of our children. I believe you when you say this. However, we have been separated now for two years, and it would be very helpful for me to understand where our marriage is going. So, I would like you to show me the sincerity of what you have been saying by cutting off your relationship with this other woman. You need not move back into the house if you are not ready. However, I believe you sincerely want our marriage to work, and this would give me tangible proof of your interest."

Pam's main purpose was to get an idea of her husband's willingness to work on their relationship. Would he respect her enough to take her request seriously?

Pam's husband was furious. "Are you kidding?" he said. "Who do you think you are, trying to take away my freedom and telling me how to live?"

Pam replied, "Wait a minute. You are the one who said you want to remain married to me. You also said you want to be the father of our children. I'm not telling you what to do. I just want to see if you want an honest partnership."

When Pam's husband said, "Forget it," she still did not act in anger. While she would not allow him back in the home over the weekends, she remained gracious to him while waiting for two months to see if he would change his mind. A phone conversation at the end of the two-month period convinced her that he wasn't interested in the marriage. He wanted his own way. The following week she filed divorce papers against him.

Pam's story doesn't have the happy ending you might have expected. The purpose of the plan that Pam and I developed was for reconciliation—but that didn't happen. Yet the strategy clarified her expectations and provided her with a realistic understanding of her situation. Our responsibility in reconciliation is not to control or manipulate the other partner. However, we can expect him to exhibit respect and commitment to the marriage if he truly wants it to work.

Pam's actions clearly demonstrated her desire to save the marriage—and they forced her husband to demonstrate his intentions. In that way, she was able to take an active role in her situation, not merely being a victim of his whims.

MAKE IT YOUR OWN

➤ What do you think of Pam's story? What would you have done differently? _____

_____

➤ How do you think her actions at this point might affect the way she recovers from her divorce? Will she feel guilty for actually filing the divorce papers? Or will she feel comfort in the fact that she did her best to save the marriage? How would you feel?_____

_____

_____

➤ Does Pam's strategy fit your situation?_____ If so, let's go through it. List all the things you want your marriage to be (and what your spouse needs to do to make this happen)._____

_____

_____

_____

_____

_____

_____

_____

_____

➤ Now go back through that list marking some with N for "necessities" and some with D for "dreams." Relist all those marked N._____

_____

_____

_____

_____

_____

➤ Now grade them A to F in order of importance. Relist any you have judged as A needs. _____

_____

_____

_____

➤ Of these, which is the first that needs to happen? What is the time frame in which this needs to happen?_____

_____

_____

_____

➤ How will you tell your spouse that you need this to happen? Write a practice speech here. _____

_____

_____

_____

_____

_____

_____

_____

➤ When and where will you talk with your spouse about this?_____

_____

_____

IN THE MEANTIME

While you're separated, you need to work out *guidelines for your emotional protection.* You are vulnerable during this time, and it is possible to open yourself up to all kinds of hurts.

For example, if you allow yourself to continue having sexual relations with your spouse (who may be having sex with others as well!), you could be setting yourself up for more pain. Yes, you're still officially married, but continuing your sexual relations can build the expectation for reconciliation. And your spouse may be using the opportunity to fulfill his or her physical desires. By sharing yourself in this way, you're allowing an estranged spouse to experience the joys of marriage without the responsibilities accompanying that commitment. You'd be sacrificing your personal emotional stability for the sake of pleasure (not to mention the health dangers if your spouse is promiscuous).

This self-sharing can work in other ways as well. For example, will you allow your spouse to come over to the house at any time? When can your spouse see the children? When are you willing to talk together? Answers to such questions form the framework for your emotional protection. I don't mean to be harsh, because it's fine for you to be as concerned for your spouse as you are for yourself. But you need to protect yourself from emotional violation. You need to develop respect for yourself—and expect it from others—before you open yourself to any more hurt.

During separation, you also need *a healthy social network.* We've already discussed the never-never land of separation, one of the greatest problems you'll face. How do you deal with the discomfort you feel with your married friends? Should you start spending time with single people, even though you don't feel single?

We all need friendships. Especially in this critical time, you need a network of safe friends with whom you can share yourself without fear of their expectations or judgment. You must find people who understand you. (Chapter 5 will help you learn how to develop and maintain healthy relationships while separated.)

But speaking of friendships, what about dating? Is it okay to date while separated?

First, you need to remember that dating is a prelude to remarriage, not a therapy for reconciliation. Yes, you need friends, but in a one-on-one relationship with someone of the opposite sex you can suddenly find yourself in an emotionally compromising situation. You may develop deepening ties to someone you're dating, and the new attachment may damage any hope of reconciliation. Your new relationship may inspire you to speed up the divorce process, even if you didn't initiate the separation.

Remember, too, that a separated person is still married. Some say, "It's only a matter of time until the legal paperwork is completed. Why can't I date while I'm waiting?" Is this just a technicality?

There are at least three stages to divorce. The first, the *emotional stage,* usually happens around the time of separation. Many see this as the true termination point of a marriage. This is when people *decide* to split up, disrupting their social lives and emotional expectations.

But there is also the *spiritual stage* of divorce. When we marry, we make a vow before God stating our fidelity and commitment. The Bible tells us that God oversees this commitment and holds people accountable to their marriage vows (Mal. 2:13–16). We must recognize our responsibility to maintain personal integrity and self-respect by being faithful to our vows, regardless of our spouses' infidelity. Until the divorce has been completed before God, we must remain faithful to this commitment.

This faithful commitment to our marriage vows can deeply strengthen the character of our personalities. When someone maintains faithfulness until the full termination of marriage, he or she forms a foundation on which future commitments can be built with full conviction and proven integrity. Faithfulness is the primary ingredient of commitment.

I've told you a bit about my first marriage, which ended painfully in divorce. Years later, God brought another woman into my life, whom I married. But after our first few dates, she began to ask me about my former marriage and divorce. Then she asked me a heavy question: "After your wife left you, did you start dating others, or did you keep your commitment to her even when she was unfaithful?" I was glad to be able to tell her I hadn't dated while I was separated. Later she said, "I know that you are a person who keeps his word. You remained faithful when it was the most difficult."

Finally, there is the *social (or legal) stage* of divorce. The Bible teaches that we are to obey the authorities over us (Rom. 13:1). Like it or not, in the eyes of the state you are still married until the divorce decree. Perhaps this is just a matter of paperwork to the government. But you weren't allowed to get married without a marriage license, and legally, you aren't divorced until the judge says so.

Therefore, until you are emotionally, spiritually, and legally divorced, you are still married. And a married person ought not to date others. However, a separated person still needs friends, and other options are available for personal support.

MAKE IT YOUR OWN

➤ What emotional guidelines do you need to set up during your separation? I list some possibilities here that you should consider. There may be many others.

Will you still sleep with your spouse?

Will you allow your spouse to visit whenever he or she wants?

How involved will your spouse be in your children's lives?

If there is "another woman" or "another man," how will you (or your children) deal with this person (if at all)?

➤ Are you always available to talk with your spouse, or are there some times when you need to turn off that pressure?_____

_____

➤ Other: _____

_____

_____

➤ What sort of social network can you develop? List the friends you can rely on for support. _____

_____

_____

➤ How do you feel about what I've said about dating? Do you agree?

_____

_____

➤ What alternatives to dating can you think of? _____

_____

_____

WHERE IS GOD IN THIS MESS?

When I got married in the church, I thought God was supposed to bless this union. After all, he created marriage in the first place. Now my marriage is falling apart. I feel that God has failed me. Where is he in all this mess?

You may be asking a question like that. It's not unusual.

Why would God allow something like this to happen?

At least since Job, people have pondered this question, but a marital breakdown takes it out of the theoretical realm and right into your gut.

If I do certain things, will God respond by pulling my marriage back together?

These are tough issues, and all the tougher because of the pain involved. We'll be looking at God's perspective on marriage and divorce in Chapter 3, but we need to make one crucial point here. *God's first concern is always for reconciliation.* God didn't design marriage to end in divorce. The New Testament makes it clear that for a Christian, the grounds for divorce are rather narrow. And even when a believer is married to an unbeliever, Paul said the general rule is for a couple to remain married unless separation is initiated by the unbelieving spouse.

Does God Promise Reconciliation?

Some teachers make you believe that your marriage will automatically be reconciled if you follow certain biblical patterns. "After all," they say, "God is pro-marriage. Therefore, your obedience will release the power of God to bring your family back together again."

I don't believe the Bible gives us this kind of simplistic answer. Note, for example, the relationship between God and his "bride" Israel as described in Jeremiah 3. God drove home the point that Israel had abandoned her relationship with him. *God experienced marital separation!*

Yes, in Jeremiah 3, God said he desired reconciliation with his "spouse." But his call for reconciliation wasn't a method of bargaining! He didn't say, "Israel, please come back to me, and I will act as though nothing ever happened."

No way! God cried out for reconciliation on the basis of correcting wrong, improper, destructive behavior. Listen:

> "Return, faithless Israel," declares the LORD,
>   "I will frown on you no longer. . . .
> Only acknowledge your guilt—
>   you have rebelled against the LORD your God,
> you have scattered your favors to foreign gods
>   under every spreading tree,
>   and have not obeyed me," declares the LORD. (Jer. 3:12–13 NIV)

God told Israel he desired reconciliation, but only on the basis of honesty. He refused to play the bargaining game, passing over the hurts and failures as if they had never happened. He demanded reconciliation on the basis of openness and integrity.

Doris Bridges separated from her husband, Mike, after nine years of marriage. "I left home because of my husband's frequent unemployment, alcohol abuse, and cocaine addiction," Doris explained. "I figured we were bad for each other since we seem to feed into each other's addictions. Since leaving, I've cleaned up my act. Now Mike wants me to come back. I know he has a long way to go, but I feel like I need him in my life again. Perhaps I can help him through his problems."

"Doris is right," Mike added. "I've been a bum. But now I know I can't go on alone. I told her if she will move back in, I'll stop the drugs and booze and get a job. This separation has made me realize how much I need her. I know when she comes back we'll work it out together."[3]

Doris moved back in with Mike, but soon they lapsed into the same destructive tendencies that caused the separation in the first place. The Bridges were trying to get back together without honestly facing their past mistakes, assuming everything would work out okay.

But God doesn't play that game. He called his estranged wife to repentance, which simply means an honest recognition of past mistakes and a commitment to accountable living in the future. Repentance is more than just remorse over the past. It implies a change of attitude and future conduct.

What does that mean for you?

God never promises a simplistic reconciliation. The Bible shows that true reconciliation happens only through repentance, forgiveness, and the commitment to work on a healthy, honest relationship. As long as Israel did not repent, God wasn't reconciled to her. And neither does he promise automatic reconciliation to separated Christians. Beware of any hyperspiritualized notions that you can force God to restore your marriage if you do some righteous act.

However, saying reconciliation *may* not happen is different from saying it *will* not happen. God is at work doing more than we can ask or imagine (Eph. 3:20). Reconciliation is not beyond his power.

Will God Heal My Marriage?

I believe God can heal people. A little girl in my church had a potentially fatal parasite infection. The doctors had tried everything, but all their treatments were unsuccessful. They were about to use a drug that could kill the parasites but might promote cancer.

The little girl's parents brought her to the elders of the church, asking us to lay hands on her and pray for healing. Now, none of the elders claimed to have the gift of healing. And we didn't promise a healing if we prayed for her. We obeyed God's instruction to pray for healing, believing that God had the power to do so if he wanted.

When she was taken for her last round of tests prior to administering the stronger drug, the parasites were gone. Who could explain it? The only answer was that an all-powerful God worked for his glory in healing her.

I have seen God heal marriages as miraculously as he healed that little girl. One man, who had recently left his wife, was driving through the rain one night when his car went out of control. When he regained consciousness, he was lying on the side of the road, his car in a ditch, flashing lights all around him. Amazingly, neither the man nor his car had any serious injuries, and he was able to drive away.

But he didn't continue to his destination. Instead, he drove back to his house and told his wife, "I've been acting like an idiot. Would you please forgive me for hurting you?" Since that day they have worked at their marriage, and today it's a strong, healthy relationship. But it all began with the "miracle" of his car going off the road.

But does God always use miracles to heal people? No. Sometimes he heals through the hard work of professionals: doctors, nurses, therapists, and others who are involved in the medical profession.

My friend Glenn broke his neck at the seashore, diving into a wave and hitting the shore bottom. After an extended period of operations and therapy, he has regained the ability to walk and maintain an active lifestyle. A slight limp is the only visible sign of Glenn's accident.

I have also seen marriages healed through the hard work of professionals: counselors, psychologists, psychiatrists, and pastors working to create understanding and renewed commitment for couples whose marriages were on the brink of ruin.

That was the case with Paul and Diane, both involved in extramarital affairs. Their separation seemed to drive a deeper wedge of mistrust and alienation until Paul asked if he could meet with Diane's counselor. Over several months, repentance turned to rebuilding. Now with renewed commitment, Paul and Diane work with alienated couples in their church, sharing a hope for honest reconciliation.

Miracles can happen. And professionals can facilitate healing. But the fact remains: not all illnesses are cured, and not all marriages are put back together.

Take, for instance, the well-known story of Joni Eareckson Tada. Like my friend Glenn, Joni broke her neck while diving. Only in her instance there was no physical healing. No miracle. Though she received excellent care from physicians, Joni did not recover the use of her limbs.

However, while Joni was not healed physically, she has expressed a message of courage and hope to millions through her books, artwork, singing, and speaking. Why? Because another miracle took place, a healing that wasn't physical. Joni's *soul* was restored. Through the power of God, she learned the strength of acceptance, and then she began to share the lessons she learned with other people. As the Bible says, she learned to "comfort those in any trouble with the comfort we ourselves have received from God" (2 Cor. 1:4 NIV).

In the same way, many Christians have gone through separation and prayed like crazy for reconciliation—but it never happened. However, through the trauma of their divorce, they've experienced an inner healing of the soul. And they're stronger persons today, not because their divorce was something good or something they wanted, but because God used their divorce to spur growth and maturity.

Where is God in this mess? God does heal the separated. He doesn't always heal the way we expect or want. We can't control the actions of the loving, caring God. Nor will we be able to put all the pieces of the puzzle together and understand the way he works. But we can hold on to the belief that he uses our present pains to make us into healthy people who can honor him.

MAKE IT YOUR OWN

➤ How has your separation affected your relationship with God?

_____

_____

➤ What sort of miracle would you like to see happen?_____

_____

_____

_____

➤ If God decides not to do that, what's your second choice? _____

_____

_____

_____

➤ If you like, write out a prayer to God in the space provided. Be honest about your desires, your frustrations, your dreams, your doubts. Be bold enough to ask for a miracle, but humble enough to yield to his ways.

_____

_____

_____

_____

_____

Hope for the Future

Separation is a time of turmoil and uncertainty. While God desires reconciliation, there are no guarantees it will take place. However, the way you handle this crisis can determine the future of your marriage and the stability of your life.

God is involved in the lives of his children who are separated. While the "all things" that work together for good (Rom. 8:28 NKJV) do not always work out the way we would like, we can call all things good because of his promise that nothing shall separate us from his love (Rom. 8:29). That separation will never take place.

Chapter 3

YOU CAN BOOK IT
BIBLICAL INSIGHTS ABOUT DIVORCE[1]

A few years ago I faced a test of personal maturity. It was my son's birthday, and he wanted a bicycle. *No problem!* I thought to myself, and off I went to one of the local toy superstores to find the right bike.

After looking over the fifty or so models available, I selected one that I particularly liked. It was a shiny black one with only one gear (none of that fancy stuff!) and two brakes—a hand brake and a foot brake.

I took a slip of paper from the display and handed it to the clerk at the cash register. "Wait a moment," she said pleasantly. "Someone will bring that right out for you." I expected someone to wheel a fancy new two-wheeler out to me. Instead a young man brought out a cardboard box.

At that moment, I noticed a sign hanging near the bicycle display: LET US ASSEMBLE YOUR BIKE—ONLY $15.

For a moment I thought, *Wouldn't that be easy?* Then I regained my masculine sanity. *I'm not going to let some runny-nosed kid with a ratchet set rip me off for $15! I'll put it together myself!*

That evening I began to assemble the bike. And what would take some runny-nosed kid about fifteen minutes went on for two or three hours! You see, as a typical American male I took one look at the directions that came with the bike and said, "No problem! This looks easy enough." Then I put the directions down and tried to assemble it on my own.

The finished product did look something like a bike. However, I never got the hand brake attached. And it wasn't until he was riding it that my son discovered that I had put the handlebars on backward! It would have been so much easier to read the instructions.

SOCIETY'S PERSPECTIVE

Unfortunately, most people enter marriage today with the same type of attitude I had about that bike. *No problem,* they think. *Marriage is natural. We love each other. Everything will work out.* It's easier to get a marriage license than a driver's license. Perhaps if we made it more difficult, people would be asking the difficult questions ahead of time.

Marriage as a Convenience

I'm not saying that our society takes marriage lightly. Most people are very serious about their commitment when they take the plunge. However, behind the decision to marry lies a disturbing attitude about marriage that dominates our culture. This attitude can be summarized in one word: *convenience.* Marriage is seen as a convenience, a way for me to get my needs met and be fulfilled as a person.

Now, there is nothing wrong with becoming a fulfilled person or with having your needs met. However, if these are primary motivations for marriage, then the opposite is also true: if this marriage does not fulfill me or meet my needs, then it must not be right for me anymore. So we often find people considering divorce because marriage is no longer convenient.

I was visiting a friend a short while ago. It was a beautiful day, and we were chatting on the front lawn. "See that house across the street?" my friend said. "Those folks have only been married for a year, but now they're getting a divorce."

"Why?" I asked.

"Oh, he says he just doesn't like the pressures of his marriage. His wife never seems to be happy, and he's tired of the negative atmosphere."

Not every divorce is so simplistic, but that could be the story of many marital breakups. When marriage stops being convenient, people stop being married. When marriage stops paying the expected dividends, we often withdraw our emotional investments.

Evaluating Marriage Quality

In the process of making the divorce decision, three broad standards are used to evaluate the quality of one's marriage. The first standard is *whether or not you feel happy in your marriage.* Of course, this depends on how you define *happiness,* which is a very personal matter. One might define happiness as the provision of creature comforts: "My husband gives me everything I need," or "My wife is a lousy cook." Others might define happiness in terms of emotion: "My wife understands me," or "My husband lacks all passion."

The second standard is *whether or not you have a better, more desirable alternative.* Here one might look longingly back at the freedom he had as a single adult. He thinks to himself, *You know, it sure was easier not having all these hassles.* And he considers whether a return to the single life would be better for him.

Another better alternative could be a more desirable person. Perhaps a woman develops a friendship with a man at the office. He seems so much more sensitive than her husband. Or he looks better. Or he has so much more drive and ambition. Before too long she starts to fantasize about living with him. She's pondering whether he might make a better alternative.

> **The prevalent view of our society is that marriage is a convenience whose primary purpose is the fulfillment of the individual.**

The third standard for marital evaluation is *whether or not there is social pressure to prevent you from getting a divorce.* This standard depends on the social context of your culture: whether or not it reinforces marriage or is lax about divorce.

We tend to consider American culture rather liberal in the areas of marriage and divorce. With "no fault," "shared custody," and other laws on the books, one wouldn't think of our country as a place that demands marital stability.

However, subcultures in our society place a great deal of social pressure on their members not to get a divorce. I remember talking to one woman who actually feared for her life because she was divorcing her husband. "Everyone in the family knows that he runs around with other women and he beats me up," she said. "But that doesn't matter. You just don't get a divorce in our community."

Many sociologists would say that if one of the three criteria I've mentioned is negative in your marriage, there is a good possibility you will experience a divorce. If two of these criteria are negative, you have a high probability for divorce. And if all three of them exist in your marriage—well, we'll see you at the domestic court!

"Divorce Is Natural"

Because marriage is viewed as a convenience, many people have come to believe that divorce is normal and natural. As a matter of fact, it is not unusual to read social scientists who describe divorce as a regular step in the developmental phases of adult life. Just as a person develops from childhood into adolescence, then from adolescence into adulthood, so adults move developmentally from one marriage into another. So say these "experts."

"After all," they would argue, "you can't expect that the wife of your twenties will necessarily meet your needs when you are in your forties." With that kind of logic, they assert that a typical person could expect to have two, three, or more partners in his adult life.

Where's the Church?

You might expect the church to counter these arguments—but that's not necessarily so. Some parts of the church only affirm what society is saying about marriage. One major denomination has changed its book of worship to provide an alternative reading in the marriage service. Instead of vowing "until death do us part," you may now substitute "until love ends." Obviously, the denomination has bought into the idea of marriage as a convenience.

MAKE IT YOUR OWN

➤ As you listen to what society is saying about marriage, which of the following messages do you receive?

❑ Marriage is a beautiful thing—when it works.

❑ Marriages should last forever.

❑ Sometimes it's tough to be married, but you should work hard to keep the marriage together.

❑ When you're growing up, marriage is a dream; after you're married, it's a nightmare.

❑ In today's society, it's normal for husbands and wives to cheat on each other.

❑ If you make it through ten years of marriage, you're a pretty noble person.

❏ People change. If you grow and your spouse doesn't, go ahead and leave the marriage.

❏ If you don't have kids, there's really no reason to stay together if you're having trouble in your marriage.

❏ Once you stop being in love with each other, your marriage is a farce and might as well be ended.

❏ Marriage relationships can grow through good times and bad.

❏ It really doesn't make sense to stay together "for the kids' sake."

❏ *Marriage* is not a word; it's a sentence.

➤ Where do you hear messages like this?

❏ *Oprah*

❏ *Newsweek*

❏ PTA

❏ *National Enquirer*

❏ Church

❏ Ann Landers

❏ On the phone

❏ *General Hospital*

❏ CNN

❏ *Wall Street Journal*

❏ The gym

❏ *ER*

❏ At work

❏ *Good Housekeeping*

❏ From your kids

❏ Other: _____

_____

_____

➤ When was the last time you picked up some message from society about divorce or marriage? What was the message?_____

_____

_____

_____

➤ I mentioned that some subcultures, especially religious groups, can be dead set against divorce. Are you in such a subculture? Do you feel a tension between this subculture and the world at large? Explain.

_____

_____

_____

➤ As you look at the three common criteria—unhappy in the marriage; better alternative; lack of social support for marriage—how many apply to your marriage?_____

_____

_____

➤ Which of the following apply to your church?

❑ Helped hold my marriage together as long as it could.

❑ Supported me following the divorce.

❑ Added pressure to my marriage that contributed to the divorce.

❑ Didn't understand what I was going through.

❑ Made clear to me the Bible's teaching on marriage and divorce.

❑ Seemed unsure of what the Bible teaches about divorce.

❑ I really have not been involved in a church.

➤ How did you feel about your church's response to you during this time?

_____

_____

_____

THE BIBLE'S PERSPECTIVE

Because much of the church holds the same position on marriage and divorce as our culture does, you might assume that the Bible reflects a similar view. But that's not the case. The Bible does not consider marriage as a convenience. Rather, it defines marriage as a *covenant.*

What Is a Covenant?

You might find the word *covenant* stuffy and old-fashioned, but it's actually quite simple to understand. A covenant is a contract—and we all use contracts. When you buy a car, rent an apartment, go to a movie, or ride a train, you use a contract! With a contract, you agree to pay a price and receive goods or services.

A covenant is a relationship contract, an agreement between two or more people. It has nothing to do with exchanging goods and services. Rather, it formally establishes or maintains a relationship.

When I was a boy, I enjoyed playing cowboys and Indians. There was a childhood ceremony I performed with my friends—becoming "blood brothers." You may remember how it went. Both you and your partner pricked your fingers. Then you pressed them together so that the blood would (theoretically!) mingle. You shared each other's blood. You were bonded together. That bonded relationship is a covenant.

In ancient days covenants were legally binding agreements. When two kings agreed to peace, they formed a covenant. When two friends were particularly close, they made a covenant. And when two families agreed to marriage, it was established by a covenant.

Every contract consists of at least three things: obligations, blessings, and curses. Say I buy a car. My obligation is to make payments. The dealership is obligated to make delivery on my car. Then I receive the "blessing" of driving the car. However, if I stop making payments, the "curses" of the contract are enforced. A "repo man" comes (probably in the night) and takes away my car!

Marriage as a Covenant

As I said earlier, God describes marriage as a covenant. When a couple are married, they receive all the blessings of the relationship, but there are also obligations. In terms of the traditional marriage vow, couples promise "to have and to hold, for better or for worse, in sickness and in health, as long as we both shall live." God expects marriage to be a lifelong covenant.

When a man and a woman are married, God says, they are bonded together. The Bible describes this as becoming "one flesh" (Gen. 2:24 NKJV). And we know what happens when that one flesh is torn apart: you go through the stages of grief! That, by the way, is one of the "curses" that come when one or both parties are not faithful to their covenant.

> ## The Bible describes marriage as a covenant commitment that's intended to be lifelong.

Since God views marriage as a lifelong covenant, divorce of any kind must be understood as a deviation from his original plan. God didn't design marriage to end in divorce. However, God recognizes the reality of divorce. When he gave his laws to the nation of Israel, he included the proper legal procedures for a divorce (Deut. 24). That doesn't imply that God condoned divorce. He just knew divorces were going to occur, so he outlined the proper methods for the courts to follow.

God understands that divorce is the end of a marriage. When the covenant is terminated, the man and the woman are no longer husband and wife. This is a legal fact. However, just because a divorce is *legal* in God's estimation doesn't necessarily mean it is *valid.* God declares that some divorces are for valid reasons and some are not. In the Bible, God allows for divorce on specific (valid) grounds. Divorces that occur for other reasons, although still legal and binding, are not valid and should not have taken place.

MAKE IT YOUR OWN

➤ Besides marriage, what modern examples of *covenants* can you think of?

_____

_____

➤ As you see it, what are the *obligations* of a marriage covenant?

_____

_____

➤ As you see it, are these obligations still binding on you? Why or why not? _____

_____

➤ What are the *blessings* of a marriage covenant that is kept? _____

_____

➤ Have you experienced them? Explain. _____

_____

➤ What are the *curses* of not keeping a marriage covenant? _____

_____

_____

➤ Have you experienced them? Explain. _____

_____

_____

GROUNDS FOR DIVORCE

The first place where the Bible speaks of a valid reason for divorce is Matthew 19. In that chapter, Jesus debated with some religious leaders about the grounds on which a divorce could occur. And in verse 9, he said that divorce is invalid except for marital unfaithfulness.

The Greek word for marital unfaithfulness is *porneia,* which is best translated "sexual immorality." Taken in context, Jesus said that ongoing, unrepentant sexual deviancy of any kind is a valid ground for divorce.

Why? Because the sexual relationship in marriage should demonstrate the whole-person commitment that two people have with each other. It's meant to be an expression of their covenant. As my Fresh Start partner Tom Jones says in *The Single Again Handbook:*

> The meaning God has given to sexual intercourse is that of the marriage union (Gen. 2:23–25; Matt. 19:4–6). Sexual intercourse is symbolic of the whole-life sharing that God requires of spouses. God invented it to be such a symbol and, in fact, a seal of that union. It was not given to humankind merely for physical pleasure; rather, it

was given to indicate in an outward way what has happened and is happening in the souls of the two people who so unite.[2]

What happens, then, when one partner of the covenant continually goes outside the marriage and gives himself physically to other persons or things? What does that say about the soul condition of covenant commitment? What does it express concerning the bondedness of that person to his spouse? It indicates a real brokenness in that covenant relationship, a brokenness that ought to be acknowledged and repaired. But if a partner is not willing to change and rebuild his one-flesh covenant relationship, Jesus said, if there is a long-term, aggravated problem in this area, the other spouse has grounds for a valid divorce.

Later in the New Testament, in a book written to the Christians in the city of Corinth, the apostle Paul responded to some serious questions about marriage (1 Cor. 7:10ff.). Apparently, the questions came in response to a previous teaching of Paul. The apostle had explained that a follower of Jesus Christ shouldn't marry a person who was not committed to following Christ. It just didn't make sense for two people with different priorities and life purposes to try to work together. It made about as much sense as trying to plow a field with a horse and an ox yoked together!

"Well," they might have responded, "what happens if a Christian is already married to someone who isn't committed to Christ? Should this person get a divorce?"

In his response, Paul first restated what Jesus had taught in Matthew 19, explaining that Christians ought not to divorce; but if they do, they ought to be reconciled. Covenant faithfulness was the standard that Jesus taught throughout his ministry, and Paul affirmed it. It can be safely assumed that Paul (and his readers) understood the one exception Jesus had given to this general rule. Therefore, he went on to address the issue of mixed marriages.

When a partner who is not a follower of Christ wants to leave the marriage, Paul explained, the believer should let him leave. It cannot be inferred that the Christian spouse is kicking the other spouse out of the house. No, Paul taught that the believing spouse ought to remain in the marriage if the unbelieving partner wants it. Paul referred to a situation in which an unbelieving spouse has made a conscious decision to abandon the marriage. "A believing man or woman is not bound in such circumstances," the apostle said (1 Cor. 7:15 NIV).

That phrase "not bound" is very important. The term was used when a slave was freed from bondage. Paul asserted that the believer is no longer enslaved in the covenant relationship when the unbelieving spouse abandons the marriage.

Believers Abandoning Believers

It's interesting that Paul's teaching on mixed marriages differs from his teaching to couples who claim to be disciples of Christ. Why did he say that the Christians ought to be reconciled?

We find an answer in Matthew 18, one chapter prior to Jesus' teaching on divorce. When two Christians have a dispute with each other, Jesus said, they ought to work it out together. When they can't resolve it, he stated, they need to go to a member of the church who will act as an arbiter and help them solve their conflict.

However, if this arbitration doesn't work, Jesus taught that the matter ought to be taken "to the church"—that is, the authority of the church—and that the elders should bring the problem to closure (Matt. 18:15–17).

Although this text applies to disagreements in general, we can certainly apply it to divorce. If a couple cannot resolve their disputes, ideally the church should be able to help them.

But what happens when one of these believers still pushes for divorce? In Matthew 18, Jesus taught that a member who refuses to submit to the intervention of the church is to be treated as an unbeliever. (Note that the church cannot say, "You aren't a Christian." Only God can say that! But the church must say, "You are acting as though you are not a Christian; therefore, we must treat you as an unbeliever.")

In cases that terminate in excommunication, the believing spouse is considered abandoned by an unbeliever and is no longer bound in the marriage.

This process of restorative discipline takes hard work. It is one of the most taxing responsibilities of the church. However, it is vital care for those who turn to their church for help in times of marital crisis.

What Is Abandonment?

The church is responsible to provide emotional and spiritual support for members who are struggling in their marriages. Further, it needs to stand alongside members who are forced to make tough decisions in the midst of a destructive marital environment.

One of these tough decisions comes in the area of defining abandonment. Traditionally, abandonment has been understood as one spouse irrevocably leaving the household. However, in our day it has been suggested that abandonment might include other ongoing, problematic situations.

For example, what about physical abuse? Shouldn't a situation where a husband or a wife beats up a spouse over a long period of time, refusing to change, be considered abandonment? Or what about two persons who live in the same house but maintain totally separate lives? Are they maintaining the covenant relationship of marriage?

Many who hear questions like this about abandonment respond by saying, "Wait a minute. When you think like that, a person could rationalize any problem as abandonment!" And that's true! Therefore, we must ask if the Bible gives any criteria for abandonment other than physical desertion.

The answer to this question is both no and yes! No, the Bible does not specifically address circumstances such as abuse and neglect. But yes, the Bible does give guidelines to interpret these problems.

The first guideline is our *definition of marriage.* If marriage is a covenant commitment, then abandonment should be defined in terms of abandoning the covenant commitment rather than simple physical desertion. So, for example, the Bible teaches that a husband ought to love his wife as he loves his own body (Eph. 5:28). If a man is continually beating up his wife, he may be abandoning his covenant commitment to her.

A second guideline is the *attitude of the offender.* Is she repentant about the problem? Or does she refuse to face the destructive nature of the situation? Perhaps even worse, does she seem repentant (desiring to stop the behavior and be responsible), yet in practice act no differently? Matthew 18 implies that discipline ought to be used in cases where a party is unrepentant and refuses to change.

A third guideline is the *objective perspective of the church leadership.* There is nothing more difficult for a person in an emotionally destructive situation than to make a reasonable, rational decision. The elders of the church ought to be available to a member in this situation to provide wise, godly counsel. Furthermore, in Hebrews 13:17, we read, "Obey your leaders and submit to their authority. They keep watch over you as men who must give an account. Obey them so that their work will be a joy, not a burden, for that would be of no advantage to you" (NIV).

A believer is responsible to submit his circumstances to the leaders for understanding and direction. And the leaders—who are accountable for their members—must respond. For a situation of marital difficulty to qualify as abandonment, elders must confirm that the actions of the unrepentant spouse have the same extreme effect as someone's physical abandonment.

Using these criteria, a Christian shouldn't be able to define *abandonment* in a simplistic way to provide an easy solution (divorce) to a complex situation.

Recently, a study committee of one evangelical denomination seriously grappled with this question of abandonment. You may find a few excerpts from their conclusions helpful:

Are there other forms of "separation" today that may be considered equivalent to this leaving of the marriage of which Paul speaks? We must be careful not to open the floodgate of excuses. On the other hand, we need to recognize the reality of the "separation." We should allow [leaders] the liberty to discern with much prayer what would be the proper response in a particular circumstance.

Several considerations incline us to agree . . . that desertion can occur as well by the imposition of intolerable conditions as by departure itself. . . . It seems to us that sins which are tantamount in extremity and consequence to actual desertion should be understood to produce similar eventualities. . . . We are quick to add, however, that the list of sins tantamount to desertion cannot be very long.

We are not unaware of the danger which lurks behind such a position in the temptation it may pose to some to spin out a vast array of marital sins equivalent to desertion. This danger, however, we conclude is best met in other ways than by an effort to forge a barrier to divorce sturdier than the Bible's own. In many more ways than this, the church's health and integrity depends upon her elders' ability and willingness to provide godly, wise, merciful and severe, and scrupulously Scriptural application of Biblical norms to human situations.[3]

What About Invalid Divorce?

If you have gone through a divorce that would not be considered valid according to the Bible, you should understand a number of points.

First, *God still empathizes with the pain that brought about your situation.* Jeremiah 3:8 states that God himself went through a divorce. He understands what you have been through and what you are facing.

Second, *divorce is not the unforgivable sin in God's eyes.* I have made it a point to read through every list of heinous sins recorded in the New Testament—and divorce is not even mentioned! Here's my point: God can forgive you of your sin of seeking a divorce for invalid reasons. "If we confess our sins, He is faithful and just to forgive us our sins and to cleanse us from all unrighteousness" (1 John 1:9 NKJV).

Third, if it is possible, *God expects you to work for reconciliation.* As I stated above, if you and your former spouse are disciples of Christ, there is no option for divorce outside of ongoing sexual immorality. If you can restore your marriage, you should.

Or if your former spouse is not a follower of Jesus but still desires a marriage, you should not have left her. You should seek to be reconciled.

However, if your former spouse has remarried or is not interested in reconciliation, there is nothing more you can do about it. You are forgiven and no longer bound.

MAKE IT YOUR OWN

➤ Based on what you have read here, along with your personal study or your church's teaching, what do you feel are valid grounds for seeking divorce?

❑ 1. Spouse has an affair.

❑ 2. Spouse has repeated affairs.

❑ 3. Spouse moves out.

❑ 4. Spouse abuses you physically.

❑ 5. Spouse abuses the kids.

❑ 6. Spouse abuses you emotionally.

❑ 7. Spouse is addicted to drugs or alcohol and will not seek treatment.

❑ 8. Love is gone from the marriage.

❑ 9. You two have grown apart.

❑ 10. Spouse does not communicate with you.

❑ 11. Spouse does not care for your needs.

❑ 12. You become a Christian, and your spouse doesn't.

❑ 13. Spouse insists that you stop going to church.

❑ 14. Spouse insists that you give up Christianity.

❑ 15. You find someone else who fulfills your needs.

Discussion

I don't presume to be the final arbiter on these things, but you might be interested in my views, and those of my Fresh Start colleagues, on the situations listed here. Let me urge you to seek counsel from your church leaders wherever possible.

1–2. An affair, especially if it's ongoing and the spouse is unrepentant, certainly qualifies as *porneia* in the biblical sense. Yet even here, repentance and restoration are the most desirable options. *Repeated* affairs indicate that there are a deeper problem and a lack of repentance (even if the spouse claims to be sorry after each one—true repentance requires behavior change, or at least a concerted effort to deal with the offending actions). This could certainly be seen as abandonment.

3. This is abandonment, pure and simple.

4–5. Physical abuse can certainly be seen as a violation of the marriage covenant. It is no sin to escape a dangerous situation. Try to deal with the problem, but if it persists, you have grounds for staying separated and perhaps divorce. Again, seek counsel from church leaders for a neutral opinion.

6. Emotional abuse is hard to define. Severe cases could be considered valid grounds for staying separated and perhaps divorce, but be careful not to draw your definitions too broadly.

7. "Will not seek treatment" is a key phrase there. Spouses can help each other overcome addictions. But obstinate denial of a problem is impossible to deal with. This can qualify as abandonment. The person is essentially having an affair with drugs or drink.

8–11. No way. Society may accept these explanations, but God does not.

12–14. The Bible is clear that a Christian should stay with a non-Christian spouse unless the non-Christian instigates the breakup. If the unbelieving spouse demands that you stop going to church, you have a conflict of commitments. If it cannot be resolved, you must ultimately obey God's orders to assemble with other believers. Certainly, if your spouse insists that you give up your faith, you cannot do that. Your spouse may, as a result, seek divorce, and in such a case you should let him or her go.

15. No.

How do you think God feels about the circumstances of your divorce? Check all that apply:

❑ He knows I did what I had to do.

❑ I was an innocent victim. He sympathizes.

❑ I made wrong choices. He has forgiven me.

❑ There is distance between God and me because of my sin.

❑ I blame him for my problems. I don't care what he thinks.

WHAT ABOUT REMARRIAGE?

The topic of remarriage is so important that in our Fresh Start alumni seminar called Second Wind we devote an entire session to it. In this chapter we'll just offer some general biblical guidelines concerning remarriage.[4]

What does the Bible teach about remarriage after divorce? This subject has been hotly debated for generations, with numerous (and sometimes complicated) answers suggested. However, we boil down the issue to a simple principle: if you had biblically valid grounds for divorce, then you have biblically valid grounds for remarriage. If you *didn't* have biblically valid grounds for divorce, you should seek reconciliation if it's possible.

Yet you need to be very careful before you go running into a new relationship. Just because you have the biblical right to remarry doesn't necessarily mean it is right for you!

When I talk with people about remarriage, I always want to cover a few key questions before encouraging them in this direction:

1. Have you worked through the implications of your divorce?

You need to work through your personal healing and recovery before you commit yourself again in a lifelong covenant relationship. When people rush back into marriage, they apply pressure on themselves that they are not prepared to handle.

What implications of your divorce am I talking about? Well, there are at least three. The first is *forgiveness.* Are you still carrying around the negative emotions of your past relationship, or have you come to closure with the pain of your past? If you haven't forgiven yourself and the significant others of your past, you will be carrying unhealthy, destructive baggage into your new marriage.

The second implication is *restoration of relationship with your former spouse.* Are you able to work together with your former spouse, particularly in the area of coparenting? Restoration implies the ability to respect each other and communicate with each other as responsible persons. You don't have to be friends. You don't even have to like each other. You do need to be able to work with each other in a sane manner without consistent tension and blowups.

Let me say that restoration of relationship may never happen with your former spouse. But have you made honest attempts at it?

The third implication of your divorce is *reconciliation.* Of course, this is often impossible. (If you skipped over the chapter on separation and reconciliation, you may want to work through it at this point just to review the issues

> ## The right to remarry doesn't necessarily mean it's right for you to remarry.

involved.) However, you need to remember that from God's perspective, reconciliation is always the first line of concern. Often, when we are in the pain of separation and divorce, we don't even want to think about the idea of reconciliation. Yet God wants us to review this step in our minds and hearts before we consider the possibilities of remarriage.

2. Why do you want to remarry?

There are many wrong reasons to remarry: escaping from singleness, seeking financial security, finding sexual relief, to name a few. Remember that rebound marriages have a higher percentage of divorce than first marriages! Why? Because people on the rebound are looking for someone else to make them whole and healed. But no one else can make you into a whole person. Two whole persons make a healthy marriage. Attempting to find another person to solve your problems and make you whole is another way of defining codependency!

I have found over the years that the person who is best prepared for remarriage is the one who would like to remarry, *but doesn't* need *to be married.* When you feel that you are a whole person who can live life fully without another person, you may be ready to commit again. You are ready to remarry when you don't need to remarry.

MAKE IT YOUR OWN

➤ Do you currently have a desire to remarry?

❑ Strongly.

❑ Mildly.

❑ Maybe someday.

❑ Are you crazy? I just got out of a marriage!

➤ When do you think you'll be ready to remarry?

❑ Right now.

❑ I have no idea.

❑ I'll know when the right person comes along.

❑ Give me another year or two.

❑ Five years.

❑ Does "hell freezing over" mean anything to you?

➤ Do you believe you have valid reasons to remarry? What are they?

_____

_____

➤ Have you dealt with the necessary issues from your previous marriage?

a. Have you forgiven your former spouse (and sought forgiveness, where necessary)?

b. Have you restored a working relationship with your former spouse if that is possible?

c. Have you done all you can to reconcile that marriage on healthy terms? (In other words, was it a valid divorce from your perspective?)

➤ What does this statement mean to you? "You are ready to remarry when you don't need to remarry." _____

_____

_____

_____

Getting on Course

If a jet pilot sets the instruments slightly wrong after takeoff, the plane will be far from its proper destination when it's time to land. In a similar way, if we set an improper course for marriage, the final result can be disastrous.

Our society has set its course by defining marriage as a convenience. The results can be seen all around in broken marriages, children without stable homes, and people who haven't learned how to maintain commitments.

The Bible sets a different course. It would be simplistic to say that viewing marriage as a lifelong covenant commitment would resolve our society's problems, but applying the biblical norm could go a long way to stabilize our social condition.

Fortunately, when planes are off course, they can make a midcourse correction. And the same is true for us. We can make the responsible decisions to define marriage biblically and to order our lives according to it.

Now, if I could only find those directions for my son's bike, I could get that hand brake connected. . . .

Chapter 4

❧

THERE OUGHTTA BE A LAW
DEALING WITH THE LEGAL ISSUES

Tim and Beth weren't getting along, though both were devout Christians. Tim owned his business, and he seldom had time for Beth or the kids. She would complain about his being a workaholic, and he would complain about her complaining. You know how that goes.

Eventually, Tim moved out. He continued to support his wife and children in their elegant home while he lived in a really inexpensive apartment near his office. For a couple of years, they lived like that, neither one seeking a divorce. As Christians, they weren't sure they had valid grounds for divorce; they just didn't want to live together.

Then Tim's business hit hard times. He tried to explain to Beth that he couldn't send her as much money anymore, but she figured he was just ducking his responsibilities. That's when she hired a lawyer, a real cutthroat guy who promised to get her every penny she deserved and then some.

The lawyer demanded that Tim *increase* the amount he paid his wife and kids, and he billed Tim extra for underpaying their support in the past. But Tim's business was going under, and he had already lost a bundle. There was no way he could meet the demands.

Beth insisted that Tim was hiding his assets, and the lawyer fueled her suspicions. Tim's finances were scrutinized from every angle, but no hidden money was found. Beth was more convinced that Tim was very good at hiding the money. After all that work for all those years, he had to have *something* tucked away.

But the truth was, Tim was practically broke. He couldn't even afford a lawyer of his own. Beth's lawyer was able to push her case through the courts, and Tim was given an ultimatum: pay up or go to jail. The amount was about $100,000, and Tim just didn't have it.

That's when Tim called me. Maybe I could talk some sense into Beth and get her to call off the hounds. I tried.

Beth was very angry. Tim had wronged her by moving out. Even more, he had wronged her by ignoring her through the twelve years of their marriage. Now he was going to pay. I appealed to her sense of mercy; surely as a Christian, she could find some forgiveness for him. But she snapped back, "Tim sinned against God and against me. And now God is using me to punish him."

How do you respond to that?

Tim didn't go to jail. He would sell something or borrow money to pay a part of what they wanted, and they would back off for a few months—but then it would start all over again. He was miserable, struggling to pay the minimal rent on his ratty apartment and scrambling to keep his business afloat with no capital. Meanwhile, Beth and the kids lived in a lovely home on the money he sent them.

Let me say that I don't minimize the wrong that Tim did. He should have paid more attention to his wife and kids, and he should have stayed with them. But Beth was letting her sense of vengeance poison her heart, and she was using the legal system to torment him. Tim's torment was far worse than he deserved, and Beth was changing into a spiteful creature. When Tim asked for a joint meeting with church leaders, she refused, on the advice of her lawyers. Meanwhile, the kids were quietly suffering in a home where all Mommy cared about was hurting Daddy.

I don't mean to paint lawyers in such an ugly hue. In a way, Beth's lawyer was just doing his job. But I feel he went too far, urging Beth to do as much as possible to hurt Tim. There are many good, decent lawyers, but the system by nature is adversarial. A case is *Someone versus Someone,* one pitted against another. Lawyers can easily make it a matter of winning and losing, hurting you before you hurt me.

You can't beat the system, they say, and that's true of divorce. You need a lawyer. Tim should have scraped up some money somehow to pay an attorney to represent his interests. He assumed that his ex-wife would be reasonable with him. He was wrong.

MISTAKES WE MAKE

When it comes to the legal handling of a divorce, Christians commonly make four mistakes.

1. *Some Christians seem to leave their faith at the lawyer's door.* Hurt and angry, they fight for every penny they can get without any attempt to be fair to their former spouses. Like Beth, they seem to be trying to administer punishment for all the pain they've been through. Revenge is their goal. If you remind them of Jesus' command to "turn the other cheek," they respond, "You don't understand what my ex did to me!"

2. Other Christians go the opposite way. Shell-shocked by the whole process, *they refuse to fight for anything.* "Here, take the house, take the kids, take the money. I don't need it." In some cases, they're stuck in denial, failing to face up to the need for fair distribution of property and rights. Or they may be playing a martyr role: "Someday my ex will see what a terrible thing this divorce is." And some Christians truly want to follow Jesus by giving rather than taking.

There is a healthy medium between these two extremes. The wise Christian will maintain a caring attitude but still seek justice. You don't need to spout venom at your ex, but you do need to make sure that you have a fair settlement. If children are involved, their needs certainly must be a high priority. But even if it's just you, you ought to make sure your legitimate needs are covered. Don't help your spouse mistreat you any more than he or she has already.

3. A third mistake Christians make is that *they sit back and let the lawyers handle it.* True, the legal world can be daunting, and you can't be expected to follow every procedural point. Yet you need to take leadership in establishing the tone and level of the divorce proceedings. Some sweet Christians hire bulldog lawyers to squeeze every dime from their ex-mates. The legal battles can go on for months, getting uglier and uglier. That is counterproductive (and expensive). Don't let the lawyers make your decisions. Take their advice, but make sure that the legal case you bring is handled in a Christian way.

A good lawyer will listen to you and respond to your desires about the case. If you want a quick settlement that's reasonably fair to both parties, your lawyer should be able to swing that (unless your ex and the other lawyer are totally unreasonable). But unscrupulous lawyers can drag a case on and keep billing you for their hours unless you exert some authority. Remember: this is *your* case. You are paying the lawyer to work for you. Don't be cowed into a decidedly unchristian strategy because your lawyer is pushing it.

4. The fourth major mistake Christians make is that *they fudge the details*. Poet Robert Frost wrote, "Good fences make good neighbors," and the same is true of divorce settlements. You need to have good boundaries in your final agreement. Yet because of all the emotions involved, people often take the details lightly. "I'll let her take the kids 'cause I'm sure she'll let me see them whenever I want." Well, maybe not. Things change; feelings change; people change. If your divorce settlement gives away some things that are precious to you, you may never get them back.

When Roger and Linda split up, the agreement divided their property fifty-fifty. They tried to sell the house so that they could split the equity, but the market was weak. Eventually, Roger bought her share of the house. But Linda and the kids didn't want to move, so he agreed to let them stay there for free. That was fine until two years later when Linda's boyfriend moved in. Roger was happy to let his ex-wife live there with their children, but he didn't want a moocher in on the deal. When he asked them to move out, the amicable divorce turned ugly, and the kids were hurt by it.

The problem was that they were fudging the details. Linda assumed the house was still hers, even though her ex-husband held the title. Roger assumed that they could always be one big happy family, even though he had moved out. The problems could have been prevented if they had come to some agreement in advance about the terms of living in the house.

Divorce settlements are designed to deal with the details, but the divorcing partners (especially Christians) often assume that niceness will prevail, regardless of what the documents say. Don't assume. If something is important to you, talk about it; get it in writing. Otherwise, you can never be sure of it.

With all that in mind, you're left in a quandary. Divorce is a legal matter, but it can't be *just* a legal matter. You will probably have to find a lawyer to guide you through the negotiations and court proceedings, and it's wise to find a good one. But you can't leave everything in your lawyer's hands. You want to be reasonable in dealing with your former spouse, but you shouldn't be too trusting. Ideally, you will show Christian love to everyone (including your ex) throughout the divorce proceedings, but the best way to do this is to seek fair and just arrangements for all concerned—including yourself.

Do you want to win your divorce case? Forget it. No one wins, except maybe the lawyers. Divorce is a bad business for both sides, and you need to recognize that. You may win a bunch of money, but you may also lose a bit of your soul. You may win custody of your kids, but you may also lose their love. This is a time when you need extraordinary wisdom to sort through all the issues and order your priorities.

MAKE IT YOUR OWN

➤ Which of the four common mistakes are you most likely to make?

❑ Leaving your Christianity at the lawyer's door

❑ Refusing to fight for anything

❑ Letting the lawyers handle it

❑ Fudging the details

➤ How can you avoid that mistake?_____

_____

_____

➤ Assuming the divorce will happen, and whether or not you instigated it, what do you wish would happen in the process of becoming legally divorced?

_____

_____

_____

FINDING A LAWYER[1]

Like it or not, you will need a lawyer. Family law varies from state to state, and the laws of each state change regularly. In recent years, we've seen an upheaval in family law, reflecting an upheaval in social attitudes about family relationships.

As a result, you need an expert who knows the law in your state and is up to date on recent changes. It would be terribly unwise to represent yourself or to turn to a well-meaning friend who has only a passing knowledge of the law. You need a real lawyer—and a good one.

How do you find the right lawyer? It isn't easy.

If you're choosing a doctor to see about a particular ailment, you can ask your local hospital for referrals to specialists in a particular field of medicine. But the field of law isn't like that. Though certain specialties—such as family law, corporate law, trial law, and so on—exist, these categories are not officially recognized. In most states, professional review boards do not give certification in specific legal fields. Once they've passed the bar exam, lawyers are free to pick any area of law in which they want to practice, without further training in that area and without any experience in it.

Not long ago, most lawyers were general practitioners, who would take on any legal need you had. But lately we've seen more and more lawyers restricting the areas in which they'll practice. As a result, fewer lawyers will handle a messy divorce. But some will, and they generally fall into four categories.

1. The new lawyer who has to take every case to make ends meet. Watch out for this one. He means well, but has little experience and may be wrong in his projections. If he works for an experienced family law attorney, someone can advise him. But if you go to a well-known attorney who refers you to his associate, be careful. The associate is probably pretty much on his own. His boss is too busy to keep an eye on him and doesn't want to.

2. The good old general practitioner. Some of these lawyers are surprisingly good at handling divorce cases. Many are not.

3. The semispecialist. This lawyer does only a few things, and divorce is one of them. This lawyer will likely be up to date and highly competent. She may not know quite as much as the true specialist, but the difference will be minimal in all but a few cases. She will also be considerably less expensive than the true specialist.

4. The true specialist. This group is growing all the time, mostly in urban and suburban areas, and it is the most expensive choice. While many true specialists are honest, reasonable individuals, some rarely try to really settle a case because their reputation is based on winning. Too many people suffering the trauma of a divorce fall prey to the image of the fighter, who won't stop until he wins their case. After spending many thousands of dollars, they finally learn that a divorce is not a battle to be won, but a complex circumstance to be settled fairly.

What to Look For

What should you look for as you choose an attorney to handle your divorce?

First, there is no substitute for *experience*. Litigation, negotiation, and counseling are all skills learned by experience, not out of a book. A minimum requirement is five years of experience in family law.

Experience also breeds the right sort of reputation, that is, how other lawyers see the lawyer. It is very important that opposing counsel respects your lawyer's competence both in and out of the courtroom. If this respect is not there, then you're not negotiating with a full hand. But be wary of lawyers with big reputations among the public at large; that sort of reputation will cost you an arm and a leg, and will probably not help you in court.

Second, there is *efficiency*. The biggest source of malpractice in this field is the inability of a lawyer to get his work done on time. Many lawyers are months behind, with work piled on their desks. Your lawyer's inefficiency problem quickly becomes your problem. A good lawyer must be able to get a day's work done in a day.

Good communication habits go along with this. You should receive a photocopy of every letter or document the lawyer gets that concerns your case, and it should be mailed to you within a day. You should also be informed immediately of every telephone call or conversation in the hallway of the courtroom that relates to your case. Obviously, only an efficient lawyer can do this.

Third, the lawyer should have the *commitment* to find the quickest, least expensive, and fairest resolution of your case, by negotiation if possible. So should you. Get rid of the idea that going to court will vindicate your sense of justice. It almost never does. The sooner a settlement can be reached, the sooner your level of emotional trauma and uncertainty will be brought under control.

You want your lawyer to be committed to *you,* someone who will listen to your unique concerns and not pursue the case in a way that might be detrimental to your life in the future. If your lawyer takes a cookie-cutter approach to your case, just going through the motions without paying attention to you, get a new lawyer.

But last, the lawyer should be able to maintain *objectivity,* which may seem like a lack of compassion and concern. A lawyer should listen to your desires, but then give you a reasonable picture of how the system works. You may not get everything you want, and your lawyer needs to tell you that. Don't think badly of your attorney for telling you what you need to hear. You don't want a surgeon bursting into tears before operating on you. In the same way, a lawyer won't help you if she gets as emotionally involved in the case as you are.

A good attorney cuts through the whole dramatic story and finds the 1 percent with legal relevance. This is a counselor *at law,* not a psychological counselor. He isn't trained to hold hands; he is trained to find solutions to legal problems.

On the Hunt

So, how do you find such a person? People seek lawyers in many ways, but the best way is to ask other lawyers. Nobody can better judge a lawyer than other lawyers who have tried cases against her and negotiated with her. If you will call three lawyers who advertise in the yellow pages that they handle family law, and ask each one to identify the most competent divorce lawyers in their locality, you will probably notice that you are hearing the same names. If the lawyer tells you that he is the best, he might be right.

Other ways of selecting a lawyer include state bar referral systems and referrals by professional organizations. The American Bar Association and state bar associations have family law sections. If you are seeking a true specialist, this may be the best source. The Christian Legal Society also maintains a list of member attorneys, including the areas of practice for each.

Word-of-mouth referrals may tell you a lot about an attorney's manner, but probably very little about true competence. Above all, don't compare your case to somebody else's. Most clients misunderstand key legal elements of their cases, and they can pass on inaccurate impressions of their lawyers.

Many Christians feel most comfortable hiring a Christian attorney, and that's fine—*if the attorney is a good one.* But don't skimp on quality. It's wiser to hire a non-Christian lawyer who will handle your case well than a Christian lawyer who won't. Still, you may find special trust and rapport with a Christian lawyer, and these feelings are valuable if you can also trust the lawyer's ability.

You need to trust the lawyer you choose, Christian or not. You can't afford to be suspicious of your lawyer's motives or ability. The lawyer who knows her client trusts her will usually work harder than the one who feels suspicion and mistrust.

Paying for It

A word about fees. Virtually all attorneys handle contested divorce cases on an hourly fee basis and require a retainer paid in advance. Rates vary; don't be afraid to shop around. But remember that a lower hourly fee usually means a less-experienced lawyer, and a flat fee from a clinic usually means a secretary will know your case better than the lawyer does. The true specialist will have the highest fee.

The lawyer you select should be able to provide you regularly with a detailed billing statement itemizing every action taken and the time and cost associated with it. It's wise to insist on this and to review it carefully. Don't expect a cheap divorce, and be prepared to pay what it costs. Many people have to borrow the amount of the retainer. Good competent legal advice can be worth many times its cost in property settlement or support figures. And what price can be put on those noneconomic factors concerning custody and visitation of minor children? It's far wiser indeed to pay now what it's really worth and not second-guess the legal services than it is to seek a bargain and later question whether you made a big mistake.

Remember, however, that whatever you resolve on your own, or mediate with a neutral party, will be less time your lawyer will have to spend on your case. The deliberate escalation of the hostilities will bring with it a high cost to all parties.

MAKE IT YOUR OWN

➤ How will you find a lawyer (if you don't have one yet)? _____

_____

_____

➤ How much can you afford to spend on legal representation? _____

_____

_____

➤ How will you ensure that the lawyer remains responsive to your needs and wishes? _____

_____

_____

MEDIATION[2]

When Craig and Julia decided to divorce, they agreed that their children would be their top priority. With that in mind, they didn't want to go through an ugly divorce case. They sought an alternative: mediation.

Increasingly, divorcing couples are seeking this calmer and cheaper way to hammer out a divorce agreement. As we've said, our adversarial legal system makes people enemies whether they want to be or not. The point of mediation is to avoid that, to reduce the hostility. Lawyers are still involved, because legal rights are at issue, but the lawyers don't drive the process. The mediator asks questions and the clients make decisions that satisfy both parties. When it works, it's a win-win situation.

If you're serious about this option, it's best to start early before the legal machine gets going. As soon as you've decided you'll seek a divorce, call a mediator to see if that process will work for you.

If you already have a lawyer you know and trust, you could ask him or her about mediation. Perhaps your lawyer could recommend a qualified mediator. The problem is, many lawyers aren't crazy about mediation. It's their competition, for one thing. But some are justifiably concerned about the quality of mediators' advice. Since the mediation business is just starting to set standards for training and procedures, some lawyers don't trust it yet.

So if you want to try mediation, call a qualified mediator first. He or she can then recommend mediation-friendly lawyers who can represent you.

Finding a Qualified Mediator

How do you know a mediator is qualified? In some states, practically anybody can set up a shingle as a mediator, but some professional organizations are setting standards. Contact the Academy of Family Mediators (4 Militia Drive, Lexington, MA 02173; 617-674-2663) or the family law section of your state bar association for names of mediators in your area. When you talk with a mediator, ask about his or her training. Be sure the person has gone through at least a forty-hour course on mediation.

Most mediators start out as either psychologists or lawyers before getting the specific mediation training. The psychologists tend to be more effective handling questions about children, while the lawyer-mediators do better with property distribution. For this reason, some mediators work as a team, offering both specialties to the same clients.

Be careful about a nonprofessional, untrained mediator. For instance, your pastor may be very wise and helpful, but mediators are trained to stay neutral and to handle many specific details your pastor may not know about. Through the mediation process, you'll be crafting a legally binding divorce document, so you want to be sure it's done right.

Craig and Julia called a mediator who works out of my counseling office and scheduled an initial meeting—two meetings actually. Most mediators will hold the first meeting with each partner separately. That helps the mediator get both perspectives on the issues and screen the couple for any red flags that would doom the process from the start.

Red Flags

Five red flags would keep a mediator from taking a case. The first is obvious: *both parties must want mediation*. If one partner refuses to come to the first session, nothing can be done. But if the reluctant spouse can be convinced to go one time, when the advantages of mediation would be discussed, he or she might be won over.

The second red flag? *A severe power imbalance*. Each person has to be able to speak for himself or herself. If one of the people can't express basic needs, the process won't work. Mediation is a needs-based negotiation, not a position-based negotiation. Both parties must communicate their needs in order to find the best way to meet the needs of both.

A third red flag is *physical abuse*. The mediation process will stir up some nasty issues, and couples often leave some sessions in anger. If there is a history of physical violence, such conversations can be downright dangerous.

Substance abuse is a fourth prohibitive problem, and *mental illness* is a fifth. As with physical abuse, there is some danger that the heated discussions could make these problems worse. But more important, these problems are probably central to the couple's breakup, and they go beyond the mediator's ability.

Exploring the Issues

At the first meetings, Craig and Julia separately filled out a questionnaire, asking about those red-flag issues; how decisions had been made in the home; what they'd like to see happen; and which issues they thought would be easiest and hardest to resolve. (The mediator would probably want to start with the easiest issues.)

Craig and Julia were together for all the remaining sessions. In their second session, they made a master list of the issues that their divorce agreement would need to cover. These included parenting, finances, insurance, property, debt, and taxes.

Beginning with the third meeting, they tackled these issues in all the nuts and bolts. Mediators are trained to ask questions, but not to suggest answers. It's up to the couple to figure out the best way to keep both happy.

Though Craig and Julia were committed to their children's well-being, their discussions got rather heated when they hit the property and financial issues. More than once, they left in anger. But they kept coming back to hammer out their agreement.

The mediators will keep scheduling sessions until all the issues are resolved. A few couples can zoom through them in four or five sessions. Others take twenty or more. The end result is an agreement that is handed to lawyers for their stamp of approval and signed by all the parties. Usually, it's a solution that sees both partners treated fairly. After all, they're the ones who created it.

Craig and Julia took about ten sessions to work out their differences, and they were pleased with the final agreement. Best of all, they remained friends through the process, cooperating fully in the care of their children. Though the letter of their agreement gives Craig every other weekend with the kids, Julia doesn't mind if he takes one of them out midweek for some quality time. They can practice flexibility in the details of their agreement because they trust each other. That trust was never shattered by an ugly legal conflict.

It's just a shame they couldn't get along that well when they were married.

Once in a while, the process of expressing needs and reaching agreement breathes new life into a relationship. They've never been able to communicate like that before, and now that they can, maybe they can make things work. A wise mediator will sense this and ask the couple if they want to drop the mediation, get some marriage counseling, and stay together.

No such happy ending for Craig and Julia, and don't count on it in your case. But at least mediation can keep you and your spouse from dragging your personal pain through the court system. It's a safer environment where you can discover solutions that will work for both of you.

MAKE IT YOUR OWN

➤ Is mediation an option for you? _____

➤ How will you find a mediator? _____

_____

What issues do you think will be easiest to resolve?_____

_____

_____

 What issues do you think will be the hardest to resolve? _____

_____

_____

Part 2

PICKING UP
THE PIECES

Chapter 5

※

SINGLE AGAIN
REENTRY INTO THE SINGLE LIFE

Let's talk chronology. We started this workbook by looking at the stages of recovery. Then we discussed separation. When do the stages of grieving start: during separation, or after the divorce, or when?

It all depends. The stages of denial, anger, bargaining, and so on may start even *before* the separation. A friend told me of her struggles with an alcoholic husband. She went through all the stages with that, and the process *ended* with her asking for a divorce. She had come to a point of accepting what she felt she had to do.

The case of Pam, from Chapter 2, is similar. She went through those stages *during* the separation. Finally, she came to terms with what was happening, called her husband to take responsibility for his role in the marriage, and ultimately accepted the situation by filing for divorce. The timing of your stages of recovery depends largely on when the shock hits you.

You may go through an entire separation blithely assuming that you'll get back together, and when that doesn't happen, that may be when the recovery process begins.

But let's say you've made it through most of the stages of recovery, and you're moving toward a point of acceptance. As I've said before, you'll slip back down the slippery slope every so often, but you have generally come to terms with your divorce. What's next?

Reentry. Somehow, you have to resume your life. And it will be a different life from what you're used to. You're single again. You're also older, wiser, and injured. The climb up the slippery slope toward acceptance is only half the struggle. Rebuilding your self-image and relationships and faith—that's what needs to happen next.

"WHO AM I, ANYWAY?"

I never had much sympathy for people who complained about "identity crises." Whenever someone would whine, "I don't know who I am anymore," I'd think it was the silliest thing I'd ever heard.

"It's obvious who you are," I'd say, and I'd go on to mention a few things I knew about the person. I had very little patience for that sort of emotional disorientation.

But then I had a massive identity crisis of my own. I didn't know who I was.

Oh, I could still fill out the forms. Name, address, Social Security number. But deep inside me, it seemed there was no bedrock anymore, no place where I could put my foot down and it wouldn't move. Everything was in transition. *This is where I want to be,* I'd think, but then it wouldn't be what it used to be.

My sense of who I was had been forged by my relationships, by my work, by my faith. With my divorce, that all had vanished. No wife, no job, very little faith, and only a couple of my old friends. Everything that made me *me* was gone.

This reaction is not unusual. Any crisis shakes our self-awareness to some extent, but the ripping apart of our most intimate relationships is devastating. This is especially true of women, who often learn to define themselves in terms of their connections with others. But when the other goes away, what's left? If you're not Mrs. Smith anymore, who are you?

The first struggle of reentry is a struggle of *identity*. You must radically redefine yourself. That takes some reorientation, some digging, some shoring up. It sounds a bit hokey these days to say you have to "get in touch with yourself," but that's the idea. You need to take the time to listen to yourself, to pay attention to your unique interests, talents, desires, and personality traits. Gain a new awareness of yourself completely apart from the old relationship.

"Am I Any Good?"

Many of us reenter with a poor self-concept. As we begin to put our identity back together, we become painfully aware of all the bad things. After all, we've just been rejected by the ones who supposedly knew us best. We must not be worth very much—or so we tend to think.

In my case, I felt like a complete failure. The most important thing in my life—my family, my home—had fallen apart. And I thought to myself, *If I couldn't keep that together, then what* can *I do? What good am I?*

I'm not talking about a week or a month after my wife left. I'm talking about *years* later. I had finally accepted my situation and was working on my graduate degrees in counseling—and *still* the self-doubt was afflicting me. I even remember thinking, *If anybody knew that I couldn't keep my marriage together, why would they ever come to me for counseling?* I felt like a total washout.

And that affected everything I did. Whenever I entered a new situation, I already felt like a failure. Have you experienced that too? You walk into a room, and you think, *These people don't care about me. They don't want to hear what I have to say. This person doesn't care how I feel. Everything I say is so stupid.* In the normal ebb and flow of life, every insult gets magnified a hundred times over, and we tend to downplay whatever praise and affirmation we get.

As we rebuild our lives, we must not only reidentify ourselves, but also accept ourselves. We may have reached the stage of acceptance by accepting our *situation*, but accepting ourselves is a different story. That may be even harder to do.

This low self-esteem hobbles us as we attempt to reenter society. We are not seeing anything—the world or ourselves or even God—as it really is. We are skewing everything to conform to our negative view of ourselves. That's dangerous. Low self-esteem can lead to twisted relationships. We can rebound into encounters with those who affirm us, but we never really trust them. We tend to use others and let others use us. These unhealthy relationships are quite common in the lives of the newly separated and divorced.

You may know people who are stuck at this point. They have never rebuilt their self-image after a divorce, and now they're bitter, timid, withdrawn, desperate, and extremely vulnerable.

So be careful. Stay away from the voices that will tear you down. Find the friends who will build you up. Start your inner pattern of encouragement. When you look at yourself in the morning, say, "I'm not a failure. I'm a unique individual, created in God's image. I have a lot to offer!"

The Elijah Syndrome

Divorce is an incredibly lonely experience. That's ironic when you consider that nearly half of the marriages in the United States end in divorce. But when you're splitting up, you're sure that no one else feels as you do.

I like to call this the Elijah syndrome. In the Bible, the prophet Elijah was struggling against an evil king and queen. Queen Jezebel was out to kill him, and Elijah was on the run. He was also severely depressed. "There is no one," he complained, "who is not worshiping idols. I am left alone, and they're trying to murder me!" (1 Kings 19:10, my paraphrase).

Well, maybe you're not dodging assassination plots, but you probably know this feeling. The irony is that with the divorce, you've lost the person closest to you. The person who *should* be there to understand you, to commiserate with and support you, is gone—and that's the whole problem! It gets worse when people try to give you advice. "What are you moping around for? It has been six weeks now. Come on. Get on with your life." And you think, *I must be crazy because it has been six weeks and I'm still heading downhill.*

And if you watch anything on television about people who have been through divorce, you feel even stranger. It's so far from reality. I just wish they'd put on a show that showed the reality of divorce. Most divorced people on TV are separated one day and then back in action the next. They seem free to enjoy a great single life. TV makes it seem as if hundreds of eligible people of the opposite sex are just dying to go out with you. No loneliness. No pain. No strings attached to new relationships.

And I'm going home to my empty house, sinking into my easy chair with a bowl of cereal, and flicking on reruns of *The Love Boat*. On the tube, every passenger is finding the love of his life in one weekend cruise. And I'm thinking, *I must be weird. My life isn't like that. I'm dying inside. There must be something wrong with me.*

Remember Elijah, sitting and complaining? Well, God answered him by assuring him that there were six thousand people in Israel who were on his side. He was not alone after all.

> ### *Every year* more than one million Americans go through a divorce.

As I speak in Fresh Start Seminars, I sometimes stop and ask whether anyone is relating to the feelings I'm describing. Invariably, a sea of hands goes up. Then I ask people to look around. "Here are people feeling the same frustrations that you are," I say. "You are not alone." That in itself is worth the price of admission.

If you've been thinking, *I must be the only one who's not out having a good time,* I've got news for you. You've been watching too much TV. I've seen at least ten thousand divorced people in the seminars I've led, and they're not going on cruise ships and finding the men and women of their dreams. They're working through recovery. And that takes a long time and a lot of work.

So relax. You're not crazy. You're not alone.

MAKE IT YOUR OWN

➤ Do you feel you are ready for reentry? That is, have you passed through the stages of recovery and reached a point of acceptance of your new lifestyle?

_____

_____

_____

➤ If not, when would you estimate that you would be ready for reentry?

_____

_____

(*Note:* It's important that you not rush things. Going through this section of the workbook may tempt you to rush into reentry when you're not ready. You may want to skim this section now and return to it later.)

➤ Who are you? Start writing some things about yourself: name, age, job, schooling, address, and so on. _____

_____

_____

_____

➤ What personality traits do you have? List three things that you like about yourself, and then three things that you don't like or wish that you could change.

Likes	*Dislikes*
1. _____	1. _____
2. _____	2. _____
3. _____	3. _____

➤ Between the likes and dislikes you just listed, which list was easier for you to write? In other words, did you find it easier to think of things you liked about yourself or things that you disliked about yourself? Perhaps your answer will give you some insight into your self-image._____

_____

_____

➤ What activities do you enjoy? What are your talents?_____

_____

_____

_____

➤ What are your most important relationships? _____

_____

_____

➤ Choose one of the people you just listed. In twenty-five words or less, how would that person describe you? Call this person and ask for a brief description of you. Write it down here. _____

_____

_____

_____

_____

➤ What is your best personal quality? (Some options, among many, are loyalty, love, humor, tenacity, good listener, intelligence, humility, spirituality.)

_____

_____

➤ Is there some area of knowledge in which you know more than the average person? What is it? _____

_____

_____

➤ On a scale of 1 to 10 (10 being extremely), how lonely have you felt since your divorce? _____

➤ Have you talked to others recently in similar situations? If so, who?

_____

➤ If we called together a hundred people at random from your town, how many of them do you think would understand how you feel right now? _____

➤ How many do you think would be experiencing the same amount of emotional pain or worse? _____

➤ How many do you think would consider themselves failures? _____

TORN BETWEEN TWO TROUBLES

So what's the cure for loneliness?

Being with people, right? Well, if you are in those early stages of recovery or reentry, you know better. There is nothing *more* lonely than being in a crowd of people and feeling as if you're totally alone. The party may go on around you, but you're not a part of it. You may even be talking and laughing with people, but inside you're thinking, *They don't really know me. I don't belong here.*

I went through that. For quite a while, I felt a tremendous sense of ambivalence. I needed people desperately—but they scared me to death.

This tension stems from two God-given instincts. On the one hand, we need to be loved. We need to be considered valuable by others. On the other hand, we need to protect ourselves. We have just been clobbered emotionally by this divorce thing, and all our instincts tell us to run and hide. People can hurt.

I would find myself at a social event, feeling very "out of it." You may know this feeling too. You walk into a room full of people, and you immediately look for the exits. You want to sit near the edges or in the back so you can always make a quick getaway if things get a little bit uncomfortable.

I dealt with others on a surface level; I wasn't investing myself in anyone. That would be too dangerous. I was terrified that someone would ask me a probing, penetrating question like "How are you?" I felt as if there was a big red *D* on my chest, and that everyone was avoiding me or pitying me because I was *divorced*.

So the whole event was unsatisfying to me. It was teasing me. People were close enough to offer the love and affirmation I needed, but I couldn't let them do that because I'd have to open up my heart, and I might get clobbered again. The two opposing instincts—my need for love and my need for self-protection—taunted me. It was like having somebody knock on the front door and the back door at the same time. You don't know which way to turn.

Often I would leave the social events early just to get out of that pressure. But then where would I go? Home? To my lonely place? No love and affirmation were there. Sometimes I drove around and around, just as my emotions were going around and around on the inside. My ambivalence had me trapped.

Do you know those feelings? A kind of weariness goes with them. It's an endless chase, and it wears you out.

The Way We're Made

What's the answer? It starts by accepting both feelings as gifts of God. You may feel very odd when you're dealing with these conflicting emotions, but that is the way God made you.

You see, the need for other people was created when God created us. The Bible says that we are created "in His own image" (Gen. 1:26–27 NKJV). What does that mean? God is a Trinity—Father, Son, and Holy Spirit, wrapped up in one Being, constantly communing with one another. (God said, "Let *Us* make man in *Our* image.") So God is a God of fellowship, a God of relationships. To be made in God's image, then, is to *need other people*. Nothing is wrong with that!

We get another clue a chapter later in Genesis. God had created the world, at each stage declaring it "good." Then he made Adam and put him in charge of it all. But suddenly, God said, "It is not good for the man to be alone" (2:18 NIV), and so he made Eve. From the start, then, God intended for human beings to relate to one another. Remember, Adam walked with God in the Garden of Eden, but he still needed other people in his life. (By the way, I don't believe this means that God wants everyone to be married; 1 Corinthians 7 indicates otherwise.)

So when people say, "All you need is God. You're a single parent. Don't worry about it. God will be there for you"—well, that's nice, but they don't understand. You need other people in your life. Not a new spouse, but *friends,* people to talk to and listen to, people who will love and appreciate you. That's a God-given need.

But God also gives us the wisdom to shield ourselves from emotional disaster. We've been wounded and we need to recover. If you break your arm, what does the doctor do? Puts it in a cast. Why? To immobilize it. It needs to heal. It needs to be out of action for a while.

Well, your heart has just taken a pounding. You might even say it has been broken. You need to put it in a cast. You need to immobilize it for a while. That means drawing back, protecting, shielding yourself from involvement in relationships.

Sometimes you'll see people who try to deal with their divorce without this self-protective instinct. They say, "Hey, I'm so glad I finally got that divorce out of the way. I can dive right into life again. I'm going to have a blast." You can see the denial a mile away. They need to pull back, protect themselves, but they're out there saying, "No problem! It's been a whole two months since my divorce. I'm okay!"

But they're not okay. In fact, they're in *more* danger because they refuse to accept their "injuries" and immobilize their wounded hearts. If you try to use your broken heart in new relationships, the result will be the same as when you try to use a broken arm—it will cause you more pain.

If you find yourself putting up walls of self-defense, great! That's a healthy option at this point. You are extremely vulnerable. Proper healing requires that you understand your vulnerability and allow for it.

Vulnerability

In my case, I was extremely sensitive emotionally. I suddenly had an overkeen *sense of justice. I* had been wronged, and so I felt moral indignation at every act of injustice I learned about. I couldn't watch the evening news. It would stir me up to hear Dan Rather talking about dictators mistreating peasants or a murderer getting off on a technicality. I'd throw things; I'd pace up and down; I'd think, *This world stinks!*

This same sensitivity crept into my personal life. I was quick to feel mistreated over the slightest misunderstanding. You may be like that now, or you may know others like that. We go around with a chip on our shoulders, daring the world to knock it off. The healing process involves a slow putting down of the boxing gloves. Slowly, we learn to give people the benefit of the doubt.

During my reentry, I was also quick to feel *sorrow*. I couldn't watch *Little House on the Prairie* without bawling like a baby. At the time, I thought, *I must be going crazy. I can't control myself.* Any little thing could push a button. All I'd have to see was a happy family, with a dog by the hearth, and right away I'd start crying.

That can be cyclical. Our emotional instability makes us think we're crazy, which further convinces us that we'll never have a home like the one on *Little House.* The healing process involves a certain distancing from those things that make us cry. *It's only a TV show,* we can learn to say to ourselves. *My life is different from that, but it's okay.*

It may sound silly, but you may need to stop watching upsetting TV shows for a while. Or avoid going to weepy movies. Don't toy with your vulnerability. As you ease your way back to health, you can resume some of these "normal" activities, but in the meantime, recognize your need for protection, and avoid stimuli that will wound you further.

Recognize also that your sense of self-protection may make you very *selfish* for a while. You will be focusing on your own needs (and probably unaware of the needs of others). That happened to me, and it strained one of my best friendships.

Through my whole ordeal, I had one friend who stayed with me. He kept calling me and didn't let me get away with locking the doors and unplugging the phone. He kept calling and saying, "Why don't you come over? You can watch TV, have dinner, talk if you want, sleep here if you want, do whatever you want. Just come over."

He kept bugging me, "Just come over. You don't have to do anything. You don't have to say anything." He hung in there with me. Little by little, I began to pour out my emotions to him—how unfair everything had been and how people had hurt me and how God was such a terrible God that he would allow these things to happen. My friend just listened.

Looking back on that, I realize that I never once said, "Well, how are *you* doing?" My whole focus was on me. That's part of the self-protection. I was very needy, very vulnerable. They must have provided me with twenty or more meals, and I never said, "Hey, how about you guys coming over to my place and I'll cook you a meal."

One of the first signs of my healing was that I became aware of my selfishness. I suddenly began to say, "You know, if I ever get healthy again, I'd like to do something for these friends of mine." I was already planning my road to recovery.

Let's go back to the arm-breaking analogy. When you first break your arm, it hurts a lot. Then, as it heals, it's in a cast, and it feels uncomfortable. You complain a lot. You're focusing on your pain, your inconvenience, but that's okay. You have a right to complain. But suddenly, you turn a corner. You start counting the days until the cast comes off. You start thinking about what you'll do when you have the use of your arm again. That's where I was as my emotions were healing.

One other expression of self-protection is *pride*. That seems illogical when so many suffer from low self-esteem. But the mind plays funny games with us. We tend to overcompensate for our internal self-hate with external self-assurance.

In my case, I found it very hard to admit that I needed help. I was hiding out at first. I was going to a singles group at the new church I was attending, and I knew about the Fresh Start program for divorced people, but I didn't go to their meetings. I was determined to make it on my own. It was safer that way. I was going to shut everyone out of my life. I was a rock; I was an island. No one was ever going to hurt me again.

I was compensating for my pain with bravado. I didn't want to admit my weakness. I didn't want to admit that I might need some help. I still felt too vulnerable.

MAKE IT YOUR OWN

➤ Of these two instincts—the need to relate to others and the need to protect yourself—which is stronger now? _____

_____

➤ When have you most recently sensed your need to relate to others?

_____

➤ When have you most recently sensed your need to protect yourself?

_____

➤ In what ways are you vulnerable? _____

_____

➤ What examples of selfishness have you been noticing in your life?

_____

_____

➤ What examples of pride have you been noticing in your life?

_____

_____

➤ Do you think these are understandable, considering what you've been through? Or do you think they're excessive? Why? _____

_____

_____

➤ As you look forward to the time when you're healthy again, what would you like to do for someone else? Be specific. _____

_____

_____

Action Point: As you think about the kind of friend you are now and compare that with what you would like to be later on when you're more healed, what do you need to change about yourself to accomplish that? Write what you specifically would like to change about the way you relate to your friends.

_____

_____

➤ Write this same goal on page 282 (Appendix A) for future reference as part of your personalized action plan.

THE BALANCING ACT

How can we deal with all this vulnerability? How do we balance our need for others with our need to protect ourselves? Basically, we need to learn how to take calculated risks. Emotional wholeness comes to those who learn how to balance proper risks with proper cautions. Let me emphasize: *proper* risks and *proper* cautions. Many take foolish risks—like rebound romances—or observe needless cautions—hiding away for years. But by keeping the two instincts in balance, we can edge our way back to wholeness.

The first risk that you may have to take, as I did, is *seeking help.* Maybe that starts with this workbook. It may involve going to a Fresh Start Seminar, getting involved with a church, or seeing a counselor. It may be difficult, but it's a risk worth taking.

As I mentioned, I was too proud (or too vulnerable) to seek help. As it turned out, I never had to. The singles pastor at my church asked me to help out at a Fresh Start Seminar, not even knowing that I had been through a divorce. (Fearing rejection, I had kept quiet about my divorce.)

"We're looking for facilitators for Fresh Start," he said. "And I hear you're a counselor, working in the schools, leading groups for children of divorce. We usually like for our facilitators to have gone through divorce, but we'd like for you to come and help out anyway."

Not knowing what to say, I gave the good Christian answer: "Well, let me pray about that and get back to you." Only later, after a lot of soul-searching, did I tell him I really was divorced. There was that needless caution again. It made no sense! The founder of a ministry to divorced people, *looking for* divorced people to lead the ministry, and I was afraid what he would think if I told him I was divorced.

When I finally told him, his face lit up. "That's great! Boy, now that I know that, we could use you in a lot more ways."

Wait a minute, I thought. *"That's great?" How can anything good come out of something so terrible?* It took a long time for that idea to sink in.

And so it was that I came to Fresh Start to help others. But as I sat there, I told myself, *Tom, you're not even close to being ready to help anyone else. You need to be here for you.* As I soaked in all the teaching, I began to process what I had been through. Even then, three years after my divorce, I had never come to terms with a lot of it.

That was another major step in my recovery, putting down my pride long enough to get the help I needed. I think it's especially difficult for men, thanks to the "macho" image our society keeps promoting. Men aren't supposed to have needs. They just get back in the saddle and ride into the sunset, muttering,

"Women, who needs 'em?" But that's stupid. Men and women alike need to take the courageous risk of reaching out for the emotional help they need.

Go Slow

So that's a proper risk. What about a proper caution? Here it is. Don't expect to make your reentry overnight. Go slow.

That will be frustrating, but be patient. Research shows that it takes three to five years to learn to trust again, to fully reenter society. (I talked about a two-year period before. That's how long you can expect to be recovering from the grief of divorce, attaining a level of acceptance. But it's usually another year or more before you can really turn your attention outward again, restoring relationships and overcoming vulnerability. It's a long, slow road.)

In a way it's like a lingering illness. You lie in bed thinking, *This is stupid. I don't want to be sick. I should go to work. Why am I not better? It's been long enough. I should be better.* You get angry at the sickness; it just doesn't make sense. But it's there. You're still sick. You just have to let it run its course.

Divorce recovery happens over a long period of time. That doesn't mean you are totally incapacitated. You can still have fun with others; you can still learn new things about yourself, other people, and relationships. But all the while you're still vulnerable. Any little thing can set you back. Don't be surprised when that happens. Don't be disappointed. Be glad for the progress you *are* making, and don't expect too much.

MAKE IT YOUR OWN

➤ What have you done so far to seek help for your divorce recovery?

❑ Talked with friends

❑ Became involved with a church group

❑ Sought counseling from a minister

❑ Sought counseling from a psychologist/psychiatrist

❑ Attended a recovery seminar

❑ Read books on the subject

❑ Other: _____

_____

➤ If you haven't sought help, why not? _____

_____

_____

➤ What specific thing could you do in the next month to reach out for help?

_____

_____

➤ How would you describe your expectations for recovery?

❏ I'll be all better in the next few months.

❏ I am getting better each day, with some relapses.

❏ It will be another year or two before I'm at full strength emotionally.

❏ I can't imagine myself ever getting over this.

❏ Other: _____

_____

ON THE REBOUND

About three years after my divorce, I started dating a woman I met in the singles group at church. I still wasn't heavily involved in the group, but it was somewhere to go, and it seemed safe. And I hit it off with this woman.

She was a very giving person. She was Italian—I don't know if that had anything to do with it, but any time I went to her house, the first thing she'd say was: "Can I make you something to eat?" It wouldn't matter what time of day it was: "Can I make you something to eat?"

It would be ten o'clock at night, and I'd say, "Well, yeah, a little something."

"How about veal cutlets? I'll just whip them up here."

Here was a person who wanted to meet my needs. And I had a lot of needs, so I was attracted to that. Psychologist Larry Crabb describes it as being like a tick on a dog. The relationship was based entirely on need meeting.

Maybe three months into the relationship, she said, "You know, Tom, I'm wondering where this relationship is going."

My answer was, unfortunately, typical: "Hey, why ruin a good thing? I'm having a good time. You're having a good time. Aah, let's not ruin it by getting serious."

Six months into the relationship, eight months, the question kept coming: "You know, Tom, I really care about you, but I don't want to get hurt. I just need to have some idea of where this relationship is going."

"Hey, don't worry about it. Let's not ruin it. Let's just have a good time. We enjoy each other. Let's not talk about anything serious."

What was going on? Obviously, I was scared. I was afraid to make any kind of commitment. I didn't want to trust this person. I wasn't trying to take advantage of her, but somehow my heart wasn't functioning right. Though I sort of knew that, I still couldn't describe what was going on. All I knew was, I was having a good time. I felt really good about it. It was nice to have somebody who cared for me. I was taking far more than I was giving. And I knew I wasn't ready for commitment.

Well, after about a year—you can probably guess how it turned out—she said, "Look, if you can't tell me where we're going, I don't know that I can continue this relationship."

And of course I responded, "Hey, I don't need that kind of pressure. If you can't just enjoy the relationship, then I'm outta here."

That hurt both of us, but I learned something. Even though it was three years after my divorce, I obviously wasn't healed. But I thought I was. Yet when I tried to use my heart again, I found out it still didn't work right.

You may be finding this out the hard way. You are in a relationship based on need, but your heart isn't healed. Sometimes we think these relationships will do the healing for us, but it seldom works that way.

You see, you're still wounded. You are a different person from the person you'll be two or five or ten years from now. Right now, your emotions, your priorities, and your needs are all twisted. You are moving back toward health, but you're not there yet.

At the moment, then, you're attracted to anybody who strokes your damaged areas. And there are lots of damaged areas. You probably feel rejected, and it's glorious to be accepted by someone, to be wanted. You may feel rejected sexually—you're afraid you're too ugly or not sexy enough. And when someone comes by who finds you sexy, that seems to be just what the doctor ordered. For the moment, it may be satisfying. Just like my veal cutlets. But the danger is that the damaged area gets too much attention, and so your relationship is tilted unhealthily in that direction.

Seek Honest Friendships

I've been talking about proper risks to take and proper cautions to avoid. Here's a pair that go hand in hand: you need to take the risk of finding true friends; you also need to avoid rebound romances.

You need people who can love you for who you are, people who can accept you. Your most basic emotional needs are not romance and sexual fulfillment, as the talk shows keep telling us, but security and significance. You need to have relationships in which you know you are accepted. That's security. And you need to have friends who care about you, whose lives you can touch. That's significance. The safest place to find these things is in honest nonromantic friendships.

And that's a risk! Your heart is still vulnerable. It's not easy to open up to others, to let them care for you, and to care for them in return. You've been hurt. There's a lot of fear in you, but this is worth the risk. Solid friendships are the most important boost toward wholeness.

But avoid romance. You may not like to read that, but romance is fraught with pitfalls for someone recovering from divorce. It is tempting because it promises to massage your wounded areas. But it will probably wound you again.

This is one pitfall of having a poor self-image. When someone starts to pay attention to you, it's hard to keep it in perspective. Either you run and hide or—voilà!—"I've found the love of my life!"

I went through that myself. If a woman paid any attention to me at all, I got heart palpitations and began fantasizing about what a great relationship we'd have. I may not have even spoken with her yet, but already in my mind we'd be marching down the aisle.

Remember the analogy of the broken arm? Well, my heart was still broken. My whole identity was broken. And I needed to immobilize my romantic inclinations, to put them in a cast. If you don't immobilize a broken arm, it's liable to heal crooked. The same is true of your heart.

Too many people these days are walking around with crooked hearts. They've been shattered by divorce, but they think, *What I need is to get back in action again*. And so they get shattered all over again.

> **You need to move forward *slowly* in the reentry process. Learn to be comfortable with yourself, and don't look to other relationships to make you whole again.**

It is even more tempting because society keeps forcing romance on you. Sometimes it's your family. I often hear people say, "My parents are always trying to set me up. They invite me over for dinner with the guy next door, or someone from the office, or the man that they think is so nice from the church group." They're convinced that you are half a person until you marry again, so they want to set you up with somebody right away. They don't understand that the emptiness in your life is far deeper than one person can fill, no matter how wonderful that person is. You need to rediscover *yourself*. You need to bandage your heart. You need to learn how to love again.

That happened to me. People at work kept saying, "Oh, you're young, and you have a full life ahead of you. There are plenty of fish in the sea. Just go out and find someone else." But somewhere inside me I was saying, *You know, that's the last thing in the world I need, to go out and find someone else. I need to get* myself *together*.

I've heard dozens of horror stories about rebound romances. "I've been in, like, a dozen relationships in five years," one woman told me, "and they all seem to go the same way. At first I figured there were just too many horrible men out there. But now I'm beginning to think, *Maybe there's something in here that's not working right*. Do you think that could be?"

I asked her to tell me more. "Well, about two months after my original divorce, I got involved with this guy, and that didn't last, and two months after that I got involved with another, and well, I've never gone more than six months without somebody. I've always needed somebody in my life. What do I do about it?"

"Go back to your original divorce," I said, "and work through those issues. If you don't, you're just going to take the same issues into the next relationship and the next relationship. You've got to stop and put your heart in a cast, and then go back and work on the original issues. Don't rely on a romance to fix you up. You have to fix yourself."

As long as you are counting on a romantic relationship to make you whole, you will not be whole. As long as you feel you *need* to be remarried, you're not ready for remarriage. When you know that you're able to live a full, healthy life on your own, only then will you be able to enter a marriage as a giver and taker, as a full partner.

MAKE IT YOUR OWN

➤ What qualities do you want in a friend?_____
_____
_____

➤ What people do you know who could provide the friendship you need to get back to wholeness? _____
_____

➤ How will you go about communicating your need to these people?
_____
_____

➤ Have you been involved in a rebound romance? _____

➤ If so, what dangers do you see? Do you find that the relationship is primarily a need-meeting one? _____
_____
_____

➤ If you are in a rebound romance now, picture yourself five years from now in a state of emotional health. How will that relationship be different then from the way it is now? _____
_____
_____

➤ What could you do to make this relationship more honest and less need oriented? _____

_____

_____

START WITH YOUR STRENGTHS

Often people who have been divorced begin to think of themselves as losers. They wear "defeat glasses," seeing their entire lives in terms of their weaknesses. They know only what they've done wrong.

In rebuilding your life, reprocessing the real you, you need to take a good look at your strengths. You need to open your eyes to what you *can* do. Ask yourself, *What kind of person do I now want to be?*

Accept where you are. You're divorced. You didn't want to be, but you are. You're hurting. You didn't want to be, but you are. Close your eyes to all that and look forward. *From this point, what do I want to become? What kind of person will I be? Once I have my act together, what will I do? Who will I be?*

After spending months in hiding, this can be a risky venture. Once you start to dream, you might be disappointed. But this is one of those proper risks that you need to take. Careful planning can result in therapeutic involvement.

Identify Your Assets

First, you need to figure out what your strengths are. Friends can help you. They often present an unbiased opinion. You may not even realize that you're uncommonly caring, especially energetic, or good at organizing things. Your friends can tell you.

Maybe there are things that you're very interested in, though you're not sure how good you are. That's fine. Commit yourself to learn all you can learn about such things. Your enthusiasm counts for something.

MAKE IT YOUR OWN

➤ Identify your strengths. List three to five things that you're good at. Include personality traits, talents, or strong interests. _____

_____

_____

_____

Hang Out with the Right People

Next, you need to look for the people who are doing what you want to do. Look for those who exhibit the traits you want to exhibit. Look for those involved in the areas you're interested in.

Then, *associate with them*. Become a part of the lives of such people.

For instance, what if you said, "I want to be a bar hound—one of those people who goes to bars all the time and hangs around and drinks too much and is always telling the same old sad stories"? If that's what you want, go to those bars and hang out with those people. You will become just like them.

Of course, you might have higher aspirations. (I hope!) But the same principle applies. If you want to be like the people you see at church, go to church. If you admire the people who build houses for poor families with Habitat for Humanity, join that group. If you want to be an actor, get involved with a community theater. If you like organizing things, volunteer your services to a community service organization. They're usually more than happy to welcome a new volunteer.

My friend Tom Jones tells of how, three years after his divorce, a friend invited him to sing with the St. Louis Bach Society Chorale. He hadn't sung classical music in twenty years, but he was interested in it. The experience turned out to be extremely therapeutic. He was doing something productive, enjoying the company of others, but not sitting around waiting for a new wife to show up.

I know a woman whose husband left her for a younger model, and she was hurting. But she had taken ballet lessons before she was married, and a friend suggested that she get back into it. She signed up for some lessons and found that she could still dance. Now that woman is teaching ballet. She has a whole new joy in life because she refused to sit around moping over her divorce.

I know another woman, devastated by a divorce, who was an extremely compassionate person. That was her strength. I suggested that she get involved with some women I knew who wrapped bandages. She didn't want to. "Listen," I said. "People are hurting, and somebody needs to wrap those bandages. Why don't you try it?"

I saw her again a few months later, and I asked, "Did you ever go and wrap those bandages?"

She gave me a look and said somewhat grudgingly, "I actually liked it. Some neat people are there, and they loved having me there. They acted like I was the greatest thing since safety pins."

It seems like such a little thing, but she began to find a new purpose in life. She was important to people. She had something important to do. Maybe that's what you need too.

MAKE IT YOUR OWN

➤ Where can you go to find people who are (*a*) doing what you want to do; (*b*) being the kind of people you want to be; or (*c*) involved in activities you want to be involved in? (Consider charities, community organizations, church groups, night school, theaters, sports organizations, singles groups.)

_____

_____

_____

_____

➤ What could you do to associate with these people? _____

_____

_____

➤ What is the first step necessary? When will you take it? _____

_____

_____

TAKE RESPONSIBILITY FOR YOURSELF

I love a "Peanuts" cartoon in which Charlie Brown and Lucy are leaning on a fence and talking. Lucy asks, "Why do you think God put us here in this world?"

Charlie responds, "God put us in this world to make other people happy."

Lucy thinks about it for a minute and then screams at the top of her voice, "SOMEBODY IS NOT DOING HIS JOB!"

Maybe you feel that way too. Whoever is responsible for your happiness is failing.

But I've got news for you. Nobody else in the world can make you happy. That's your job. If you don't decide to take responsibility for yourself, happiness will always elude you. You'll always be upset at somebody else. You'll always blame someone else for where you are. You'll always complain and be bitter on the inside.

But the person who says, "This is my life; I'm going to be responsible for myself," is going to begin to grow. He is going to put his life back together. He is going to turn things around.

You may have been waiting years for your ex-spouse to come back and make everything better. He or she got you into this mess, and he or she will have to get you out. You have been convinced that your ex would see the error in his or her ways. But it hasn't happened. You've been waiting for the other person to fix things, and you've been disappointed.

Here's what you must realize: nobody can fix you but you.

Your healing is your responsibility. Don't wait for a person or anything else to come along and fulfill you or even heal you. You need to make the tough choices now for your recovery.

If you're a Christian, you may be saying, "God can fix me." Yes, that is true. I wholeheartedly believe that. God can turn people around. He can fill you with power and work wonders in your heart. But God rarely (if ever) does that to anyone who is not ready to accept responsibility for his or her life.

My healing didn't start until I said to myself, *I'm going to stop lying in bed feeling sorry for myself. I'm going to stop waiting for someone to come along and heal me, and I'm going to begin to move on with my life.* Yes, God was the one doing the healing, but it's a lot easier to steer a moving car than one that's standing still. I had to accept the responsibility for my life and decide to move forward.

And when you do move forward, let me suggest that you move in the direction of love. Not romantic love. We've discussed those dangers. I'm talking about friendship, giving, sharing, serving. Don't rush it. It will be difficult to trust others, even your closest friends. But slowly move in this direction.

Doing this, too, is risky. You're putting yourself on the line. You can't blame anyone else. It's just you now—and you might fail. But this is another of those proper risks you need to take.

➤ Which of the following statements are true of you?

❏ My divorce has messed up my life.

❏ I still hope that my ex will come back to me.

❏ I'd like to be happy, but bad things keep happening.

❏ I'm upset with God because he has not brought me happiness.

❏ I feel pretty stagnant right now. My life isn't going anywhere.

❏ It's high time I took responsibility for my life.

❏ I have recently begun to move forward in my recovery.

❏ Life is still tough, but I'm heading toward happiness.

➤ Finish this sentence: My life would be a lot happier if only _____
_____.

➤ In what way can you take responsibility for your life? What specific action can you take? _____
_____
_____

➤ When will you take this action? _____
_____

➤ In what way can you begin to show love to others? _____
_____
_____

Action Point: You have just written a specific goal for how you will begin to take responsibility for your growth and healing. Write that goal on page 282 (Appendix A) where you are recording these action points for future reference.

LEARN HOW TO LOVE AGAIN

The last step you'll take in your recovery is learning how to trust again, commit again—all the necessary ingredients for learning how to truly love others. We've already talked about developing healthy friendships and learning how to be self-sacrificial, but this kind of love goes beyond that. Now we're talking about *agape,* an unconditional love. (*Agape* [pronounced uh-GAH-pay] is a Greek word for love used often in the New Testament.)

After what you've been through, you're going to have a hard time in trusting, committed relationships. So if you're cringing at the mere thought, it's okay because that's all part of the self-protection that is necessary for a while. But you don't want to stay there. For complete healing, you need to reach a point where you can love others in a committed way.

This kind of love will be new for many—you may not have had it in your marriage. *Agape* love is the way God loves us, as only he can, but it's something we can strive for. God loves us just as much on the worst day of our lives as when we are acting our best. His love doesn't change, whether we are in the midst of having an adulterous affair or sitting in church in our very best outfits.

Let me illustrate this point by telling you about my two weddings. At my first marriage, I was young, but I had all the answers. (Just like you at age twenty, right?) People would ask me, "Aren't you nervous? Are you sure you know what you're doing?" I would confidently answer, "Yes, I know exactly what I'm doing, and I'm not nervous at all."

That was true. I wasn't nervous, and I really thought I knew what I was doing because I was going to trust in God, and he would always take care of me.

When I said my marriage vows at my first wedding, I said with confidence that I would love my wife no matter what happened, and I would always be there for her no matter what the circumstances, and I would put her needs before my own. Do you remember saying those things? But did we really have any idea what we were saying?

If you were like me, what you were thinking while you were saying those vows was more like, *Look at all I'm getting—a fine-looking wife who's going to help me get through school, and be there for me, and . . .* You see, my focus was generally on what I was *getting,* not what I was *giving.* I knew I had responsibilities and all that, but like most people, I was focusing on my needs.

Now contrast that with my more recent remarriage. After being single again for about eight years, and learning to be very content as a single, I was faced with the decision to commit myself to another person, to trust again, and to love unconditionally. That was scary! And well it should be. As I thought about taking those vows, I was thinking about the awesome responsibility I was about to take on.

I was going to promise to love, even when I was treated poorly, to communicate, even when I didn't feel like talking, and to put my wife's needs before my own. Is there anyone who believes he or she can do that on a regular basis? If so, I'd like to meet you.

I was nervous about getting married again, not because I loved my new wife less, and not because I didn't trust her or God, but because I knew I was setting myself up for a lot of hard work and failure. Failure? Yes. I knew I would come home from some difficult days expecting to relax, only to hear my wife say, "Good, you're home. I need you to . . ." At that moment, would I be able and willing to love unconditionally?

It's a difficult task, but I believe that with God's help, we can love others that way. Not all the time. Yes, we'll fail. But that's where the work comes in—as we constantly recommit ourselves to the task of loving others.

MAKE IT YOUR OWN

➤ Look at this list of self-oriented versus love-oriented characteristics. On a continuum between the two, where would you rate yourself? Put an X where you think you would fall.

Self-oriented person:

a. You see only your needs.

| |

Love-oriented person:

a. You see your responsibility to others.

| |

b. You expect others to fulfill you.

b. You know fulfillment is your responsibility and is available through God.

| |

c. You want pleasure without commitment.

c. You know that satisfying relationships require commitment.

| |

d. You can't be fulfilled, can't commit, and can't truly love.

d. You're fulfilled through serving God and helping others.

| |

As you've filled this out, you may have had the fleeting thought, *Boy, if I ever get married again, I want to find someone who is love oriented*. Obviously, the point of this whole exercise is for you to come to the place where you say instead, "Lord, help me to *become* a love-oriented person."

Chapter 6

SHOW ME THE MONEY
DEALING WITH YOUR FINANCES[1]

Chuck and Vicki lived in a modest apartment, and they both worked at modest jobs. An aspiring filmmaker, Chuck had spent more money than he had yet made on that career. Vicki worked in a store and taught piano on the side.

Then Chuck left Vicki for another woman, moving out of state, out of reach. Vicki was emotionally devastated, but when she stopped crying long enough to look at her checkbook, she saw that she was in big trouble.

In between film projects, Chuck had always been able to pick up short-term jobs to pay the bills. Without his income, Vicki wasn't sure she could keep up the payments on her rent and her beloved piano. To make things even worse, Chuck was using their joint credit cards for some of his film expenses, and he also charged some gifts for his new girlfriend. Vicki was getting the bills for those charges, but had no forwarding address for him. She begged the credit company to take her name off the account, but it wouldn't without written permission from both parties. When Vicki finally contacted Chuck through a relative, she learned he was in his own financial crisis and had no money to pay the bills anyway.

The credit charges made an already tight budget impossible. Vicki sold her beautiful baby grand piano, trading it in for a cheaper piano, so she could still give lessons. She added new lessons to her schedule, working four nights a week in addition to her day job. She cut her expenses as much as she could. And still the numbers didn't add up.

Reluctantly, she declared bankruptcy. It was a moral quandary for her. Vicki had always believed in owning up to her responsibilities, but she also realized she was saddled with her ex-husband's irresponsibility. If she could be free from the credit card debt, she could just barely make it.

And Vicki did make it, slowly but surely. When her lease was up, she moved to a nicer, but cheaper apartment (thanks to a landlord friend who gave her a break on the rent). She got a better-paying day job, and two years later she became a manager with even better pay. Gradually, she was able to increase her giving to her church and even to put some money into savings. Six years after her divorce, she actually bought a new car.

It has been tough for Vicki. There were many nights when she fell into bed exhausted from working fourteen-hour days. Sometimes she forced herself to go to work sick because she couldn't afford the day off. And she had to forgo having many things she wanted because she just didn't have the money for them.

Things are better now. Vicki may never be rich, but at least she can breathe a little. After biting the bullet for a few years, she can relax a bit. Like so many people who have gone through divorce, she tumbled into a financial pit, but she has finally clawed her way out.

SIMPLE ECONOMICS

Two can live as cheaply as one, they say. When people marry, they generally pool their resources, sharing their housing, food, insurance, credit cards, and cars. With two incomes and combined expenses, the new couple can look at buying a nicer home, saving for the future, paying off old debts, or starting a family. Or perhaps one partner may quit a job or cut back to part-time in order to raise a family or do volunteer work. Wage earners starting a home together have lots of options.

That's not to say married couples automatically have all the money they need. They frequently get into trouble by aiming too high, overspending, over-charging. The bachelor was fine with his cheap studio apartment, but as a married man, he needs a split-level with a two-car garage. The single woman was satisfied driving her beat-up Ford Escort, but now she wants something with a bit more comfort.

The simple economics of marriage look good on paper: income times two, expenses times maybe one and a half. But marriage is also a rite of passage that propels many young people into adulthood, along with all the expensive perks of adulthood. Your expenses balloon to fill your income and then some.

And if a couple have children, expenses go through the roof. Any disposable income pays for disposable diapers, or baby-sitters, or braces, or dance lessons, or college tuition. As years go by, the parents may see their income go up, with promotions, raises, and cost-of-living adjustments. But expenses usually stay way ahead, at least until the kids graduate from college, get married, or move out (and lately that's been happening when they're thirty-five or so).

REVERSE GEAR

Divorce throws everything into reverse. The problem is, life doesn't come with that gear installed. Suddenly, one household becomes two. Two rents or mortgages. Two cars. Two insurance policies. Expenses soar without any rise in income. Add into that the legal fees involved in a divorce and perhaps counseling fees for you and/or your children. Consider that your emotional crisis may make you less productive at work. Count on sick days, lost accounts, or fewer commissions that may reduce your income. With all that in mind, if finances were tight before a breakup, they will be suffocating afterward.

Best case, financially speaking, is two gainfully employed partners with no kids. But even these couples feel a strain as they go back to living in individual households. A far more common situation is when one partner makes significantly more than the other. The lesser-earning spouse will have to scramble to maintain anything close to the quality of life he or she has been used to. Alimony may equalize things, but that's never a sure bet.

If kids are in the picture, the financial needs are greater, and the problem can be much worse. Even if child support is paid properly, the partners will feel the strain of adjusting to the double household. And of course, there are many stories of deadbeat dads (and a few moms), who abandon their families with no financial support.

STRATEGIES FOR GETTING BY

What's your situation? Best case or worst case, you *will* have financial problems in the wake of a divorce (or even a separation). But these problems don't have to cripple you. They may require a period of frugality, but wise planning and crisp discipline can get you through the worst of it in about five years.

What can you do?

Accept Your Losses

Your initial success strategies have nothing to do with penny-pinching or investing. They involve your attitude. You need to accept the fact that your lifestyle will change.

And that's easier said than done. We've already discussed your penchant for denial in the wake of your divorce. You don't want to accept that it's happening *at all,* so you certainly don't want to accept the changes you'll have to make. Yet your financial survival depends on it.

Face it: you will not be able to maintain the lifestyle you had before your divorce. You will have to dine at less ritzy restaurants (or at home), buy fewer and cheaper clothes (or recycle last year's outfits), and maybe even move to a more affordable home. Get used to thrift shops and yard sales. Start clipping coupons. Make sure your car gets regular oil changes because you'll be driving it for a while. This is your new life, at least for the next few years.

You'll want to make the fewest changes possible, but your best plan is to cut back radically now and restore some things as your budget allows.

If you refuse to accept that you're poorer now, if you try to maintain your standard of living, you will be selling out the future for the present. Ultimately, you'll be delaying your financial recovery.

HOW TO LIVE ON LESS

Minor cuts

Shop at yard sales and/or thrift shops.

Recycle your wardrobe.

Reduce your food budget (clip coupons and eat in).

Use the library, not the bookstore.

Find low-cost or no-cost entertainment sources.

Eliminate magazine subscriptions.

Cancel cable TV.

Resist impulse buying.

Give friends creative gifts of time or handmade objects.

Major cuts

Move to apartment or cheaper condo.

Trade in your sports car for a sub-compact.

Sell or pawn your luxury items.

Cut up your credit cards.

Take Charge of Your Situation

Are you a victim? Well, if your spouse left you with a divorce you didn't want, of course you are! Does that mean you have to suffer the rest of your life? No.

Another key to financial recovery is to forget your victimization and take charge of your situation. In modern parlance, you need to be *proactive,* not just *reactive.*

Victims are everywhere. You hear them complaining about how expensive everything is, how little they get paid, and how much people have cheated them. And it's understandable for you to feel like a victim, especially if you're still in the anger stage of your emotional recovery. "Look what my ex did to me!"

But you can't stay there very long. Financially, victims keep slogging away at low-paying jobs, keep paying too much for everything they buy, keep getting fleeced by credit card companies, and keep complaining. You have to get past that. How? By deciding that it's up to you to change things.

Can you make more money? Maybe. What would it take? A different job? More hours? A second job? How would you go about doing that?

Can you spend less money? Probably. What major or minor cuts do you need to make in your lifestyle?

Can you make a budget and stick to it? Absolutely. Can you plan things so you'll have some money to spare in a few years? I think you can. It's up to you, but you need to decide to take charge of your finances. No one else is going to do it for you.

HOW TO MAKE MORE MONEY

A little more

Work overtime.

Hold a yard sale.

Baby-sit for neighbors on week-ends.

Give lessons in something you know how to do.

Do other odd jobs.

Ask church leaders about support services you could do for pay.

Substantially more

Ask your boss for a raise.

Take a second job.

Find a better-paying job.

Start taking classes for better employment in the future.

Rent out a room in your home.

Start a secondary work-at-home business.

Balance Short-Term Living with Long-Range Planning

You need a bifocal view of your situation. With bifocal glasses, you see distant things clearly through part of the lens and then use another part for close objects. Similarly, you need to make sure your day-to-day needs are met while always keeping an eye on the distant future.

Today, you need to eat. You need a place to live and clothes to wear. Scrimp and save all you can, but you have to pay for these basic things.

Still, every penny saved today is a penny earned for the future. If you can cut back on extraneous expenses now, you can improve your future financial outlook.

"Savings?" a friend once told me. "I can't afford to put money into savings. It's all I can do to stay current with all my bills. In a few years, I'll be making more. Then I'll start saving." He told me that a few years ago. Now he is making more, but his expenses have also grown. He is still not saving.

As tight as your budget may be now, you've got to lay some groundwork for the future. And I'm not just talking about socking some money away in a savings account or IRA. It's a matter of wise foresight in many areas: getting job training now so you can earn more later; paying for an oil change now so your car will last longer; buying a condo instead of renting a house, so you'll be earning some equity. Don't go chasing wild pipe dreams, but make solid investments in the future to balance your present needs.

Don't Give Up Hope

At this point it would be natural for you to put down this book and sigh, "How do they expect me to do all this? I'll never get out of this money trap." Go ahead. Sigh.

You can do it. It's a long road back to financial security (even solvency!), but you can start taking the steps that will get you there. Vicki was sighing, too, and crying, and cursing her lousy ex-husband, but she got through it one day at a time. You can too.

Ask for Help

Chances are, you know people who would like to help you get through this tough time. They may even offer you a financial gift or a loan to tide you over. It's hard to ask for help, but swallow your pride and do it. An act of kindness always helps both the giver and the receiver.

Go to your *family* first—parents, siblings, rich uncles. Always be very clear on the terms of the transaction. If it's a loan, put it in writing: how much, for how long, and what interest (if any). If it's a gift, be very sure about any strings that may be attached. Families often have an unspoken currency, transactions that stay under the surface, and misunderstandings that can cause bitterness at some later point.

If you have a few *close friends,* let them know of your needs. They may offer financial help or other services (baby-sitting? transportation? computer?) that will help you in your efforts to get by.

In one church, a single mom gave a gift of one hundred dollars to a newly divorced woman in a time of dire need. She attached one stipulation: *when you're able to, pass it on to another needy person.* A few years later the recipient did pass it on, with the same stipulation. Think of all the blessing that one hundred dollars will bring before it stops circulating!

Let *church leaders* know your needs too. Often churches have special funds for temporary needs in the congregation. Even if no official assistance is offered, leaders may put you in touch with individuals who could help you with money, services, or job possibilities.

This is a tough one, but your *ex-spouse* may be able to help. Don't be too proud to ask. Especially if children are involved, he or she may be willing to help (beyond any mandated child support). If your ex has put you in this situation, he or she may be feeling guilty about it anyway. It may be worth a try.

If you do go this route, however, be *very* careful about any assumptions or conditions that come along with the money. Don't let your ex use this gift as a way of controlling you or sabotaging your emotional recovery.

Barney left his wife and young children to move in with his mistress. The move could have been financially devastating because his wife, Leslie, had always been a homemaker. But Barney grandly offered to continue supporting them all, so Leslie could still be at home for the kids.

It sounded like a good plan, and it started out all right. Barney, a corporate CEO, ran the family like his company. Any major expenses needed to be submitted in advance for his approval. As a result, he kept control of the family, even though he no longer lived with them. Leslie felt trapped, unable to earn any money for the family and stripped of her parental authority. She came to regret accepting his help.

You may seek help from various *community services*. Support groups for divorced people and other agencies may offer emergency aid.

Then there's *welfare*. Many people who have never been on welfare have an emotional aversion to it as if it's morally wrong to accept government help. But that's what it's there for: to provide temporary aid for citizens like you who have fallen on hard times.

Look into job training possibilities through the welfare system. Especially if your marketable skills are limited (or just untapped), it would make a lot of sense to go on the dole for six months or so, learn a career, and then get a job that pays more than you'd otherwise get. I haven't done the math, but I'd guess that in your years of greater earnings (and taxes on those earnings) you'd pay back the welfare system for whatever you got out of it.

Demystify Money

Money makes the world go 'round. They say it can't buy happiness, but TV commercials keep telling us it buys the things that bring us happiness. Money is power in our society. It buys respect.

If you had lots of money but now you're struggling, you know all about that. You got used to buying the best, and now it's tough to be shopping with the Kmart crowd.

The New Testament clearly warns us about the dangers of money. "The love of money is a root of all kinds of evil," Paul said (1 Tim. 6:10 NKJV), indicating that rich people tend to trust in their riches and not in God. "You cannot serve both God and Money," Jesus said (Matt. 6:24 NIV), and some translations use the godlike name mammon. Yes, we easily worship this false god. The rich young ruler wanted to follow Jesus but walked away when Jesus asked him to give up his wealth. His love of money was just too great.

"Blessed are you poor," Jesus said on another occasion (Luke 6:20 NKJV). Financial poverty seems to go along with spiritual poverty—that is, humility.

When you struggle to make ends meet, you need to trust God to give you your daily bread. You know you can't buy it yourself.

So why are you so worried about money? Granted, you had more and now you have less. It's tough to make that adjustment. But could it be that God is using this time to get your priorities straight? Is he weaning you away from the worship of money and forcing you to trust in him?

In this chapter, I've been talking about financial recovery, but let me clarify that the goal is not great wealth. Your goal may not even be to return to the standard of living you once enjoyed. The goal is simply this: to meet your obligations, to provide for your family, and to trust God for your daily bread. It's wise to plan for the future, but I've tried to resist talking about financial security, because we need to get our security from God. If we ever let our IRAs and our savings accounts and our stock holdings keep us from trusting God for our livelihood, we've gone too far.

So put aside your dreams of trumping your ex by rebuilding your fortune. Stop fantasizing about fancy cars and lavish vacations. You don't need those things. Instead, rejoice in your renewed trust in God, and trust him as you put your accounts back in order.

Say No to Your Kids

Many a Christian has started adulthood with a solid determination to resist the lure of materialism. Simple living has a certain appeal when you're young and not earning that much anyway. But for many, the ideal dies out, and they eventually join in the worship of the Almighty Buck.

What happens? In many cases, marriage does it. If not marriage, it's the raising of a family. Even when people don't care about their creature comforts, they want their kids to have it all. People who live simply by themselves become raging consumers when they're buying stuff for their children.

It's good to provide for your family, and you can buy things as expressions of your love, but don't buy into the idea that you *must* spend lavishly on your kids. There are many cheaper ways to show that you care.

Some parents want to shield their children from the effects of divorce by maintaining the same standard of living, even if financial realities make that nearly impossible to do. They'll do without new clothes and impulse purchases *themselves,* but they'll keep spoiling their kids. Some parents, guilt-ridden about the divorce, spend *more* on their children as if to bribe them into feeling okay about the whole thing.

Don't kid yourself: the kids know. Their lives will be changed by the divorce, no matter what you do. It won't help to throw money at them. Financially, the best thing you can do for them is to make them partners with you in creating a new lifestyle. Teach them responsible buying habits. Teach them self-discipline and delayed gratification. Above all, teach them that money is not a measure of love.

Get Tough on Yourself

It goes without saying, but I'll say it anyway. You have to practice self-discipline. It's not easy to live frugally, but the better you do at it, the better off you'll be in the future.

Learn to redefine some things you considered necessities as options. Rename some reasonable expenses as luxuries. Don't let TV commercials tell you what you need. Don't try to keep up with the Joneses. Don't measure your personal worth by your net worth. Take some pleasure in living on the edge.

Go into some parties and you'll hear folks dropping the information that a particular dress cost $800, or they just bought a new car for $30,000, or they're taking a $10,000 cruise. At other parties, guests will brag that they got this $200 outfit marked down to $25, they talked the dealer down to $2,000 for that used Corolla, or they got into the theater free by volunteering to usher. You need to start going to the second kind of party where people forgo conspicuous consumption in favor of bargain hunting, finding joy in the adventure of getting the most for the least.

That's a paradigm shift. You need to stop putting yourself down for being poor and start taking pride in your ability to control your spending.

Kill Your Credit Cards

Credit cards do exactly the opposite of what you want to do. They sell out the future for a better present. You want to scrimp in the present for a better future.

It sounds appealing: "Buy what you need now and pay for it in the future when you're better off." But if you put a lot of charges on your credit cards, you won't have a better future.

Most credit cards charge 15 to 20 percent annual interest, and the minimum payments are intentionally low to keep you from paying off your debt. So let's say you need a new couch for your living room and you buy one for $1,000, putting it on your VISA card. They'll probably bill you $25 a month. But at 18 percent, you're getting charged $15 each month in interest. So your payment is just reducing your debt by $10. At that rate, it would take you eight years to retire that debt. That couch ends up costing you more than $1,800, almost twice its cash price.

The answer is simple: stop using your credit cards. Destroy all but one (which you may need for car rental, ticket purchases, or emergencies). If you can budget it, pay twice the minimum payment on existing balances. (And if you must put new charges on that one card, be sure to pay off all new charges plus the interest plus the minimum payment.)

As Vicki discovered, credit cards can be a sticky issue in a divorce. Most couples have joint accounts; they're both responsible to pay any debt, no matter which one incurred it. Debt repayment should be considered in a divorce settlement, but some dirty tricks can still go on.

As soon as possible, you should get your name off any joint account. I recommend this even in the case of separation. If you are maintaining separate households, you need separate accounts, credit, checking, and savings. If you can discuss this rationally early in your separation, agree together to contact the credit companies and make the necessary changes. (If you get back together, you can always merge accounts later, but this can be a thorny problem if it's not addressed early.)

Find a Trusty Adviser

As you make the adjustment to divorced life, you will face changes in your tax situation, insurance, investments, debt, and possibly housing. There are too many details for you to master on your own. Find someone who can steer you through the maze.

Some people do financial planning for a living, but they charge handsomely for it (since most of their clients have a lot of finances to plan for). If you're lucky enough to know such a professional, ask for free advice. If not, perhaps your pastor could suggest someone in the church or community who might help.

It would be smart for you to get professional help with your taxes, at least in the first year after your divorce. There may be deductions or credits you don't know about.

As for insurance, be wary of the advice of professional salespeople. Their job is to sell you stuff, so they may not give you an unbiased perspective. Even if you're dealing with a friend or church acquaintance, get a second opinion. (I'm not saying they'll lie to you, just that their perspective is probably tilted toward buying more than you need.)

But you do need health insurance, and the divorce will change your policy. If you don't have a work-based plan, ask around at church or in the neighborhood for a group policy you can buy into.

Consider Moving

Maybe this decision has been made for you, but maybe not. You may be in the same house or apartment you shared with your ex, but now you don't need all the space. Moving to a cheaper place is one of the most effective things you can do to improve your budget.

But this involves your emotions as well as your bank account. With all the other upheaval in your life, can you deal with a new home as well? On the other hand, does your current home hold too many sad memories? Do you need a fresh start, geographically speaking?

If you have children, their well-being is crucial. But don't assume that a move would do them damage. They may have bad memories of your current place too. Still, I'd recommend looking for a new home within the same school district and within range of the same church. You don't want to shatter your children's social networks.

The moving question has no easy answer. Weigh the pros and cons, get good advice, and pray about it.

Should You Declare Bankruptcy?

It's an increasingly popular option, but I recommend it only in extreme cases. Christians ought to pay their debts, and wriggling out of them in this way can be irresponsible and unfair to the rest of us who pay our bills.

However, if there is no way out, if your credit trap is inescapable, if you've cut expenses to the bone and you still can't pay up, then go ahead and look into it. Get sound legal advice and see if it's right for you.

Bankruptcy experts call it reorganization, and that's a good concept. It's also protection from creditors. It's a way to get your feet on the ground and become a productive citizen again. Use it if you need to, but don't abuse it.

And don't underestimate the power of God to give you the wisdom and discipline you need to get out of this mess. With his strength, you can work through this difficult time and find your feet again. God can use these trials to build your character, to teach you patience, to give you hope, and to show you what's most important in life.

MAKE IT YOUR OWN

➤ Which of the following attitude adjustments will be the greatest challenges for you? (Rank the hardest three.)

___ Accept your losses.

___ Take charge of your situation.

___ Balance short-term living with long-range planning.

___ Don't give up hope.

___ Ask for help.

___ Demystify money.

___ Say no to your kids.

___ Get tough on yourself.

➤ Do you see any way to increase your income (if you need to)? If so, what?

_____

_____

➤ In what ways can you limit your expenses? _____

_____

_____

_____

_____

➤ What people could help you with money, advice, or referrals?

_____

_____

Budgeting is a crucial element in taking charge of your situation. Here we list two sample budgets, one for a single parent making $15,000 a year and another making $30,000.

> **It is critical that you budget your funds, that you stick to your budget, and that you get help from friends and family. Help comes in many forms, but it is important that you speak up about your specific needs. As the New Testament says, "You do not have because you do not ask" (James 4:2 NKJV).**

SAMPLE BUDGETS

Example #1: Income of $15,000/Year

Gross Income	= $15,000/year	$1,250/month
Taxes	= about 10%	$125/month
Church/Charity	= about 10%	$125/month
	Net Spendable Income =	$1,000/month
Housing	= 30% to *40%*	$400/month
Utilities	= 10% to *15%*	$150/month
Food	= about 15%	$150/month
Automobile	= about 10%	$100/month
Insurance	= about 5%	$50/month
Clothes	= 5%	$50/month
Entertainment	= 5%	$50/month
Savings	= whatever you can	$50/month
Balanced Budget		$1,250/month

Example #2: Income of $30,000/Year

Gross Income	= $30,000/year	$2,500/month
Taxes	= about 20%	$500/month
Church/Charity	= about 10%	$250/month
	Net Spendable Income =	$1,750/month
Housing	= *30%* to 40%	$525/month
Utilities	= *10%* to 15%	$175/month
Food	= about 15%	$250/month
Automobile	= about 10%	$175/month
Insurance	= about 5%	$90/month
Clothes	= 10%	$175/month
Entertainment	= 5%	$90/month
Child Care	= 10%	$175/month
Savings	= whatever you can	$95/month
Balanced Budget		$2,500/month

The second budget gives you a little more for living expenses, food, and clothes. It even has an allotment for child care. Get help in whatever area you can to provide more money for savings. Notice that the more you make, the more taxes you pay.

Now it's your turn. If you already have developed a budget, review it now, and see how it compares with our average percentages. Are there any new cuts you've decided to make? How will they affect your budget?

If you've never made a postbreakup budget, this is the place to start. Use our percentages as a guideline, but fit in your own numbers where they're different. You'll want to grab your checkbook and analyze what you've been spending on various items.

Your Budget: Income of $_____/Year

Gross Income	= $_____/year	$_____/month
Taxes	= 10% to 20%	$_____/month
Church/Charity	= 10%	$_____/month
	Net Spendable Income =	$_____/month
Housing	= 30% to 40%	$_____/month
Utilities	= 10% to 15%	$_____/month
Food	= 15%	$_____/month
Automobile	= 10%	$_____/month
Insurance	= ____	$_____/month
Clothes	= 10%	$_____/month
Entertainment	= ____	$_____/month
Child Care	= ____	$_____/month
Savings	= ____	$_____/month

Chapter 7

WHAT'S THAT YOU SAY?
COMMUNICATION AND CONFLICT

What are the two biggest problems in marriages today?

The textbook answer is "sex and money." That's what I learned in school.

But the more I talk to people whose marriages have broken up, the more I find that there is *one* major problem instead of two, and it isn't sex or money. It is lack of communication. Even where sex and money seem to be the culprits, the problem usually is that the people are not *talking* properly about sex and money.

Think about it. Say one partner or the other is dissatisfied sexually—but no one talks about it. The frustration builds until it affects other parts of the marriage, or perhaps the one partner seeks satisfaction in someone else's arms. Or suppose they fight over money. Why? Because they've never discussed how to make mutual spending decisions.

How can we learn to talk and listen to each other?

"Too late now," you may be muttering. "Maybe communication principles could have saved my marriage, but that's dead and gone." I'm right there with you. I look back to the years before my divorce and realize how little I really knew about communication. I made some mistakes, and it's too late to undo them.

But there are many other relationships in our lives, and all of them need good communication. Children. Relatives. Friends. A new spouse. Even your ex. It's never too late to learn to have healthy communication with the people all around you. You can't undo the past, but you can thrive in the future.

LEVELS OF COMMUNICATION

Let's start by considering various levels on which we communicate. Obviously, there are times and places for all of these—but we'll never deepen our relationships unless we move our communication to deeper levels.

1. Nonpersonal conversation. You engage in this every day. "I'll have a Big Mac and a Coke, please." You are not divulging anything beyond simple, nonthreatening facts.

"My name is . . ."

"It's raining outside."

"The Phillies lost again last night."

I had a friend visiting from Europe a few years ago. He came out of a store once, all smiles. "What are you so happy about?" I asked.

"What a nice country you have!" he answered. "The clerk just told me, 'Have a nice day.' She was actually interested in my life!"

I had to assure him that she probably had no interest in his life, that it's just a phrase we use. He was getting his levels of communication mixed up.

2. Facts about others. You probably know people who *live* on this level. "Did you hear about Joe and Fran? Well, their niece is marrying some guy from Boston, and they never invited Aunt Helen because they thought she was going to Bermuda on that senior citizens' cruise thing, you know?"

This level can get very involved, but it's not very personal. It's all about others. You don't have to divulge anything about yourself.

3. Self-judgments, ideas, opinions. At this level, you discuss your opinions about external matters.

"I support the independence movement of the Congo."

"My favorite author is Walker Percy."

"I'm pulling for the White Sox to win the pennant."

Suddenly, you're expressing your*self*, what you feel and think. But it's still focused on outside issues. For people who feel insecure about their opinions, moving into this level can be a big risk. All it takes is for an insensitive listener to say, "That's the dumbest thing I've ever heard," and that will chase them back to level two.

But those who are confident in their intellectual ability can "hide out" at this level. While they think they are opening up to others, they are really just revealing their thoughts. Their deeper feelings remain hidden.

4. Feelings and emotions. This can be difficult. At this level we expose our true selves, not what we think, but how we're feeling.

"I'm very concerned now about my health."

"Seeing Ted again brought up some painful feelings. I cried all night."

"I feel very happy whenever I see you."

"I know this sounds crazy, but I get a bit depressed whenever the Yankees lose. Bear with me."

Our emotions are closer to the core of our being. That can make this a threatening level for some. Often, when negative feelings are expressed, a listener will say, "Oh, there's no need to feel that way. Don't feel sad. Don't be concerned. Don't cry." And the person who has just expressed his emotions feels embarrassed. "Oh," he figures, "I guess it's not right to feel that way. I shouldn't have said anything." And once again communication regresses to a safer level.

Emotions need to be accepted, reinforced, and nurtured at this level. And—here's a generalization for you—men tend to have a harder time expressing emotions. We tend to get stuck at level three. For some reason, in our culture women are allowed to have emotions, and men aren't. To progress to deeper levels of communication, a couple will have to overcome that tendency.

But it's not just a gender-based problem. Much of it depends on the patterns you learned while growing up. How did your parents communicate? What patterns did you pick up at school or church? Some families are very emotional. Others are more intellectual. Some share freely. Others are more guarded. Some cultures are more open about emotions. In my church background, which was fundamentalist and decidedly noncharismatic, there was great emphasis on the supremacy of facts over feelings. I still believe that Christian faith is based more on the facts of Christ's death and resurrection than on our feelings about them, but somehow this seeped into the rest of my life as well. Feelings, I assumed, could not be trusted, and therefore, they should not be talked about. This is something I have had to work at overcoming on the road to more intimate communication.

5. Intimate communion. This is the feeling of oneness often felt in a marriage or in an extremely close friendship. It involves emotional, spiritual, and sometimes physical intimacy. Communication is open and honest at all these levels.

Interestingly, this level of communication often results from some sort of conflict. Researchers have found that conflict tends to *increase* communication. You have to work things out. Perhaps you have experienced this—a sharp disagreement that results in a greater understanding. You want to hug the person you were fighting with just moments earlier.

It takes work to stay at this level. It involves regular sharing, regular giving, regular talking. A marriage relationship, or even a good friendship, can bounce through various levels in a short time. Researchers have found that most marriages spend most of their time at levels one to three. You must be vigilant to stay at the more intimate levels of four and five.

MAKE IT YOUR OWN

➤ How do you feel about this workbook right now? _____

_____

_____

➤ Looking back at your marriage, about what percentage of time did you spend in each of these five levels of communication?

_____% Level One (Nonpersonal)

_____% Level Two (Facts about others)

_____% Level Three (Ideas, opinions)

_____% Level Four (Feelings, emotions)

_____% Level Five (Intimate communion)

➤ Often one partner will try to pull the other toward deeper levels of communication. In your marriage, who was the puller—you, your ex-spouse, or neither? _____

➤ As you grew up, which level of communication was practiced most in your home? _____

➤ Which of the following statements are true of you? Check all that apply.

❏ I feel hesitant to express my opinions.

❏ I am good at talking with others on nonpersonal levels.

❏ I have been hurt by people who criticized my opinions.

❏ I find it hard to express my true feelings.

❏ I spend more time talking about others than about myself.

❏ I feel more secure in my ideas than in my emotions.

❏ I think I have experienced a level five intimacy.

❏ I have been hurt by people making fun of how I felt.

❑ In my relationships, I usually pull the other person toward deeper levels of communication.

➤ Look back at the first question in this section: "How do you feel about this workbook right now?" Did your answer express what you *thought* or how you *felt*? _____

➤ This can help you learn something about yourself. If you answered more about how you *thought,* it may indicate that you tend to stay around level three and resist efforts to move to level four. Is this true of you? _____

➤ Choose one of your closest relationships right now—a friend, a child, a sibling, a new romantic interest. About what percentage of time do you spend in each level of communication?

_____% Level One (Nonpersonal)

_____% Level Two (Facts about others)

_____% Level Three (Ideas, opinions)

_____% Level Four (Feelings, emotions)

_____% Level Five (Intimate communion)

(You may want to monitor this relationship for a few days and come back to this question.)

➤ What is one thing you could say to this person that would deepen this relationship?_____

_____

CONFLICT

Conflict can make or break your communication patterns. Consider the following examples:

Couple #1 fight a lot. They express their feelings quickly and heatedly, but they make up rather quickly too.

Couple #2 never fight. They have disagreements, but they never talk about them. They're afraid of conflict, so they try to keep the peace by shoving their problems under the rug.

Couple #3 fight a lot. They always seem to be disagreeing, nagging, proving a point. They don't listen to each other, and they never back down. This marriage is in trouble.

Couple #4 fight sometimes, but not often. Occasional disagreements are voiced, discussed, and dealt with. They keep the peace by talking through their problems.

Recognize anyone you know? Most couples would fall into one of these patterns. To a great extent, the strength of a marriage is based on how the partners deal with conflict. As you might guess, Couples #1 and #4 have the healthiest relationships.

We must understand a few basics about conflict.

Conflict is natural and unavoidable. Life is full of conflict. Driving on the expressway, waiting in a bank line, lobbying for a promotion at your job— you can't live in this world without experiencing some level of conflict. The best you could do would be to shut yourself off as some sort of hermit, but what kind of life is that?

> **While we tend to want to avoid all conflict (particularly after a divorce), we need to view it as a natural and necessary part of life. We need to work on improving our communication skills in order to resolve our conflicts in a healthier way.**

This leads us to a second fact: *conflict creates an opportunity for increased communication and, therefore, learning and growth.* I desperately needed to learn this in the years following my divorce. I'd had my fill of conflict. I didn't want to see any more conflict for the rest of my life. That's why I isolated myself: I didn't want to be with people. I certainly didn't want to communicate with people beyond that "Have a nice day" level. That would be to risk conflict.

What I didn't know was that in saying, "I don't want any more conflict," I was indirectly saying, "I don't want to learn. I don't want to grow."

Everything we learn in life is indirectly a result of conflict. In first grade, when we don't know how to read, the teacher writes a word on the board, and that creates conflict in our minds. *What does that mean? I don't understand. I want to know what those symbols stand for!* The conflict motivates me to figure out what those letters mean.

It's the same way with relationships. *Why does she always seem cold to me just before I go off on a business trip?* There's a conflict. Talking about it, however, you can learn that she has a deep-seated fear of rejection, which is triggered by your departure, so she "rejects" you first. The conflict gives you an opportunity to assimilate new information.

To shut out all conflict is to shut out all learning, all growth. What we really want, I think, is an optimal amount of conflict—just enough to keep growing without causing undue stress.

Obviously, it's not just the conflict that causes growth; it's what we do with it. That pre-business-trip coldness could go on for years. It's not until you talk about it that you learn those new things about each other.

This leads us to another truth: *unresolved conflicts interfere with growth and destroy relationships.* Let's go back to that first grader seeing the words on the board. Unless he resolves his mental conflict by beginning to learn what the words mean, he will be frustrated and stagnated in his mental development. This may be what happened to you in calculus class. The teacher started writing odd symbols on the board and you experienced conflict—*I don't understand this.* But for some reason, you may have let the conflict go unresolved—*I don't want to understand this.* Your mental growth stagnated, your relationship with mathematics was destroyed, and that's why you're not a rocket scientist today.

Apologies if you *are* an engineer or a computer scientist, but many of us gave up on math at that moment. Essentially, we said one of two things: (1) my relationship with mathematics is not worth the resolving of this conflict; or (2) it's just too hard to learn this stuff.

The same goes for relationships with people, even spouses. If the commitment to the relationship is strong, it's "worth it" to resolve the conflict. But if the circumstances are against you or if the other partner is obstinate, you may decide it's "too hard" to resolve that conflict. In such cases, the relationship stops growing, stagnates, and often moves toward dissolution.

So conflict gives us that classic fork in the road. We can seek to resolve it and gain greater closeness, or we can ignore it and move apart.

MAKE IT YOUR OWN

➤ In your relationships, when has conflict led to greater intimacy?

_____

_____

➤ What unresolved conflicts led to your divorce? _____

_____

_____

➤ Do you tend to deal with conflicts or ignore them? Why? _____

_____

_____

_____

➤ Of the four couples presented at the start of this step, which did your marriage most resemble? _____

_____

_____

ATTITUDES—LOVING MYSELF

We need to learn how to resolve conflict in positive ways, and that requires communication skills. As we develop these skills, we can grow in our relationships, we can feel better about ourselves, and we can feel better about others. This takes work. We need to be aware of our communication habits. If we let them slip, our relationships will slip too.

Good communication starts with our most basic attitudes. And the first attitude we should examine is our attitude toward ourselves.

As I have already implied, one of the greatest hindrances to intimate communication is insecurity. If I am afraid my feelings are stupid or inappropriate, I won't share them. If I think my opinions will be laughed at, I won't talk about them.

You can be the most tender, loving person in the world, hanging on to every word your partner utters, but unless you take the risk of sharing *yourself* in a relationship, you will not find true intimacy. Many relationships are lopsided in this way. One partner does all the thinking and feeling for both. That's not healthy.

Getting a better attitude toward yourself is not easy, especially if there are forces around you putting you down. For some, it is the spouse or ex-spouse who subtly (or overtly) discounts what a person says. For others, it may stem from their upbringing. Many people's self-attitudes are formed in adolescence. That can be a cruel time. And unfortunately, even the church can sometimes send the wrong message. An emphasis on Christian love urges us to put others first, and that's great. But sometimes that can be carried to the extreme of total self-abasement. The fact is, Jesus affirmed the commandment: "Love your neighbor *as yourself*." There is an evenness of attitude that needs to underlie our relationships. Yes, I should put the other person first and even love others in a sacrificial way. But if I deny the value of my God-given personality, what do I have to give? Make no mistake. To appreciate yourself is not pride; it is gratitude to the God who made you. To deny your value is not humility; it is blasphemy.

If you have a bad attitude toward yourself, you need to work on it. Get up every morning and tell yourself that you're a unique individual, made in God's image, that you have a lot to offer. Even if no one else is telling you this, tell it to yourself. This world is not known for its encouragement. Encourage yourself. Even if you don't really feel very unique or valuable, keep telling yourself that you are important. Soon you will begin to believe it. (See Article 1 at the end of the workbook for more help in developing a positive self-image.)

MAKE IT YOUR OWN

➤ How would you describe your attitude toward yourself?

___ I am God's gift to humanity.

___ I like myself a lot. I'm glad God made me like this.

___ Some days I enjoy myself. Other days I hate myself.

___ There are a lot of things I want to change about myself. Once all that is taken care of, I'll like myself just fine.

___ I really wonder why God made me this way. I can't stand myself.

___ Other: _____

_____

➤ How much affirmation do you get from those around you?

___ A great deal

___ A fair amount

___ Very little

___ None at all

___ I get a lot of de-affirmation, tearing me down.

➤ Who affirms you the most? _____

_____

➤ Can you spend more time with this person? How? _____

_____

_____

➤ Who tears you down the most?_____

_____

_____

➤ Can you spend less time with this person? How? _____

_____

_____

➤ In this space, write a statement thanking God that he has made you the way you are. _____

_____

_____

_____

_____

ATTITUDES—LOVING OTHERS

The flip side is true too. We need to *love others* as we love ourselves. Some people fail on this point. They love to hear themselves talk. They're totally sold on their opinions, and they don't care about anyone else's. They must get their own way. They tend to see everything from their own narrow perspective. They are quick to judge, quick to take offense, and slow to give in.

You have probably known people like that. But we all move into this behavior from time to time. And just as a lack of appreciation for *myself* results in lopsided, ineffective communication, so does a lack of appreciation for *others*.

For true intimacy to occur, you need to develop a *nonjudgmental* attitude toward others. That doesn't mean you can't sort through and analyze your thoughts and feelings. But underlying all that must be an appreciation for who that person is, and where the thoughts and feelings are coming from. You could say, "The White Sox win the pennant? How stupid can you get?" Or you could say, "Well, you've been right before, but I just don't see that happening." Which statement is more affirming?

Your words can tear down or build up. If you adopt an accepting, non-judgmental attitude, you can disagree (even on more important issues than baseball) and still build up the other person. That's an expression of love.

> **We need to have a proper attitude about ourselves and others in order to communicate effectively.**

Intimacy also requires a *forgiving* attitude. "You always hurt the one you love"—so goes the song. And it's true. The closer you get to someone, the greater the chance for pain. We'll deal with major issues of forgiveness in another chapter, but the fact is that close friends or marriage partners can hurt or disappoint each other in a lot of little ways. If one of them holds a grudge, that will automatically hinder their communication. I won't share with you if I think you're mad at me. You won't listen to me if you're thinking about how I've hurt you. Good communicators offer forgiveness and understanding.

Intimate levels of communication can be reached by those with *humble* attitudes. Suppose you have a simple disagreement—say, over what color to paint the living room. Maybe you put off the discussion for a while, but you come back to it and you're still disagreeing. "I don't see how anyone could like off-white instead of blue. It's just so dull!" And before long you're arguing not about colors anymore but about yourselves. It's not blue or white: it's *who's going to win.*

I know you've been through that because it's the most natural thing in the world. It's hard to give in. But that's what love demands. Take a look at the Bible's famous Love Chapter, 1 Corinthians 13: love "is not rude, it is not self-seeking, it is not easily angered, it keeps no record of wrongs" (v. 5 NIV).

Jesus told his disciples that the way of the world was to seek first place, but they should seek to be servants (Matt. 20:25–28). That attitude freely expresses a disagreement, but willingly gives in, in deference to the other person. And if the other person is giving in, too, so much the better. Then the conversation can get back to what color to paint the walls, and maybe a suitable compromise will be reached.

➤ On a scale of 1 to 10 (10 being best), how good are you at putting others first? _____

➤ When have you found it most difficult to act with love toward others?

_____

_____

➤ As you seek to develop an attitude that is nonjudgmental, forgiving, and humble, which of those would you say is most difficult for you? Why?

_____

_____

➤ What person has been the most loving toward you? What did you appreciate most about this person's attitude? _____

_____

ACTIVE LISTENING

Have you ever had a friend you just enjoyed talking to? You walk away from each conversation feeling very satisfied—you said everything you wanted to say, you got to know the other person better, and he or she got to know you.

That person was probably practicing *active listening*. Active listening is simply a way of practicing love in conversation, a way of caring for the other person by paying attention, by interacting, by supporting.

Many of us think we practice active listening when we don't. Example 1: Mary comes home from a day of teaching school and says, "I had an awful day. The kids were bouncing off the walls and the principal came to observe . . ."

John says, "What's for dinner?"

Is John practicing active listening? Of course not. He isn't listening at all. He doesn't care about her. He cares only about his own needs.

Example 2: Mary comes home and says the same thing. John says, "Yeah, that's rough. I know what you mean. I got stuck in traffic and was late for an appointment and then I . . ." And he keeps talking about his day. Is John practicing active listening?

You might think so. John probably thinks so. After all, he interacted with her. He heard about her rough day and told about his own. But notice how he turned the conversation toward himself. Instead of drawing her out and learning more about her feelings, he wanted to hear himself talk.

In my job, I practice active listening all day. I get paid to do that. But I'm amazed at the number of people who leave a counseling session saying, "I feel like you're my best friend. You're about the closest person to me. I can tell you anything." Why do they say this? They don't know a thing about me! Yet active listening is such an act of giving that these people feel *loved*. Perhaps if more friends practiced active listening, we'd need fewer counselors.

The skills are simple. You merely need to put yourself in the other person's place. Imagine the feelings that he or she may have felt, and then get the person to talk on that level. What did you think about that? How did you feel? Be interested in what's inside the other person, and let your questions flow.

MAKE IT YOUR OWN

➤ Have you ever practiced active listening? If so, when?

_____

_____

➤ Has anyone else actively listened to you? Who? When?

_____

_____

➤ How have you felt when someone else was actively listening to you?

_____

_____

➤ How have you felt when you were actively listening to someone else?

_____

_____

➤ What do you think is the hardest thing about active listening?

_____

_____

SELF-DISCLOSURE

A flip side of active listening is self-disclosure. If all I do is listen, that's not a true friendship forming—it's more like a counseling relationship. I need to reveal what is going on inside me. If a friend of mine hurts me in some way, I need to commit myself to let him know that he has hurt me—and to do so in a loving way. That's how our friendship will grow.

Self-disclosure isn't always easy. Many good listeners out there are terrified to self-disclose. That makes them vulnerable, leaving them open to judgment, to analysis. Maybe the other person won't like how they think or feel. But to build an intimate friendship, they must take that risk.

Many other people self-disclose in negative ways. They feel no hesitation to tell you exactly how they feel at any given moment. Some of them self-disclose through *nagging:* "You didn't do this. You made me feel awful. If you were really a friend, you'd do this." And when you complain about their nagging, they say, "Hey, I was just being honest about my feelings. Can't we be honest with each other?" Well, yes, but the Bible talks about "speaking the truth *in love*" (Eph. 4:15 NKJV, emphasis added). We need to self-disclose in loving ways.

Other people self-disclose only *in self-defense*. That is, if they are criticized (by someone else's self-disclosure), they shoot back a list of ways the other person has hurt them: "Well, what about the time you did this, and this, and this . . . ?" Yes, it is self-disclosure. Those things probably need to be said. But the timing is bad.

We need to self-disclose when the relationship is at its best. That's tough to do because it may ruin the mood. But the time to bring up negative points for fixing is when things are going well. "I appreciate you very much, but when you said such and such the other day, it really bothered me. I really felt that you were putting me down." At the right moment, in the right spirit, that problem can be dealt with positively and the relationship strengthened.

If you don't take advantage of these good moments for healthy self-disclosure, the problems will squeeze out in unhealthy moments. You need to make it a point to self-disclose on a regular basis, to be honest about how you're feeling at all times in the relationship.

MAKE IT YOUR OWN

➤ On a scale of 1 to 10 (10 being best), how good are you at self-disclosure?

_____

➤ When was the last time you made a significant statement of self-disclosure to a loved one? What was it? _____

_____

_____

➤ About what percentage of your self-disclosure statements are said in the wrong way or at the wrong time? _____

➤ How could you decrease this percentage (move toward the positive side)? _____

_____

➤ Are you better at active listening or self-disclosure? What could you do to become better in your weaker area? _____

_____

_____

➤ Is there a statement of self-disclosure you need to make to someone soon? What is it?

I feel_____

when you_____.

➤ And here's what I'd like us to do about it: _____

_____

_____

PATTERNS OF CONFLICT

Often, in our relationships, we experience the same old conflicts again and again. Maybe the subject matter changes, but the patterns remain the same. One partner gets hurt, but doesn't say anything. Instead, he carries it inside and adds to it until six months later he blows up. And the other partner doesn't take it seriously because at the time it seems so trivial.

Or maybe one partner stonewalls the other and just grows cold. The other goes crazy trying to please the cold partner, bending over backward until that person snaps and starts yelling, which breaks down the wall but makes the yeller feel guilty.

We all have our crazy patterns. We need to avoid the bad ones and find the good ones. We need to break our bad patterns at the opportune moments and develop new habits that will improve our relationships.

I tend to fit into that first pattern, letting things build until I blow up. I have been trying to learn (with some success) how to let off steam earlier, so I never reach that boiling point.

I've appreciated one research report based on a study of couples who got along well and other couples who were breaking up. The researchers found three common patterns of conflict: agenda building, arguing, and negotiating. Both the happily married and the unhappily married went through these stages. But the unhappy couples spent most of their time agenda building and arguing, while the happy couples majored in negotiating. (This is further evidence that healthy relationships are not devoid of conflict, but the partners *work through* their conflicts.)

The report showed that the happy couples had one partner (usually the wife) who took responsibility to stop the arguing before it got out of hand. She would blow the whistle and move into negotiation. Take note of that. It takes *one partner* to stop the arguing and start the problem solving. Of course, the other partner has to be somewhat cooperative and committed to the relationship. But it takes two to keep a fight going, and only one to stop it.

As I read that report, I kept thinking about a similar report issued about three thousand years earlier. It's in the book of Proverbs: "A soft answer turns away wrath" (15:1 NKJV). Do you want to stop the pattern of building your own agenda (figuring out how to get your own way) and then fighting about it? Then give a soft answer and start negotiating.

"Let's calm down and talk about this honestly."

"You're right. I was wrong. I'm sorry."

"I care about you too much to argue like this. Let's start over."

Soft answers like this can defuse arguments and get you headed toward good patterns of problem solving.

Now you tell me! Is that what you're thinking? Now that you're divorced, it's hard to apply these words to your marriage. But you are probably now developing new relationships (not necessarily dating relationships, though that day may come, but new friendships). Be on the lookout for people with whom you can develop good patterns of problem solving. Listen for those soft answers.

MAKE IT YOUR OWN

➤ How would you describe your pattern of conflict? _____

_____

_____

➤ In the space below, draw a graph of your normal pattern of conflict.

➤ When you are in conflict in your closest relationship, what percentage of your time would you say you spend in the following areas?

_____% Agenda building (figuring out how to get your way)

_____% Arguing

_____% Negotiating

➤ What can you do to break your negative patterns and establish good patterns? _____

_____

_____

➤ In the space below, draw a graph of how you would like your pattern of conflict to be.

➤ Is there one person in your closest relationship who usually defuses the argument? Who? _____

_____

_____

➤ Have you ever been in an argument when a soft answer defused it? When? What happened? _____

_____

_____

_____

Action Point: When you think about the way you communicated in your marriage, what are some of the areas you now see you need to improve before you get into another serious relationship? _____

_____

_____

_____

_____

➤ Write here, and on page 282 (Appendix A), the skills that you need to work on most in order to be an effective communicator.

_____

_____

_____

_____

_____

_____

_____

_____

_____

_____

_____

_____

_____

_____

_____

_____

Chapter 8

EVERYTHING YOU ALWAYS WANTED TO KNOW ABOUT…
SEXUALITY FOR THE SINGLE AGAIN[1]

I am supposed to be a mature man now, about half a century old. The general presumption seems to be that people my age know all about sex and sexuality, but generally, I don't believe we do. Even though we are living in a time thought to be awakened and free in regard to sexuality, I find that I'm not alone in feeling that my education in sexual matters has been everything but complete and correct.

GROWING UP

I can't remember exactly when sexuality became interesting to me, but I know it was early. I was only ten years old when a little girl in my class at school sent tremors of fascination and desire all through me. I didn't think very much about the nature of that state of trembling back then. I just enjoyed it. But what was beginning to happen to me then has continued to influence my life ever since.

The kids of my generation had a head start on our parents in understanding sexuality, but we still lived in sexual ignorance. Nobody really talked about sexuality when we were growing up. Oh, sure, there was a sprinkling of "sex talk" in almost every conversation, but it never really got serious. Nobody ever sat down with us and explained anything sexual in a meaningful and helpful way. We were pretty much left at the mercy of the literature on the rest-room walls and the library's anatomy books.

There was health class, but that was about biology. It was good to find at least one place where we could take a legitimate look at the facts of life. The facts about the sexual anatomy and the reproductive system and the venereal diseases were important, but you had the feeling that there were other facts you should know too. If others knew those other facts, however, they weren't talking.

Then along came Hugh Hefner and his magazine, which drew a lot of attention. He began to publish *Playboy* when I was fourteen, but he didn't help much. Even while we boys were going out of our minds "reading" *Playboy,* somehow I think most of us knew that we weren't getting a fair shake from Hefner either. The morals of our homes and the general negativism of the church were too strong for us to accept Hefner without question.

Then there were the real girls we knew.

Real girls were so different from the pinups. The pinups just stood there without their clothes and smiled at you. Real girls kept their clothes on and didn't always smile (at least, not at me). Real girls could talk, too, and they never talked about sex. When we started dating, sex was the last thing we ever talked about. Certainly, it was on our minds. (I assume it was on the girls' minds too. I can't be sure because I never heard anyone say so.) But you didn't talk about sex on a date. You just acted very knowing and groped around in the dark.

When or where did anyone dare to talk honestly? Who ever dared to say right out loud, "I really need some help understanding sexuality; do you understand sexuality?"

No one.

Even when we got married, most of us didn't talk about sexuality. We had sexual intercourse, and we enjoyed that, but a cloud of confusion covered many things. Most distressing of all, we still didn't know where to turn for help. The doctors talked only about biological facts, the social organizations talked about diseases and unwanted pregnancies, and the church just didn't talk. Any thinking you did concerning sexuality, you did *all alone*!

Finally, however, we had the sexual revolution of the 1960s. People rebelled against the old traditions and threw off their clothes. Suddenly, everything was discussed. The shock was almost too much for us, especially Christians. What should we think? What should we do? Most of us probably felt some inner gladness that finally it was okay to talk about sex in public,

but it was scary. It seemed as if society was going too far. Mere nakedness and sexual conversation were not enough in themselves. If the new sexual revolution didn't produce helpful insight into the meaning and nature of sexuality, we might be worse off than before.

The new openness produced a flood of literature on sexuality (even books *without pictures*). And now even the church is talking. What a relief to be able to read about and discuss this side of our lives!

But do *you* understand sexuality? You may be very much like me—still groping along, trying to put a number of undefined questions into meaningful form, still listening hard to everything that's said in the hope that some answers really do exist.

MAKE IT YOUR OWN

➤ How does your experience match up to the author's? Consider the following statements:

As I grew up, my family

❏ talked freely about sexuality.

❑ joked about sexual matters.

❑ spoke very seriously about sexual matters.

❑ never talked about sexuality.

❑ Other: _____

_____

I learned most about sex from

❑ my parents.

❑ health class.

❑ friends.

❑ experimentation.

❑ graffiti.

❑ Other: _____

_____

As I look back, I think I

❑ knew too much about sex too soon.

❑ knew a lot about sex, but I'm glad.

❑ didn't know much about sex, but that was okay.

❑ didn't know as much as I should have known about sex.

❑ Other: _____

_____

My attitude toward sexual matters now is:

❑ I think about sex all the time.

❑ I am generally embarrassed about the whole subject.

❑ I talk pretty freely about the subject.

❑ It's a private thing, so I talk about sex only when it's appropriate.

❑ It rarely enters my mind.

❑ Other: _____

_____

_____

➤ Is there something that you wish you had known about sexuality when you were younger? If so, what is that? _____

_____

_____

_____

DEFINING *SEXUALITY*

It may seem a bit bold of me, having just admitted that I'm still groping after the truth, to burst into print on the subject of sexuality. So allow me to say emphatically that I don't think of myself as an authority on the subject. I am a learner, like you. I'm looking for answers too.

Some things, however, are becoming increasingly clear to me, and I want to share them with you because I know how difficult it can be to get a proper perspective. I'll begin by developing a definition of sexuality. To do that, let's look first at some things that sexuality is *not*.

Sexuality Is Not a Substitute for God

Sexuality is not a substitute for God.

"Who in the world ever thought it was?" you might ask.

True, few people in our society would consciously worship sexuality as a god (though in some cultures sexual activity, considered a method of communion with God, has been part of the worship ceremony). But many treat sex as a kind of idol. Ours is a sex-obsessed society. Our books, movies, music, clothes, and a tremendous amount of media advertising consistently beat a sexual rhythm into our brains. We are being told that life aims largely, if not entirely, at sexual fulfillment. The assumption seems to be that if we seek it with all of our hearts (not to mention our time and money), we'll soon achieve the atomic sexual experience and finally be fulfilled and complete. That attitude, I submit, is idolatrous.

You see, when anyone tells you that anything other than God himself can make you a fulfilled and happy person, that person is encouraging you toward idolatry. Idolatry, after all, is nothing more or less than placing something other than God in first place in your life. No matter what it is, if you give something first place in your life, that thing has become a god to you, and you have become involved in a form of false worship.

Two very significant things occur whenever people turn to idolatry, no matter what the false god is. First of all, *they expect the false god to do for them what only the true and living God can do*—they expect it to complete and fulfill them. They assume they will achieve the greatest happiness by seeking and serving the false god. The result, of course, is disappointment and emptiness. People have obviously done this with sexuality in our society. Millions have swallowed the *Playboy* philosophy only to end up burned out and disillusioned.

The second thing that happens when people turn to idolatry is that *they lose the meaning and significance of the thing they have chosen as their idol.* When the idolater puts an idol in the place of highest significance and importance, he or she has thereby removed it from its proper place. Now it can't provide the good for which God designed it.

You see, all things were created by God with good purposes inherent in them, and that includes sexuality! God designed it for our blessing. However, that good can be obtained only by those who keep the proper perspective. When we take sexuality out of its proper place, we lose the right perspective and, consequently, the blessing that God wants it to give us.

> **Sexuality must not be put in God's place. If it is, it will lose its power to bless and ultimately will always disappoint us.**

Sexuality, like all other created aspects of human nature, is only part of our createdness and must therefore be subordinated to God like everything else. However, while sexuality is not God and cannot provide our ultimate happiness, it is indeed a marvelous and wonderful part of the way God has made us. It is his gift to us, and when it is properly understood and enjoyed, it provides us with much good.

➤ As you look at society, in what ways do people make sex an idol?

_____

_____

_____

➤ Have you done this in your life? If so, how? _____

_____

_____

➤ In what ways (if any) has your worship of sex hurt your worship of God?

_____

_____

_____

➤ In what ways (if any) has your worship of sex diminished the true value of sex in your life?_____

_____

_____

_____

Sexuality Is Not Love

Here's a second negative definition: sexuality is not the same thing as love. It has something to do with love and cannot be correctly understood apart from love, but it's not the same thing. People often express their sexuality in ways that aren't loving.

An obvious example of unloving sexual expression is rape. Clearly, rape is sexual, but it's not love. Prostitution is also sexual, but only a very confused person would think of it as love. In addition, there are many selfish and, therefore, quite unloving ways in which even married people sometimes use sexuality.

Many people have found themselves in great confusion and pain because they have mistakenly supposed that sexuality was identical to love. Many a young woman has yielded to a young man's sexual demands, all the while assuming that his sexual desire for her meant that he loved her. How wrong we are to use the term *making love* as a synonym for sexual intercourse! Sexual intercourse can be a wonderful way to express love, but it can express many unloving things as well. There is a great difference between sexuality and love, and we'd better learn the difference!

It would be wrong for me to assume that someone loves me just because she has sexual interest in me. And it would be wrong for me to assume that I love a woman just because I have sexual desire for her. My inability to discern this difference caused me many problems when I was growing up. If I became attracted to a young woman sexually, I found it very easy to think that I was in love. What I loved, however, was not the girl, but the surge of sexual need and desire within myself. In many cases, I didn't even know the girl.

It's rather simple to determine if I have sexual desire for a woman, but it's much more complicated to find out whether or not I love her. I have to ask myself many questions beyond the subject of physical pleasure. I must concern myself with her whole being, *not just her body*. To love her, I must want her whole personality, her mind's peculiar way of thinking, her varying moods, her attitudes, and her interests.

Beyond that, if I love her, I must be willing to make some commitments to her. I must commit myself to her, not only for the moment, but for the future. Consider the familiar concepts of the marriage vows: "for better or worse . . . in sickness and health . . . for richer or poorer." Such thoughts go beyond sexuality to the whole of life.

Other kinds of love don't include sexual expressions. One may love his parents, for example, or his brothers and sisters, or children, or friends. Such relationships commonly involve physical expressions of affection—warm handshakes, hugs, and kisses. Yet these expressions are not sexual in nature. Physical touch is legitimate in its own right and plays an important part in all love relationships, but it's not always sexual. Neither is the desire for physical touch necessarily a sexual desire.

This last distinction is very important for a variety of reasons. Many people carry around a tremendous burden of false guilt because they're affectionate persons who enjoy touch. Other people often mistake these innocent touches for sexual overtures, and that can lead to serious misunderstandings. Sometimes these high-touch people can even misunderstand *themselves*, thinking they must have an overeager sexual appetite when really they just want to be hugged.

➤ Do you like the term *making love* as it is used by our society? How would *you* define it? _____

_____

_____

➤ What are the dangers of equating physical sexuality with love?

_____

_____

_____

➤ List ten expressions of love that are not sexual.

1. _____   6. _____

2. _____   7. _____

3. _____   8. _____

4. _____   9. _____

5. _____   10. _____

➤ Have you tended to equate sexuality with love in your relationships? Why? _____

_____

➤ Have you dealt with others who have done this? Explain what happened.

_____

_____

_____

> ### *What Sexuality Is Not:*
> ### A substitute for God
> ### The same thing as love
> ### Merely a biological function

Sexuality Is Not Merely a Biological Function

A third thing we often confuse with sexuality is biological sex, or sexual intercourse itself. Your sexuality is much, much more than a biological thing.

Our society does a lot of talking about sex without saying anything about sexuality. Most of the books on sex today are about biological sex—what to move; how, when, and where to touch. The purpose, by and large, is to produce that atomic experience I spoke of earlier. Everyone assumes that sex is about one thing—physical pleasure.

But true sexuality is not merely physical, biological, or genital. It's not even *primarily* physical, biological, or genital. *Sexuality is spiritual and personal!*

Sexuality Is Spiritual

If you've had any degree of sexual experience, I don't have to prove to you that mere biological sex can be an extremely frustrating and empty experience. It is quite possible to have intercourse, even to the point of explosive, vibrant, physical climax, without having much personal satisfaction. Many married people experience a lot of negative feelings about their physical sexual relationship, and I believe that it's often because they're ignoring the spiritual aspect of sexuality. For genuine fulfillment and satisfaction, you must recognize the mental, emotional, and spiritual dimensions of your sexuality, along with the physical.

The movie *Annie Hall* forcefully makes this point. In one scene, Woody Allen and Diane Keaton are in bed together having sexual intercourse. Then a very strange thing happens. Suddenly, a second Diane Keaton appears, a rather ghostly one. She gets out of the bed, steps across the room, sits in a chair, and stares at Woody and the other Diane in bed. The look on her face shows clearly that she's bored.

Then Woody looks over at the Diane in the chair and says something like, "That's what gets me about you, you never put yourself into this." The ghostly Diane responds that he should be happy because he's got all he really wants there in the bed. He has her body.

It's a very funny scene, but deep down inside we all know the loneliness, hurt, and anger that often accompany sexual intercourse. A man and a woman can unite sexually and still feel very far from each other in personal ways.

Look more closely at what Woody and Diane are saying. Diane is hurt and angry because she believes that all Woody wants from her is the use of her body to satisfy his physical desires. Woody, however, is hurt and angry because all Diane will give him is her body. Diane wants more than Woody's body, and she wants him to want more than her body. Woody wants more than Diane's body, and he wants her to give him more than her body. Both Woody and Diane know that sexuality is not a mere physical, genital relationship.

> **Sexuality is our God-given potential to share our whole selves—body, soul, and spirit—with another person. Sexual intercourse is the symbol of that sharing and whole-life commitment.**

This illustration helps us move toward a working definition of sexuality. *Sexuality is the human potential for the sharing of one's whole life with another.* It is the ability and need imprinted upon our nature by the Creator to give ourselves completely to another human being. It is also the ability and need to receive another person into our lives in a total and complete way. The romantic expression "body and soul" perhaps says it best. I have the ability and need to give myself, all of myself, the body and soul of myself, to another person. I have the ability and need to receive another, all of another, the body and soul of another, into my life.

The Meaning of Sexual Intercourse

This understanding of sexuality helps us to gain a correct understanding of sexual intercourse. Sexual intercourse is the symbol of the total-life sharing that God requires of those who marry. In sexual intercourse, one person actually enters into the body of another, an outward expression of what exists between the souls of two people who are totally committed to each other. This spiritual aspect is what makes human sex unique in all of God's creation.

Understood in this way, then, intercourse is lifted out of the merely physical realm. Without the deep commitment to whole-life sharing, sexual intercourse loses its meaning because it stands alone as a merely physical involvement between two persons.

➤ It has been said that a relationship should develop in the following order:

- Social

- Mental

- Spiritual

- Emotional

- Physical

➤ Is that a good order of progression? Why or why not? _____

_____

_____

➤ Answer the next two questions only if you have experienced these things.

➤ How does it feel to have sex without spiritual commitment?

_____

_____

➤ How does it feel to have sex with spiritual commitment?

_____

_____

➤ What does the following quotation from Lewis Smedes mean to you: "Sex without interpersonal intimacy is like a diploma without an education"?

_____

_____

_____

SEXUAL MORALITY

This understanding of sexuality as a whole-life sharing—and sexual intercourse as a symbol of the total union of husband and wife—helps explain

Christian morality. It provides an important part of the rationale for viewing sexual intercourse between unmarried persons as sin.

Because extramarital sexual intercourse violates the true meaning of sexuality, it therefore violates the very humanity of the two persons who commit the act. People who decide to have sexual intercourse without also having mutual commitment to whole-life (and lifelong) sharing are, in effect, deciding against their own wholeness and happiness.

You see, you just can't separate sexuality into parts without human pain. When people seek to enjoy the physical pleasures of sexuality without the spiritual pleasures, they will find the physical sexual experience becomes empty and hurtful.

What do I mean by the "spiritual pleasures" of sexuality? I mean the pleasures that accompany the knowledge that I am loved honestly; the assurance that my sexual partner is devoted to me alone; the certainty that my sexual partner loves me as a whole person and not merely for my body's attractiveness. The spiritual pleasures of sexuality also include the joy of knowing I'm loved regardless of how well I perform in physical sex on a particular day, and even on days when there is no sexual intercourse. Underpinning all such assurance and comfort is the certain knowledge that my sexual partner is personally committed to loving me in all the variety of life's experience *through my whole life*. Only the marriage promise can provide that certainty and pleasure!

The Importance of Commitment

In our day many will argue against the need for the marriage commitment. Two people can enjoy the pleasures of sexuality without marriage, they will say. There are two common arguments along this line. First, people will say it's possible to separate the two aspects of sexuality, enjoying physical, genital, sexual pleasure without the spiritual and personal assurances.

Well, of course, it's possible! But without those spiritual and personal commitments, our sexuality cannot be fully satisfied. In addition, people who have intercourse outside the marriage bond guarantee for themselves the experience of inward spiritual pain.

That pain includes fear, guilt, and loneliness. All of these grow directly out of the absence of the mutual commitment to whole-life sharing and support. The woman (or man) who wonders, *Will he/she respect me in the morning?* is fearing that she/he is not loved honestly and certainly.

The guilt of uncommitted sex has little to do with our social or religious views. Its deeper and more real cause is the soul's awareness that *love, to be real, must be committed love,* and we have not given it. We have not committed our whole selves to the other person, and we know instinctively that we should.

Those who manage to avoid the fears and guilt (and I sincerely doubt that anyone can completely avoid them) will never escape the loneliness that accompanies unmarried intercourse. The more a person insists on physical sexual pleasure without the undergirding of personal committed love, the more that person builds a wall around himself that no one can penetrate, not even himself.

Yes, one can enjoy the physical pleasures of sexuality apart from the spiritual pleasures, but not without denying some very basic needs. Every person needs the joy and satisfaction of committed love, and the longer a person goes on telling herself that she doesn't, the more personal guilt, fear, and/or loneliness she will create for herself by continuing to have sexual intercourse while unmarried.

The second argument against marriage has to do with other personal commitments *short of marriage* that couples make—such as moving in together. But such arrangements don't prove that commitment is unnecessary—on the contrary! Unmarried partners who live together are recognizing that a certain kind of commitment *is* necessary for the full and proper expression of their sexuality. Although they do not take the final step of formal marriage, they are demonstrating that they know that sexuality is more than merely a physical pleasure. All that they lack is the willingness to make a public commitment that would bind them together legally in a marriage recognized and honored in society.

In the final analysis, however, lovers who live together are failing to give each other the ultimate assurance of committed love. At any time, one or the other could get up and move out. Nothing binds them on a permanent whole-life basis. "Will you still respect me in the morning?" has merely become "Will you still respect me in six months or a year?"

Marriage, and marriage alone, is able to provide the solid foundation and framework necessary for the full expression of sexuality. Let me emphasize that I am speaking of marriage in the historic Christian sense of a *permanent* whole-life commitment between two people.

That's right—"till death do us part!" Nothing else but that absolute promise will do. This is true because any other view of marriage is susceptible to the same weaknesses as living together. If we say marriage is valid and binding only up to a point that one party decides to get up and leave, then we don't have what our sexuality cries for most deeply. We don't have committed love.

Some people will argue against marriage precisely on the ground I've just given. How can anyone possibly know himself or his spouse-to-be well enough to make a permanent lifelong commitment like that? No one knows how things will go a few years down the road. People change; feelings change.

But *you can't know for sure unless you decide to commit for sure.* Marriage cannot possibly be safe for anyone if it is based on things that change. That is why the vow of commitment is so important. Marriage, to be safe, must be based on unconditional promises of love. The marriage vow says, "I will love you even if you change," and further, "I will love you even if I change." Only the people who are willing to make that kind of commitment to each other, to become that vulnerable to each other, have the right to the delights of sexual intercourse. Without that commitment, sexual intercourse is a mere shell of momentary physical pleasure.

MAKE IT YOUR OWN

➤ According to the author, why should sexual intercourse be restricted to marriage relationships? _____

_____

_____

_____

➤ Do you agree or disagree with his reasoning? _____

_____

_____

➤ What pain can result from sex without commitment? _____

_____

_____

➤ Do you think divorced people are, in general, more or less tempted to engage in extramarital sex than the never-married? Why? _____

_____

_____

_____

➤ How do you respond to the following statements?

a. You really can't know if you'll be good marriage partners unless you live together first. _____

_____

b. As long as you're not a virgin anymore, it doesn't matter if you have sex. _____

_____

c. Sex is just for fun. Why get so hung up about commitment?

_____

_____

d. Why bother with all this fancy reasoning? God's Word says, "No sex outside marriage," and that's enough for me. _____

_____

e. We can experience the fullness of sexual intercourse only when it is expressed within the spiritual commitment of marriage. _____

_____

_____

f. The prevalence of divorce proves that marriage is an outdated institution. To reserve sex for marriage is archaic. _____

_____

_____

For your assistance, I'll add some thoughts on each of these statements. They are not definitive answers, but they'll help you weigh the issues.

a. The permanence of marriage is a unique factor that no live-in arrangement can test. You must enter by faith. People should go into marriage with their eyes wide open, knowing a great deal about their prospective spouses. But sexual intercourse should still be reserved for the relationship of permanent spiritual commitment.

b. Some religious subcultures have made a big deal about virginity, which is fine except for this backlash. Nonvirgins sometimes feel they can no longer be sexually pure, so why not live it up? Obviously, this applies to many divorced people—you saved yourself for marriage, the marriage broke up, so what's there to save yourself for anymore? Well, God's mercies are "new every morning," and so is your purity—and your responsibility. Each day you make new moral decisions. If you're in Christ, the past doesn't matter; today's choices do.

c. As I've said, to divide the spiritual aspect of sex from the physical is to vandalize one of our most precious gifts. Sex without commitment can be fun, sure, but it's not what it's supposed to be, and it's ultimately dangerous.

d. Well, yes. God says it, I believe it, and that settles it. But God says things that make sense. He has given us minds to understand his commands. Especially in a world that increasingly thinks Christian morality is crazy, it helps to figure out the sense of it. As we're bombarded by temptation, our minds can help us to obey God rather than lead us astray.

e. That's what I've been saying.

f. Old is not necessarily bad. The prevalence of divorce doesn't prove anything. It may be that certain modern factors contributing to a high divorce rate—no-fault divorce, our sex-crazy age, materialism, and so forth—are the problem. Marriage is a God-given, time-honored institution. Maybe things would be better for all of us if we honored it more.

> **Sex without commitment brings spiritual pain.**

SINGLE (AGAIN) SEXUALITY

For the person who has been divorced, this study of sexuality may seem like an exercise in utter frustration. What possible sexual fulfillment or wholeness can I now expect? Apart from remarriage (and there may well be many reasons why remarriage is not in the picture for me), I'm condemned to a life of sexual emptiness.

No, not necessarily. While the road to sexual fulfillment and wholeness is difficult and treacherous for the person who is single again, it's possible to travel that road successfully by God's grace and with God's guidance. I am writing to you as a person who has traveled that road. I've stumbled and fallen into many of the pitfalls. I've learned hard lessons about my weakness and emptiness. I've also found that there are sexual fullness and wholeness for the single person who will commit himself to the pattern God has given us. Let me offer some suggestions for your guidance.

Develop a Positive Attitude Toward Your Sexuality

The first thing we need is to feel good about our sexuality. We can begin to accomplish this by recognizing that our sexuality is God-given and that God designed us as sexual beings for the furtherance and strengthening of our lives.

If you go back and study the definition of sexuality I've given, you'll recognize that your sexuality has to do with your whole being. You are a person created with the God-given ability to seek and find fullness and wholeness in others. You are able to give yourself to others and to receive others into yourself.

Don't let yourself be tripped up by guilt or fear in regard to your sexuality. Perhaps you've made a lot of serious mistakes of a sexual nature. Perhaps others have abused you sexually. Undoubtedly, you've experienced pain and disillusionment. Still, your sexuality is God's good gift to you, and if you'll take the time to learn well how to understand your sexuality, it can lead into wholeness.

Set the Goal of Self-Sharing for Your Life

Sexuality demands self-sharing, not just body sharing. We were created as persons capable of giving more than our bodies to others. That is the fundamental truth about sexuality, but perhaps you haven't learned it yet.

Here, then, is a good starting place for becoming a fulfilled and whole person: learning how to share yourself, your real, personal self. Intimacy with others is absolutely necessary if you are to become what you ought to be as a sexual being.

At this point, however, one of the sexual pitfalls lies in wait. How is it possible to develop personal intimacy without physical sexual involvement? Good question, and there are good answers.

In the first place, make clear in your mind the distinction between personal intimacy and physical sexual (genital) intimacy. It is possible—indeed, it is very important—to learn to become an intimate person in ways that don't involve physical sexual touch. For many people, the very word *intimacy* means drawing close to another person in a sexual way. But many ways of being close don't involve sexual touching. Anytime I reveal my true self to you and trust you with that knowledge, I am being intimate.

The best road to intimacy is *talk*. To develop as a self-sharing person, I must learn to talk about my true self. I must therefore learn to be very honest. I must recognize what I truly am like and develop the courage and trust to disclose the truth about me to others.

A necessary corollary to self-revealing talk is *trust*. To be a self-sharing person, I will have to learn to trust. Lack of trust causes us to be cautious and self-protecting. We all fear that if we honestly reveal ourselves as we truly are, others might reject us. But if you don't develop the trust necessary to reveal yourself, then no one will have the opportunity to love the real you.

For the person who has been deeply injured in a love relationship, this step of trust will be extremely difficult, but it's an essential step toward wholeness. Trust is also the only pathway of escape from loneliness. If I don't trust anyone and never reveal my true self to anyone, no one will ever be able to be my friend. I may have many superficial relationships, but I will have no honest ones.

Loneliness is one of the greatest causes of our sexual distress and sorrow. Loneliness, far more than mere physical desire, drives single strangers into bed with each other. Here again, we must see that the spiritual side of sexuality comes into play. As sexual beings, we long to share ourselves with another, seeking fulfillment in that person. However, because most of us have learned far too little about self-sharing, we are tempted to move quickly past the spiritual side of sexuality and to plunge headlong into the physical sharing of our bodies.

An important caution is therefore necessary. The person who is recently single again may find herself stricken with terrible loneliness. It's very easy for those so stricken to misinterpret their personal longing for intimacy as a merely physical sexual need. This confusion is a primary reason why so many divorced people so quickly land in bed with partners they hardly know. And there's an even greater danger: a rebound relationship that includes sexual intercourse may ultimately produce an even greater mistrust and unwillingness to share oneself, which in turn will only deepen the loneliness.

I suggest, then, that a person who is single again go very slowly and cautiously in developing his ability to trust others and reveal himself. At first it's probably best for women to seek other women and for men to seek other men for self-sharing friendships. Gradually, those who are learning to share again will develop the strength to reveal themselves to others of the opposite sex without great vulnerability to physical sexual temptation.

As we learn to reveal ourselves to others in deep personal ways, other healthy characteristics will develop in us. First of all, *we'll learn to understand ourselves*. Talking honestly with others requires us to think about what we really want and what things are motivating us. It will also allow us to ask questions we might never have asked ourselves while alone. One of the healthiest things a person can do is to discover that there are attitudes and behavior patterns in his life that he has never honestly analyzed and, therefore, never understood.

This matter of learning to understand ourselves has a lot of bearing on our sexual behavior. Many people play sexual games with members of the opposite sex without ever realizing they are doing it. One reason for such games is the simple fact that these people have not examined their thoughts and motives honestly.

A man may, for example, put on a great show of tenderness and understanding for a woman when he really just wants sex. The tenderness is a superficial veneer. In cases like this, the man is often very lonely, aching to love and be loved, but doesn't know how to understand his personal needs in anything but physical, sexual terms. The greater tragedy may be that the poor fellow doesn't even know the game he's playing. He hasn't learned to know himself honestly. He needs *talk* far more than he needs sexual intercourse.

A second healthy characteristic that develops when we reveal ourselves to others is that *we'll learn how to let others reveal themselves to us*. The process is reciprocal. When I take the time to reveal myself honestly, I'm going to learn about the process of self-revealing. That will, in turn, help me to understand what's happening when others honestly share themselves with me. It will also help me see the truth when others are only being superficial and manipulative with me.

A third thing that happens is that *we'll begin to develop a greater control over our actions*. We'll find that we know much better than before who we really are and what we really want. We will have become much stronger persons who know how to say yes and no seriously. Perhaps no quality of life has greater value to us morally than the ability to say yes and no with personal strength. What a devastating thing it is to discover that, no matter what I think I want, and no matter what I say, I cannot honor my own principles and cannot keep my word. Self-sharing helps us to develop into people who can honor our own words. This, obviously, will be a great help in keeping ourselves free from the control of others, but more important, it will keep us full of inner peace. I will find that I am becoming much happier with myself because I am making decisions that I am also sticking with. More deeply than that, I'll be growing in true self-knowledge.

Perhaps this last thought is obvious, but let me underscore a fourth result of self-sharing. As we learn to share ourselves, we'll be learning how to do the one thing that's most important to sexual fulfillment. *We'll be growing into people who have the ability to commit ourselves to others*. Remember again my definition of sexuality and the importance of personal commitment in finding sexual fulfillment. Many people never find personal sexual fullness because they have never learned to give themselves. They have given only their bodies. We can learn to give our whole selves.

➤ How positive is your attitude toward your sexuality? Check all that apply.

❏ It gets me in trouble all the time.

❏ I am regularly frustrated by it.

❏ I enjoy my sexuality, within limits.

❏ I don't feel like a sexual being at all right now.

❏ Other: _____

_____

➤ On a scale of 1 to 10 (10 being best), how good are you at sharing yourself with others through *talk*? _____

➤ On a scale of 1 to 10, how good are you at trusting others? _____

➤ What effect did your divorce have on your ability to trust others?

_____

_____

➤ Which of the following best describes you?

❏ I share myself deeply in conversations with others.

❏ I tend to rush right past talking and get sexually involved with others.

❏ I'd like to talk with people more, but I'm never sure what to say.

❏ I talk with people, but I don't trust people enough to reveal much of myself.

❏ I'm afraid to reveal myself to others.

❏ Other: _____

_____

> **Sexuality demands self-sharing, not just body sharing.**

LEARN SELF-CONTROL WITHOUT SELF-CONDEMNATION

In the previous section I emphasized that as a person grows in self-knowledge, she will also grow in the ability to control herself. As she learns better who she is and what she honestly desires for her life, she will grow in her ability to say yes and no. The ability to control oneself is an extremely important part of healthy single sexuality.

While I believe it is very important to develop into a self-sharing person, I must stress that sexual intercourse is absolutely out of the picture for the single Christian. I hold wholeheartedly to the biblical morality that forbids sexual intercourse outside marriage. I believe that a serious Christian single person must willingly accept that truth as a binding moral principle for his life. And he must do so because he sees and understands the true nature of human sexuality as a whole-life (and lifelong) sharing of two persons. Unless he reaches the point of being willing to share himself on a whole-life scale with someone who shares that same commitment, he will never possess the privilege of physical sexual union with another.

The single Christian must, therefore, practice self-control of his physical sexual desires. That, of course, is easier said than done. There are many temptations to sin along this part of the Christian's journey, but it's possible for the sincere Christian to control himself if he honestly wants to.

Let me mention something here that gets at a tremendous problem in our contemporary society. I don't believe that the satisfaction of physical sexual appetite is a basic life need. This statement may surprise you if you've seen many movies or read many sex books recently. The prevailing view of much of our society seems to be that our physical sexual appetite *must be satisfied.* We're told that normal, healthy life requires it. To survive, we have to eat, we have to drink, and we have to have intercourse. That is simple falsehood. It's possible to live a fully normal, healthy, and happy life without sexual intercourse. You will die if you don't eat and drink, but you won't die if you abstain from sex. The failure (perhaps I should say *refusal*) to recognize this fundamental fact makes it difficult for many people even to consider sexual self-control. Yet self-control is not only possible, it's required of the Christian single person. This is God's rule of life for us, and we must seek it if we want to walk with God.

Let me suggest some things that will help in the struggle for self-control.

First of all, self-control is impossible for the person who refuses to make a commitment to it. Self-control begins with a hard and clear decision to be a certain kind of person. The single person who toys around with his commitment is guaranteeing his failure at self-control, but the person who honestly determines that he'll refrain from sexual intercourse is going to have success.

I want to emphasize the *certainty of success* for those who make a personal commitment to refrain from sexual intercourse. A real commitment made by a person who knows himself well will bring success. I am talking about determination—a life-and-death determination.

"Wait!" you might say. "I might try to control myself sexually, but you know how it is. I get with that perfect person, and one thing leads to another. How can I possibly fight temptation when it's that strong?"

All right, let's take that scenario and put it in a different light. Suppose you're with the one you love, the mood is right, and things are moving along physically to a point where you're about to have intercourse. Most people would assume that self-control would be long gone by that point. But now suppose your partner announces, "Oh, by the way, have I told you that I have AIDS?"

Now let me ask you again: Do you have self-control at that moment? Sure you do. Why the difference? Probably because now you see it as a matter of life and death. Suddenly, your determination is raised to a satisfactory level.

To maintain sexual self-control, you need a determined commitment that includes several ingredients. It includes *being fully honest with oneself*. The person who is committed to not having sexual intercourse, for example, will not lie to herself about her relative strength and weakness. She'll be honest, acknowledging the temptation she faces and her vulnerability to it. One wonders how many sexual tragedies might have been avoided if people had only known how to be honest with themselves.

Such honesty will help you with the second ingredient: *staying out of tempting situations*. Avoid any temptation and anything that leads toward a greater vulnerability to temptation.

A number of examples are obvious. A person who is working on self-control needs to have the good sense to turn off the myriad influences that draw people toward sexual activity. Certain types of music are powerful sexual stimulants. The same is true of TV programs, movies, magazines, and books. The person who is determined to control himself should also stay out of the kinds of social gatherings that are designed to be sexually supercharged. Singles bars and nightclubs are not suitable places to learn self-control.

Also be careful about being alone with members of the opposite sex. I suggest strongly that recently divorced people not date at all until they have good reason to believe they are strong in self-control. There is really no substitute for good sense, you know. Even the strong person needs to watch out for one-on-one situations.

The final ingredient of successful self-control is *having the support of others*. You don't need people who will tempt you or point you toward temptation, but you still need people. You need friends with whom you can (and will) be honest about your weakness and who will, in turn, encourage and support you in your commitment to self-control. In my life following divorce, I found that I began to grow in self-control precisely at the time that I began honestly to share my struggle with a close friend. The mere fact that he knew the nature of my struggle was a constant help to me. In addition, he was able to pray for me and encourage me regularly.

No Condemnation

Sexuality is a battleground for many people, especially Christians. As we think about our sexuality, we can easily fall into patterns of guilt and self-condemnation. But we need to keep reminding ourselves that our sexuality is God's gift, intended for our development as whole and fulfilled persons. I may be weak, and I may be struggling for self-mastery; but that is no reason to feel guilt. I should seek the cleansing and strength that God offers me in Christ.

Furthermore, I would be wrong to approach my sexual nature as if it were an evil part of myself that deserves condemnation. The struggle for sexual self-control ought to be viewed in the same way we view any other kind of personal growth and development. It is positive and healthy and right to learn and grow. The process of sexual self-control is one kind of personal growth. The more we set the right goals for ourselves and honestly strive for sexual self-control, the more we will become the strong, fulfilled persons God wants us to be. As we gain more self-control, we'll feel better about ourselves, and we'll be more able to commit ourselves to others. Commitment, you see, requires self-control.

Place Marriage in the Hands of God

It's not always God's purpose for us to marry. Every single Christian must consider this fact. Every divorced Christian must accept the thought that you might not marry again.

Many single people make marriage an unqualified personal goal for their lives, and that's a mistake. Such people may have great difficulty in learning what they need to learn about themselves and, in particular, gaining a healthy understanding of their sexuality.

The person who makes marriage her only goal may easily short-circuit the lessons about self-sharing that I described earlier. Suppose, for example, that you get involved with someone romantically, and after six weeks, that person suggests marriage. If you have made marriage your primary goal, you may say yes without giving any serious consideration to what you're doing. There are many good reasons some people ought not to marry, and you may be ignoring many that apply to you.

For example, have you become a person who is able and willing to share yourself on a whole-life basis? Have you learned how to reveal yourself honestly and how to trust others with the knowledge of who you are? Does your new love interest really know you well enough to make a whole-life commitment to you? Many people will not ask themselves these questions if they are committed to marriage as an unqualified personal goal.

Unexamined motives and reasons may drive people toward marriage. A man may desire marriage merely to solve the problem of his loneliness. A woman may marry because she needs help with raising children. Some people get married to solve financial problems. And some marry just to satisfy the genital urge. All of these are entirely selfish and, therefore, unacceptable reasons for marriage.

If you haven't proved that you've learned how to share yourself honestly, how to trust another fully, and how to make and keep promises, you shouldn't even be considering marriage. In the end, the happiness and wholeness of every marriage depend on the ability of the two people involved to make and keep a promise of personal commitment.

The single Christian must accept the possibility that he will never marry. It is quite possible to become a fulfilled and happy single person. You need to take the responsibility of developing your life, becoming the kind of person who can share deeply with others. As you do this, you'll be developing the very aspects of your nature that must be developed if you'll ever have a balanced and whole sexuality.

An interesting thing will happen to the person who accepts singleness and determines to grow as a self-sharing person. Instead of concentrating on marriage as a goal, he or she will focus on personal wholeness, developing self-knowledge and self-control as well as a strong positive attitude toward sexuality. The satisfied single Christian will learn to see sexuality as a gift from God and will willingly submit his or her sexuality to God, letting God call the shots about any future marriage.

Sexual Fulfillment

Ironically, the only people who ought to consider marriage are those who have become happy and fulfilled persons *without* marriage. Perhaps the worst thing that two people can do to each other is to get married *in order to be fulfilled*! If you enter into a marriage as an unfulfilled person, you are very likely to remain unfulfilled. Marriage requires a great amount of giving and sharing. It therefore requires a great amount of mature personal strength.

That's why I say that marriage should not be an unqualified goal for anyone. Marriage ought to be considered only if God leads two people to the point of honest life sharing and personal commitment.

One final word ought to be given about sexual fulfillment. Earlier I mentioned that single people can find sexual fulfillment if they follow God's sexual rules. What did I mean by that?

Obviously, I didn't mean that a single Christian will be able to have everything that his sexuality desires and promises. He will not have the privilege of sexual intercourse while he remains single, but that will not keep him from personal fulfillment as a sexual being. Because he possesses understanding of his sexuality as a spiritual as well as a physical dimension of his life, he will be emphasizing his personal growth in self-sharing and self-control. Within boundaries of responsible self-sharing and self-control, he will discover a tremendous potential for personal fulfillment and satisfaction as a sexual being.

> **The satisfaction of your physical sexual appetite is not a basic life need. If you're single again, the need for fulfilling relationships needs to be your focus.**

Let me summarize the characteristics of the sexually fulfilled person. As I understand sexuality, no single person is ready for marriage without these qualities, nor can any marriage work without them.

The sexually fulfilled person does not deny but affirms the basic goodness and beauty of her sexuality. She sets the goal of self-sharing for her life, and she works toward that goal with a whole heart. She accepts her responsibility for sexual self-control and honors the guidelines of God in the choices she makes regarding her sexual relationships. She sees marriage as a possibility for her life only if God leads her and a potential mate to the place of whole-life commitment. She is fulfilled in life because she has learned what and who she is as a sexual creature, and because more and more she is becoming the whole person she wants to be.

➤ On a scale of 1 to 10 (10 being best), how good are you at sexual self-control?_____

➤ Some suggestions were presented here. Which do you think could help you the most?

❑ Make a commitment to self-control.

❑ Be confident of success.

❑ Be honest with yourself.

❑ Avoid tempting situations.

❑ Avoid privacy with people of the opposite sex.

❑ Get support from others.

➤ What tempting situations do you especially need to avoid? Be specific.

_____

_____

➤ How will you avoid them?_____

_____

➤ What other people could you get support from? _____

_____

_____

➤ Consider the following quote: "You grow by learning how to endure (resist, not repress) sexual tension without transforming it immediately into pleasure. The more you learn to stand up under tension, the more energy you set free in order to be mature" (Walter and Ingrid Trobisch, *My Beautiful Feeling* [Downers Grove, IL: InterVarsity, 1976], 33).

➤ Do you agree or disagree? Why?_____

_____

_____

➤ In their book *The Divorce Experience,* Morton and Bernice Hunt make a rather shocking indictment of those who would take a position of moral and sexual purity. They state:

> In a society that has become increasingly tolerant of premarital sex, and in a "formerly-married" subculture that is thoroughly tolerant of post-marital sex, those formerly-married who abstain on the grounds of belief usually have some underlying emotions or sexual problem that makes them shun sexual activity. . . . Most, though not all, of the others who ascribe their celibacy to moral convictions seem to have similarly pathological inhibitions for which their beliefs serve as a disguise. (Pp. 136, 138)

➤ What do you think about their comments? How would you respond?

_____

_____

➤ Compare the Hunts' statement with the following quotation from the Bible:

> It is God's will that you should be sanctified: that you should avoid sexual immorality; that each of you should learn to control his own body in a way that is holy and honorable, not in passionate lust like the heathen, who do not know God; and that in this matter no one should wrong his brother or take advantage of him. The Lord will punish men for all such sins, as we have already told you and warned you. For God did not call us to be impure, but to live a holy life. (1 Thess. 4:3–7 NIV)

➤ What differences do you note between the Hunts' perspective on sex among singles and that of the apostle Paul? _____

_____

_____

_____

_____

➤ Why do you think that Paul would so closely tie together the sexual use of one's body with holiness?_____

_____

_____

Action Point: After reading this section, what is one thing that you will do differently? _____

_____

➤ Use the space provided to write a prayer or statement of commitment, stating the sexual principles by which you will live your life. Write your commitment here and on page 282 (Appendix A) for future reference.

_____

_____

_____

_____

_____

A final word: God accepts us where we are in order to take us where he wants us to be. Perhaps you've made some sexual errors in the past. God will forgive you if you ask. Perhaps the standards I've set forth seem far away from you, unattainable. God will give you power to live by them. God promises to forgive and heal the past as well as to restore us to a life of wholeness: "If we confess our sins, he is faithful and just and will forgive us our sins and purify us from all unrighteousness" (1 John 1:9 NIV).

Chapter 9

PARDON ME
WORKING THROUGH BITTERNESS AND LEARNING TO FORGIVE[1]

You probably know the cartoon character Ziggy, who can never seem to do anything right. One Ziggy cartoon that really tickles me portrays him on a psychiatrist's couch. The shrink is saying, "Sir, you have a low self-esteem. It is very common among losers."

I suppose we all feel like losers sometimes. But how do we handle it? We can learn from our letdowns and roll with the punches—or we can shut down our hopes and wallow in our bitterness.

The biggest problem I've seen among people who've gone through divorce is *not* that they're losers, *not* that they're incapable of carrying on a relationship, but that they've never fully dealt with what's happened. They haven't forgiven their ex, themselves, or God. And as a result, they're very bitter.

UNDERSTANDING BITTERNESS

Life can cheat us and hurt us. I heard one radio commentator put it succinctly: "One big step toward maturity is learning that life just isn't fair."

As a divorced person, you have probably felt that your life has been shattered, perhaps beyond repair. I know I felt that way. The anger, disappointment, and pain of divorce remain long after the ink on the documents has dried. Bitterness can actually shape your personality so that you approach life with a hardened, negative attitude. Anger that won't let go—that's bitterness.

But it's one thing to go through a bitter experience; it's another to become a bitter person. Some people go through the pain of divorce and come out rather sweet-spirited. Their hard times have made them better people. But many others never recover, remaining angry about past events and resentful about their current problems. Blaming everyone else, they nurse their emotional wounds for the rest of their lives.

Our Attitude Is Our Choice

People who become bitter make choices to become bitter, though they may not realize it. They think of themselves as victims of other people's crimes, but they're *choosing* to think this way. As a result, they never accept responsibility for the kind of people they've become.

What causes a person to become bitter? When anger and resentment solidify into a bitter attitude, a number of things take place inside a person. First is the *fear*—or even the prophecy—*of future failure*. This fear is exhibited in comments like:

"Oh, why should I go there? I wouldn't enjoy it anyway."
"And why should I try that? I probably wouldn't be any good at it."
"That's the way things go. Everything turns out wrong."

Bitter people learn to expect failure to the point that they define the future in terms of it.

Second, a bitter person can become extremely *distrustful*, expecting the worst of others. Bitterness magnifies the mistakes that others make and minimizes the positive, helpful things they do. It's one thing to have your trust broken—many divorced people know what that's about—but it's quite another to distrust everyone all the time.

Third, a bitter person *develops a cynical attitude*. Cynicism is the approach to life that says, "Nothing is really what it's cracked up to be. Everything is really evil in disguise." The cynic looks for the lead lining in every silver cloud, never believing in anything.

One of the most beautiful passages in the Bible is in the book of Lamentations, written by the prophet Jeremiah while sitting in the ruins of Jerusalem. Known as the weeping prophet because of the despair, heartbreak, and constant unhappiness he experienced, Jeremiah said,

> I remember my affliction and my wandering,
>   the bitterness and the gall.

I well remember them,
  and my soul is downcast within me.
Yet this I call to mind
  and therefore I have hope:
Because of the LORD's great love we are not
  consumed,
    for his compassions never fail.
They are new every morning;
  great is your faithfulness. (Lam. 3:19–23 NIV)

You might be thinking, *Jeremiah must be some kind of a nut. Or at least he was in major denial.* No, Jeremiah was quite realistic. He said, "Look, I feel terrible. I'm downcast and depressed, disillusioned and angry. But when I remember the Lord's mercy, I have hope. Because I know God—what he is like and how he works—the whole picture isn't bleak. My bitterness is not the whole picture; it is only part of the picture."

The problem with the bitter person is that he looks at all of life through the framework of that bitter experience. Jeremiah shows us that bitter experiences can be put within the framework of God's love and compassion. God's mercy is always real, new every morning.

I have a poster at my house that says, "When life gives you lemons, make lemonade." There is some wise, homemade philosophy in that little line, and it can help us understand how to deal with bitterness. It has to do with our attitude. We all go through some pretty tough moments. And the way we choose to go through them will affect the rest of our lives. So this poster is saying, when you have the sour experiences in life, mix them with some sweet stuff and turn them into something better. Some of the very best things we ever learn come through hardship and difficulty.

MAKE IT YOUR OWN

➤ How would you define *bitterness*?_____

_____

➤ How bitter are you right now?

❏ Very bitter. I am constantly snapping at others and putting them down.

❑ Somewhat bitter. Some days I feel that the universe is stacked against me, but other times I'm okay.

❑ A little bitter. Occasionally, those feelings will poke through.

❑ Not bitter at all. I have forgiven everyone involved, and I've put it all behind me.

➤ When was the last time bitterness affected something you said or did? What happened? _____

_____

_____

_____

➤ As you see it, have you *chosen* to be bitter (or not bitter)? Why do you say this?_____

_____

_____

_____

➤ What do you think would happen if you decided you would not let the negative events of your life give you a negative attitude? If you lived that way tomorrow—having a positive attitude in spite of everything—how would that change your day?_____

_____

_____

_____

➤ Jeremiah said God's mercies are "new every morning" (and in light of that, he could give up his bitterness). Do those words mean anything to you? How would you express them in your own words?_____

_____

_____

_____

Key Definition: *Bitterness* is anger that won't let go.

HANDLING BITTERNESS

You can handle bitterness in many ways, but the worst possible way is to decide that it is not there. Look at it for what it is—recognize it, identify it, and decide to deal with it.

Once you've recognized your bitterness, get rid of it. How? Let's find some clues in the Bible. In Paul's letter to the Ephesians, we find some "sweet stuff" to turn the lemons to lemonade: "Get rid of all bitterness, rage and anger, brawling and slander, along with every form of malice. Be kind and compassionate to one another, forgiving each other, just as in Christ God forgave you" (Eph. 4:31–32 NIV).

First, "Get rid of all bitterness." The little phrase "get rid of" was used in ancient Greek documents for taking out the trash. Once I went on a vacation for two weeks in the hot summer. When I came home, I put the key in the

lock, opened the door, and was almost knocked out by the stench coming out of my house. I had failed to take out the trash before I left, and after two humid summer weeks, it had stunk up the whole place!

That's what happens when we don't clean out our bitterness. It stinks up our lives. So the apostle Paul said, "Take out the trash." In the next verse he explained how to do it: through the process of forgiveness. Forgiveness can turn bitterness into lemonade.

> You may not be able to choose the things that happen to you, but you can choose how to respond to them. Your attitude is up to you.

Silverware and Sacrifice

We can learn a few things about forgiveness with a brief foray into the world of literature. Consider the ancient Greek tragedies. Play after play depicted the ongoing rivalries of the ruling families. This king killed that king, so that king's son had to kill this king, whose son had to kill the other guy's brother. . . . You get the idea. It's the law of vengeance. As you read these stories, you keep wanting someone to stand up and say, "Stop the violence! I forgive you!"

A couple of thousand years later, we find that very thing happening in Victor Hugo's classic novel *Les Misérables*. (Perhaps you've seen the stage musical.) The hero, Jean Valjean, gets out of prison after several years. He had stolen bread to feed his starving niece. Under strict parole requirements, he must carry papers that identify him as an ex-con, but that keeps employers from hiring him. It's a crazy catch-22 situation. He has supposedly paid his debt to society, but apparently, the society still harbors bitterness against him. No one wants to trust a man who has been in jail. After being rejected in town after town, he lands at the home of a local bishop, who puts him up for the night.

He eats his dinner from the bishop's silver plates and begins to think how this silverware could launch him into a new life. Desperate, he sneaks away early in the morning with a sack full of the bishop's silver. He doesn't get far. The police find the ex-con fleeing with his loot and haul him back to the bishop's home. "Sorry to awaken you, Father," they say, "but we caught this crook with your silverware. He has this crazy story that you gave it to him as a gift."

Under normal circumstances, Jean Valjean would be tossed into prison. By refusing to forgive him for his original crime, society would have forced him into another crime. And if he ever got out again, the whole cycle would continue.

But here's where the surprise occurs. The bishop was moved with pity for Valjean and said, "That's right. I gave the silver to this man. But, my friend, you forgot to take these candlesticks." After the police left, the bishop urged Valjean to use the goods to start a new, righteous life for himself. Valjean does so. In a simple act of mercy and forgiveness, the wise bishop stopped the downward spiral of bitterness and mistrust.

And the story goes on. Valjean builds a new life, becoming a respected citizen and business leader. But the old police captain has been hunting him down, seeking to arrest him for parole violations. The captain, Javert, is so intent on enforcing the letter of the law that he is blind to its spirit. Valjean must be punished, he figures, no matter what he has become. Knowing nothing of forgiveness, Javert hounds Valjean throughout his life. Finally, Valjean, gun in hand, has an opportunity to kill the helpless Javert. Valjean can do away with his persecutor forever—but he lets him live.

> **If you choose to let go of your bitterness, you're the one who benefits. If you don't let go of it, you can suffer a lifetime of consequences.**

Forgiveness wins out again. Valjean lives his whole life as one who has been forgiven. How can he fail to forgive others? Ironically, Javert does himself in. Unable to deal with the forgiveness he has just received, clinging to the importance of a letter-of-the-law justice, he kills himself. Valjean goes on to spread his mercy to others.

As we deal with our bitterness, each of us has a choice. We can be like Javert, the police captain, nitpicking at technicalities, driven by the need for retribution. "This is the third time this month she's been late picking up the kids; how can I get back at her?" And maybe it's not so trifling: "His affair with that woman has messed up my life. I'm going to make both their lives a living hell!"

Or we can be like Jean Valjean, who realized every moment that he was a forgiven person and so he had to forgive others. This attitude keeps us from piling up grievances and frees us to build a new and productive life.

MAKE IT YOUR OWN

➤ If you are bitter, why? List the person(s) you are bitter at and as many reasons for your bitterness as you can think of. (Perhaps you will need several more sheets of paper.) _____

_____

_____

➤ Look back over this list of reasons. Are they valid? Do you have a legitimate reason to be upset? Have you been wronged? About what percentage of your bitterness is valid? _____ Cross out any reasons that don't make much sense.

➤ Now look at the remaining reasons. How many of them do you think the person would like to be forgiven for? Circle them. If the person has apologized, asked forgiveness, or would ask forgiveness if given the chance, circle that reason. Now, what is keeping you from offering forgiveness for the circled offenses? _____

_____

➤ How would you go about forgiving the person for those wrongs? Do you need to do so in person, or can you just do so in your head? _____

_____

_____

(There may still be uncircled reasons on your list. We'll deal with them later.)

FORGIVENESS: A STRATEGY FOR LIVING

Every so often, you'll see a story in the news about major U.S. banks forgiving the debt of a developing nation. As you know, some of these nations are hopelessly deep in debt. With the flick of a pen, a bank can wipe the slate clean. Billions of dollars of debt can be erased in an instant.

You might applaud the generosity of these financial institutions. And maybe there's a germ of kindness somewhere. But don't kid yourself. The banks write off that debt because they feel it's to their advantage. It doesn't do any good to keep it on the books anymore. The debt will never be paid anyway, and in the interweaving fortunes of the world economy, the bank benefits more by giving the poor nation a break.

I'm no monetary expert, as my checkbook will attest, but we can learn a lesson here: *forgiveness is good for you.* Sure, it's moral and godly and the right thing to do—but it also helps you put the past behind you and move into the future. For your sake, if nothing else, let your grudges go!

Forgiven and Forgiving

Amazingly, as you watch the thrilling musical *Les Misérables,* it comes as no great surprise when Jean Valjean restrains himself from shooting Javert.

That's because Jean—and we viewers—can never forget who he is, a man who has been forgiven for a great crime. Forgiven, he must forgive.

Remember that line in the Lord's Prayer: "Forgive us our trespasses [or debts] as we forgive those who trespass against us"? A great truth is expressed there, and it works on both human and divine levels.

If you have ever ridden on a crowded bus or subway, you've had a sense of trespassing. As the vehicle starts and stops, the passengers sway and jostle one another. You could have one of two attitudes in such a situation. You could be very bothered every time someone jabs an elbow into your personal space (or your personal stomach). Or you could recognize that you're jostling others as well, and they're forgiving you for that, so you must forgive others. On public transportation, there *is* no personal space.

Well, life is like a crowded subway. We all trespass. We all invade each other's space. We jab each other. And if everyone takes offense at every jab, we wind up with a Greek tragedy. You've probably had moods like that, though, where you tally up the wrongs that everyone has done you. Your ex bounces a check, the checkout clerk is slow, and a careless driver cuts you off. When you get steamed at every little thing, who gets hurt? You.

But look at it another way. Each of us is forgiven a dozen times each day by people we unwittingly offend. If we have the humility to realize that, we will be more ready to forgive others.

The Best Revenge

Did you ever see the snooty ad that boasted, "Living well is the best revenge"? That line may actually be going through your mind in the wake of your divorce. You dream of the day when you will rise above it all and your ex-spouse will rue the day he or she rejected you.

Here's a new wrinkle on that old adage: "Forgiveness is the best revenge."

> **Bitterness is bad for you. It can hurt your health, your relationships, your work, and many other things. Get rid of it.**

Think about it. Normally, revenge ties you up in knots. If you are bitter toward your ex-spouse, he or she is still controlling your emotions. Bitterness hurts you far more than it hurts the other person. It keeps you from living a happy, productive life. It hardly touches the other person.

But I have more biblical wisdom to share with you, this from Proverbs: "If your enemy is hungry, give him bread to eat; / And if he is thirsty, give him water to drink; / For so you will heap coals of fire on his head" (Prov. 25:21–22 NKJV). When the apostle Paul quoted that in the New Testament, he added the postlude, "Do not be overcome by evil, but overcome evil with good" (Rom. 12:21 NKJV).

Bitterness is an evil response to evil things. You probably have good reason to be bitter. Evil things have been done to you. But a bitter attitude doesn't help. It just allows you to be "overcome by evil." Forgiveness allows you to regain control of your emotions. It helps you to win, to overcome. That is, by far, the best revenge.

MAKE IT YOUR OWN

➤ In what ways has bitterness hurt you? Check all that apply.

❑ Bad attitude/never happy

❑ Anxiety-ridden

❑ Bad health

❑ Hurt relationships

❑ Other: _____

_____

➤ As you think over the last month or two, what have other people forgiven *you* for? _____

_____

➤ How do you feel about this? How does it feel to be forgiven?

_____

_____

➤ What good things could you do toward the main object of your bitterness, to overcome evil with good? _____

_____

_____

DIVINE PERSPECTIVE

I would be remiss if I left our discussion of forgiveness on a merely human level. Yes, it's true that "forgiveness is the best revenge," and that we all forgive each other for a million little things. But those reasons seem flat compared with the most powerful reason of all—God forgives us.

If you're a Christian, you're well aware of this fact. If you're not, I still urge you to pay close attention to the next few pages. We're going to look closely at the nature of God's forgiveness and how we can apply it to our own relationships. This God talk may be unfamiliar to you, but you may find some revolutionary concepts that can lift you out of the pit of bitterness.

Understanding God's Forgiveness

When we talk about forgiveness, we have to be careful. There are numerous books on the subject with many superficial approaches presented.

Some teachers encourage the offended to absorb their pain and release the offender. Others urge those who are hurt to turn to God and confess it. Then, they are assured, God will resolve the pain, and everything will be fine. A third approach is to tell those unable to forgive to examine their lives. They should see what mistakes they have made—even if the mistake is carrying pain toward those who harmed them—and seek forgiveness from the ones they can't seem to forgive.

There is a problem with these approaches (and many others like them): they all contain certain elements of healthy forgiveness, but they present only part of the forgiveness process. They leave out basic steps that must take place for the forgiveness process to be authentic and complete.

Forgiveness was a crucial turning point for my friend Kathy. As she realized that she had been forgiven by God, she was more able to put aside her bitterness. "As a result of the forgiveness and love I experienced from God," she says, "I had the power and security to make necessary changes in my life. Part of this was taking the difficult experience of my divorce and utilizing it to help others who were going through separation and divorce. Another part was learning how to forgive others the way I was now forgiven by God."

Kathy's experience reminds us of Ephesians 4:32. This is how we "take out the trash" of bitterness—"forgiving each other, just as in Christ God forgave you" (NIV). God is a forgiving God who has made forgiveness available through Jesus Christ. And the way God forgives us forms a pattern for the way we are to forgive others.

Just as a coin has two sides—heads and tails—so the forgiveness of God has two sides. One side can be called the *legal* side of God's forgiveness; the other can be called the *relational* side.

The Legal Side of Forgiveness

Ask anyone who has been caught in a speed trap: if you break a law, then you must legally pay a penalty. Or if a spouse is delinquent in childcare payments, he is supposed to be penalized. In the same way, the Bible teaches that God—who is holy and righteous—can legally accept only perfect people. However, we can't live perfect lives! Since we have broken his law, a penalty must be paid to make us acceptable.

The good news is that Jesus Christ lived a perfect life. He is the only person who ever deserved acceptance by God. Yet by his death he paid the penalty for our failures. He offered his perfect life to be credited to our account. Since the penalty we deserved has been paid by Christ, we can legally be considered perfect by God.

The Relational Side of Forgiveness

But if God's forgiveness is available to everyone, then is everyone in the world forgiven? Unfortunately, the answer is no. Just because forgiveness is available doesn't mean it is always accepted.

For Christ's forgiveness to be real in our lives, we must receive it. That's exactly what happened to my friend Kathy. The relational side of forgiveness is what happens when we accept God's verdict and receive God's legal solution for our condition.

MAKE IT YOUR OWN

➤ Do you feel that you have done things that God needs to forgive you for?

_____

➤ On what basis are you *legally* forgiven by God?_____

_____

➤ What would you have to do to claim *relational* forgiveness from God?

_____

➤ How do you think this might change your life? _____

_____

_____

FORGIVING ONE ANOTHER, LEGALLY

One of my favorite stories in the New Testament is the parable Jesus taught in Matthew 18:21–35. A servant owed the king the equivalent of several million dollars. When the king called in his note, the servant had no resources to pay the debt. Just when the king was about to throw the man and his family into debtors' prison, the servant cried out for mercy. The king took pity, canceled the debt, and let him go.

With the weight of his debt relieved, the servant walked out and spotted a fellow servant who owed him a few dollars. Immediately, he grabbed him, choked him, and demanded repayment.

When his fellow servant cried out for mercy, the man wouldn't listen. He had the fellow thrown into debtors' prison.

When the king learned how the man acted, he harshly reprimanded the ungrateful servant and put him in jail.

At the end of his story Jesus explained, "So My heavenly Father also will do to you if each of you, from his heart, does not forgive his brother his trespasses" (v. 35 NKJV).

> ## As forgiven people, we must forgive.

Remember Jean Valjean's lesson: *forgiven people forgive others.* As we recognize how much God has forgiven us, we must offer that same level of forgiveness to others. We have no right to hold a grudge. No one can hurt us any more than we have hurt God. On the legal side of forgiveness, we give up our rights to retribution. We must forgive others freely, as God has forgiven us.

Jesus said, "Whenever you stand praying, forgive, if you have anything against anyone; so that your Father also who is in heaven may forgive you your transgressions" (Mark 11:25 NASB).

Imagine you are praying and God brings to mind your feelings toward your former spouse. You know that, before God, you are much like that unforgiving servant in Matthew 18. Jesus died on the cross to forgive you, yet you haven't been willing to forgive your former spouse. Remember, the unmerciful slave had forgotten about his forgiven debt and focused only on the debt owed to him. In the same way, when you get caught up in feelings of anger toward your former spouse, you forget your condition before God and what it took for him to forgive you!

Jesus said we must do business with God before we do anything else. We must remember the depth of forgiveness he has given us and consider the problem we have with another (in this case a former spouse) as just a few dollars in comparison to the problem we had with God. We cannot be ready to deal with the relational side of forgiveness until we have come before God and worked through the legal side.

At this point you may be wondering why the legal side must come before the relational. Well, have you ever had your former spouse confront you when he or she was angry and bitter? You know how you feel under these circumstances. Your ex seems to be acting like a judge with a verdict already in hand—not really wanting to resolve the problem, just showing you what you have done wrong and making you feel bad about it. No respect here—just condemnation.

How well can you work through your problems with someone while you have that attitude? Do you even *want* to work through them? However, if you go before God and deal with your attitudes and feelings, you are humbled before him. The result is what the Bible calls a gentle spirit. This spirit diffuses your bitterness and helps you focus on the real issues. You no longer have to win to feel good.

MAKE IT YOUR OWN

➤ Take another look at that story Jesus told of the unmerciful servant. Which character do you resemble most?_____

_____

_____

➤ Why was it wrong for the first servant to demand payment from his fellow servant? _____

_____

_____

➤ How do you think the second servant, the one who owed a few dollars, felt when payment was demanded from him?_____

_____

_____

➤ Was there some way that the first servant could have gently asked for payment of the few dollars? What *should* he have said to his fellow servant?

_____

_____

RESTORING RELATIONS

In the legal side of forgiveness, we get our attitude right before God. We also give up our rights of retribution. No matter how much we have been wronged, we can't take the moral high ground because we have wronged God in worse ways.

Yet we still need to deal with our relationship with that other person, and that requires another side of forgiveness. Forgiveness doesn't mean we act as if nothing has ever happened. A breakdown in a relationship demands an honest dealing with the facts and feelings involved. Jesus addressed this when he said, "If your brother sins against you, rebuke him; and if he repents, forgive him" (Luke 17:3 NKJV).

Now, let's look at this verse piece by piece. First, Jesus said, "If your brother sins against you." That assumes there is brokenness in a relationship. Jesus said the one who has been violated in a relationship is responsible to go and rebuke the one who has sinned.

Going to the one who has hurt you can be hard. And the word *rebuke* makes you think you should sharply reprimand the person. But the word is gentler. It actually means to go to a person, share your side of the problem, and seek clarification of your understanding. You may not know for sure that a reprimand is deserved until you hear the response of the other person. So, you gently reveal the facts as you see them. You must be willing to hear any new evidence and also to give this "brother" the benefit of any doubt. Your motive is to define the problem and decide what to do about it. If the person has truly wronged you, he or she needs to see that and to understand how to restore the relationship with you.

This happened to me once when I was in college. Working as a youth volunteer in a church, I occasionally sneaked into a pastor's office to have a quiet place to study. Once I jostled things around on the desk and happened to pull some pages of his good Bible out from its binding.

Later, I told the pastor, "I accidentally pulled the pages out of your Bible. I hope this isn't a problem and that it's okay."

"No, it's not okay," he replied calmly.

What that pastor said was a rebuke. He didn't say it with anger or bitterness. He was showing me that something was wrong and we shouldn't just pass it off. We needed to talk about it. His rebuke helped me understand the seriousness of the situation.

Jesus said, "If your brother sins against you, rebuke him." That is, if there is brokenness in a relationship, be honest about it. Go and reveal it to this person. Allow it to be seen for what it is. Don't live in denial. Don't act as though everything is okay when it isn't. Rebuke him—that is, reveal it to him.

Then Jesus said, "If he repents, forgive him." He put a condition on forgiveness—repentance—implying that if he doesn't repent, you shouldn't forgive.

But didn't we just read in Mark 11:25 that if we have something against a person, we should forgive?

Here's where the two sides of forgiveness come into play. On the legal side, I have to deal with my attitude before God, facing my anger, bitterness, and frustration, recognizing my need for forgiveness. By the time I approach the relational side of forgiveness, I'm ready to reveal and discuss the relational problems with humility and gentleness, not condemnation.

If the other person recognizes the problem and repents, I should genuinely forgive him or her. The repentance and forgiveness bring closure to the problem and renew the relationship. Legal forgiveness brings me to the table with a humble attitude, and relational forgiveness restores the relationship.

But suppose the person won't listen, or laughs it off, or gets angry. What if she refuses to recognize there is a problem—or, even worse, sees what she has done but won't accept her responsibility for the broken relationship?

What am I to do? Smile and say, "That's all right! I've worked everything out with God, and our relationship is fine whether you like it or not"?

No, that wouldn't be honest. At best it would be playing the old denial game: close my eyes and act as if the problems aren't there; maybe they'll go away. But I know they won't go away.

We must recognize that the relationship is still broken. The problem is unresolved. There is still pain. We may need to take protective measures for ourselves, redefining the relationship so that we won't be hurt so much again. A close relationship that has had a major offense without any repentance or relational forgiveness will never be as close again.

But at least we can come to some closure. Before God we'll be able to live with the fact that we've done everything possible to resolve the problem. We'll also feel relief and freedom in choosing to speak the truth instead of saying only what we think will please others.

"And what happens," you ask, "if this person comes back later, accepts his or her responsibility for our problem, and asks forgiveness?"

The model of God's forgiveness answers that. God's offer of forgiveness is always available for the asking. Our forgiveness must be available as well.

Working on Ourselves

Finally, you may wonder, *What if my relationship with this person remains broken for an indefinite period of time? What do I do in the meantime?*

Many people attempt to rush forgiveness to avoid the painful work of dealing honestly with others and themselves. They think forgiveness is a shortcut to feeling better. That's just not true. When we work both sides of forgiveness and a relationship remains broken, we must work on ourselves. And if we want to be healthy, growing people, we need to do this anyway!

I love to tell the story about my friend Grace. I met her when she was in her mid-seventies, and she was so disabled with arthritis that she couldn't move any of the major joints of her body. She could just barely move her arms, her knees were locked in position, her ankles wouldn't move, and her toes were frozen. Attendants had to move her about, and she was in terrible pain most of the time.

When I first visited her, she was facing the other wall. Her daughter introduced me, and this woman, with a bright, cheery little voice, said, "Well, come around here where I can get a look at you."

I walked around and got a look at her. Grace's eyes were just as bright as could be. "Well," she said, smiling, "you're not half as bad looking as they said you were."

I thought, *There's somebody special living here.*

And she was special. I went to see her many times, and she was always an encouragement to me. Eventually, she was put in a nursing home. There the head nurse said, "If we ever get a crab in here, we put her in the room with Grace because Grace will cheer her up."

On my way to see her, I'd often wonder, *What can I say that will brighten up Grace's day?* But Grace never seemed to have a dull day. I never heard her complain. She never said, "How long must this last?" or "Why has God done this to me?"

Grace knew God. And by knowing God, she found something that you and I often fail to find because we look only at the pain and injustice in our lives. We don't look at the opportunity that has been given to us to grow.

As a matter of fact, sometimes pain is the greatest opportunity to make lemonade. You see, for the most part we don't ever really learn the great lessons of life until we learn how to deal with pain. I don't learn very much of spiritual value when everything is going well for me. I learn it when I'm hurting. That's when I ask about the real meaning in life. That's when I ask who I ought to be. And that's when I grow.

Chuck Swindoll tells the story about the violinist Paganini who, while playing a concert, had a string break on his violin (*Strengthening Your Grip,* 205–6). As the crowd went, "Ooh," he kept playing. Then, "Bonk," another string broke. But he kept playing the music. Finally, a third string popped! But Paganini kept playing like mad.

Finally, the master finished the piece, and you can imagine the crowd's response. They went wild with enthusiasm. But Paganini wasn't finished yet. He came out and played an encore on one string! In life we break strings. For us, divorce has been one of the more traumatic of these times. However, as Swindoll says, there is one string in our lives that can never be broken or taken away. And that string is the right and power for us to choose our own attitude. We will always have the choice of how we're going to approach life. And what we become depends not so much on how many strings break as on what we do with the one string that remains.

I still look back on what happened to me, and I hate it. I didn't want my divorce. And I'm sorry about the pain it brought into the lives of my family and others. I wish those things had not happened—but I wouldn't go back to being the person I was before it happened. And I wouldn't trade anything for what I've learned in the process. I'm a wiser and better man today as a result of my divorce.

You have a choice to make. You can decide to feel sorry for yourself. You can simmer in your pain and anger and be bitter the rest of your life. Or you can say, "I'm going to become fruitful in the land of my suffering. I'm going to learn the process of forgiveness. I'm going to play on that string. I'm going to make some lemonade."

MAKE IT YOUR OWN

➤ Go back to the list you made of the people you have bitter feelings for and the reasons why. You should have circled some of the easier problems. These are cases where the person is sorry for wronging you.

➤ As you look over that list, find one of those circled things and choose, right now, to clear it up. In the next week, what specific thing can you do to resolve that matter and restore that relationship? _____

_____

_____

➤ Now look at the uncircled things, problems that the person seems unrepentant for. Write one to three of those things here.

1. _____

2. _____

3. _____

➤ Have you "rebuked" the person(s) for these matters? (Remember, that means merely to present your case clearly.) Put a check mark beside the item if you have.

➤ If there are matters in which you have not confronted the person, where and when will you be able to do it? _____

_____

_____

➤ If you *have* presented your case, and if the person doesn't want to clear up the matter with you, you need to put the matter aside. Don't dwell on this matter. Let it go. Your offer of forgiveness is on the table. The person refuses to restore the relationship on the proper terms. There is nothing else you can do.

Action Point: Is there some symbolic action you can take in the next few days to put this matter behind you? It could be as simple as throwing away a picture, donating to a charity, or taking yourself out to dinner. It merely needs to be your way of saying (to yourself, mostly), "I will not live in bitterness. I will move on from here."

➤ What is that symbolic action? _____

_____

➤ When will you take it? _____

_____

➤ Write these actions and strategies here and on page 282 (Appendix A) for future reference. _____

_____

_____

Key Definition: *Rebuke:* to go to a person, share your side of the problem, and seek clarification of your understanding. Gently reveal the facts as you see them. You must be willing to hear any new evidence and also to give the other person the benefit of any doubt. Your motive is to define the problem that exists and decide what to do about it.

God's offer of forgiveness is always available for the asking. Our forgiveness must be available as well.

Part 3

OTHER
ISSUES

Chapter 10

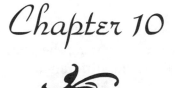

KIDS IN THE MIDDLE
HELPING CHILDREN OF DIVORCE

"I was five or six when I first remember my parents fighting a lot. I remember that Dad was working more and more, and that I missed him. There were times when Dad was gone for weeks at a time. When we asked my mom where Dad was, she would always say, 'Away on a business trip.' I now know that my dad and mom were separated. Whenever they tried to reconcile, my mom would say that Dad was home for a vacation. This went on for about two years. It didn't matter what my mom said anymore, my brother and I knew there was something wrong, and we knew we didn't like it. When Mom finally told us the truth, that she and Dad were getting a divorce, it was only because he was getting married to someone else and wanted my brother and me to be in the wedding.

"I wish my mom had told us the truth two years earlier. Then we could have started the grieving process and maybe been more accepting of our new stepmother and stepsister. That was really tough for us to swallow" (a fourteen-year-old boy).

BREAKING THE NEWS

Kids usually know "there is something going on" long before you think.

I don't know the specifics of your situation. I can't tell you exactly what to say to your children. Certainly, the example at the beginning of this chapter is *not* the way to break the news, but you may have unique challenges. This chapter may sound like a cookbook of dos and don'ts. Keep in mind that

I'm presenting a list of guidelines, some of which you can implement and some of which you can't.

Have you ever heard of the Serenity Prayer? "God, grant me the serenity to accept the things I cannot change, the courage to change the things I can, and the wisdom to know the difference." That could be renamed the Single Parent's Prayer, since it so aptly describes the attitude you need to adopt while raising your children. Keep in mind that there are no secret formulas or even standard methods of operation. Your child is an individual, and you'll need to tailor the information to fit your situation and your child's.

"How Do I Tell My Children?"

In the book of Ephesians, the apostle Paul wrote that we're to speak the truth in love (4:15). That's the best way I can describe the communication that should take place between all parties involved in a separation or divorce. It may be near to impossible at times, but it needs to be our goal.

If possible, both parents should sit down with the kids and together tell them about the separation or divorce, before one of the parents leaves. If the separation happens abruptly, the parent with the children will need to give them some preliminary information right away. But as soon as it can be arranged, both parents need to come together to tell the children what will happen to the family.

This method is important for several reasons. First, with both parents present, there's the greatest possibility of a balanced and honest presentation. Second, if the children have any questions, they need to address them to the parent who is better able to answer. And third, the united front makes it clear that both parents are in agreement on the decision. That helps to reduce the splitting of loyalties, the playing of one parent against the other, and the fantasy that "my parents will work this out." If one parent is missing, the children are likely to think, *Yeah, that's what Mom says, but I know that's not what Dad told me.*

If one parent is not present, it's even more important that the parent who tells the children remembers to speak the truth as lovingly as possible. Representing both sides of the issue is very difficult when you're so emotionally involved. Even though you're irate with the other parent, you want to let the children know that it's an issue between the parents and that you both still love them.

If your child has questions about the other parent or his reasons for leaving, try to answer as honestly as possible. Don't attribute motives or make judgments about the other parent. Just state what you know to be true, as nicely as you can.

Don't say: "Your father left because he's irresponsible. He'll probably move in with his girlfriend and forget all about us."

Try this instead: "Your father loves you very much, but he doesn't seem to love me. Even though he doesn't want to live with me anymore, he wants to visit with you whenever he can."

By taking the "high road," you will end up better off, even if you have good reason to drag your spouse's reputation through the mud. Remember, the children will know the truth sooner or later, and it would be better for you if they remember you as the one who chose the most loving course.

"When Should I Tell Them?"

It's important to tell the kids what's going on as soon as both of you know. If you're just having marital problems, you need to get help, but don't feel compelled to tell the children anything of a personal nature between you and your spouse. If the children are older, they will know something is not right and may even know you're seeing a counselor. If they ask, use the opportunity to demonstrate the proper way to handle problems. "Your mother and I are having some personal problems that we need to work out. Because we're committed to each other and to the family, we want to get help in resolving these problems as quickly as we can." If your children are too young to understand the problem, or if they don't ask, there is no need to share your personal conflicts with your kids at this stage.

Once the problem reaches a point where divorce or separation is imminent, it affects the whole family. The children need to be told as soon as it can be arranged. This should be delayed only if you need to work out some of the details or if it happens to fall on a day such as Christmas or one of the children's birthdays. It's reasonable to wait until some of the details are worked out, such as: Where will Mom live? Where will Dad live? Where will the kids stay? And how often will we see each parent? You need to present a scenario that is well thought through and reassuring to the children if possible. If these matters cannot be settled and it looks as if the children are going to find out, you may need to sit them down and tell them as much as you know.

Many parents tend to protect their children from the truth as long as possible. One study found that 80 percent of the preschoolers questioned had received no information about their parents' separation. But parents do a disservice to the child by withholding such information; that merely creates anxiety about the future and distrust toward the parent.

"What Should I Tell Them?"

When deciding how much you should tell the kids, you must consider the developmental level of your child. Get the key points across, and then allow for open discussion. If the child knows enough to ask the question, he or she is old enough to get an honest answer.

The key points to cover include:

- How did this happen? What are the reasons?
- Do you still love me? Does my mother/father still love me? Am I wanted?
- How will my life be changed? Where will I live, go to school, church, and so on?
- Am I part of the reason for the breakup? Could I have done something to avoid this separation or divorce?

It's vital to cover what will happen to the children. Reassure them of your love for them, and be prepared to back it up with actions. Give the children permission to love *both* parents. For preschoolers, reassure them that they will be cared for, and then explain the divorce in terms they can understand. For example:

"Mommy loves you very much, and Daddy loves you very much. You're going to live with me, and we'll stay in this house, where you will eat, sleep, and play, just as you do now. Daddy is going to live in an apartment nearby so he can come and visit you every week. In fact, he will pick you up this Saturday and show you where he lives. You'll eat lunch there, and then he will bring you back home where I'll be looking forward to seeing you. We are separating because Daddy doesn't want to live with Mommy anymore. But Daddy still loves you and wants to spend time with you."

Children who are elementary age or older need more specific information, particularly about where they will live and the visitation arrangements. They will also require more specifics about what went wrong. You need to be as honest as you can without discussing sexual problems overtly. (You may want to say something like, "Daddy is acting like he is married to someone else.") If possible, avoid placing blame since it's true that divorce is rarely, if ever, all one person's fault.

Don't expect children to understand your explanations or to ask all their questions the first time you talk about it. Be prepared to explain the situation and answer questions over and over again. Stress that separation or divorce is an adult decision. It wasn't their fault, nor can they do anything to get the parents back together.

If the truth is particularly ugly or hard to talk about, you need to tell them in as loving a way as you can. The earlier they hear the truth, the sooner they can start to deal with the problem and begin the healing process. You need to use discretion in light of the age of the children and how much they really can understand. But once again, if they're old enough to ask the question, they're old enough to hear an honest answer. For example, if Dad is leaving because he has a girlfriend or he is a homosexual, you may not want to give them all that information in the first meeting. Soon thereafter, however, you need to tell them what is really going on. Eventually, the kids hear the whispers and innuendos, so it's best that they hear the truth in a straightforward manner from their parents. If possible, the information should come from the one with "the problem." That way, they would know they were hearing firsthand information, which is usually more reliable. They would then have the opportunity to discuss openly their questions and concerns.

> **When breaking the news of separation or divorce to your children, it's critical that you tell them the truth as lovingly as you can.**

If that parent isn't available or willing to talk with the children, it obviously falls to the other parent to present as balanced an explanation as possible. Then if they have questions, you may want to offer to let them discuss the issue with someone more neutral. That might be an aunt or uncle they trust, a counselor at the school or church, or a relative on their father's side whom they might view as being more objective. Your children may not want to do that, but it's important that you at least offer since it allows them the opportunity to seek a second opinion without feeling they're betraying you.

In cases where the child is actually abandoned by one of the parents, it's difficult to speak the truth in a loving way. This is not only because it's hard to be loving, but also because you rarely know what the truth is. I don't believe you can tell the child that "Daddy doesn't love you" or that "Daddy's not coming back," because there is much evidence to indicate otherwise. Many parents, both mothers and fathers, who apparently abandon their children will later try to contact them and reestablish a relationship. In addition, their leaving does not prove their lack of love. Studies have shown that many times the leaving parents feel so bad about themselves that they believe the most loving thing to do is to get out of their families' lives.

Therefore, in cases of abandonment, the remaining parent needs to balance his or her comments so that the children don't have undue hope or despair. "I don't know if your father is coming back or not. We need to go on with our lives as if he will never be back, but you never know; he might realize what he's missing someday and decide to come back to see you."

Another critical reassurance needed is the child's lovability. "I don't know if your father loves you, but I do know you're a very lovable child. He is not thinking properly right now and has to work through some problems, but I know that if he ever works through them he'll realize what a wonderful child you are." Or, "I know your father loves you. He just is not able to express it or show it right now because he's trying to figure out his own life. That doesn't change the fact that you're a wonderful and lovable child. Your father's problems have nothing to do with you."

To summarize how to break the news about your divorce to your children, let me suggest the following guidelines:

- Be honest and open in the way you present the information. Give explanations, not defenses or opinions.
- Focus on what will happen to each child. Assure them of their continued well-being in spite of difficult transitions.
- Make sure the children understand they were not the cause of the divorce.
- Give clear and definite statements of mutual love and acceptance. Be prepared to back this up with actions such as hugs, interest in their world, and a listening ear.
- Let them know they can't get their parents back together. Encourage a realistic view of what life will be like after the divorce.
- Expect that you will have to reinforce this information by opening discussions with your children about the divorce at regular intervals throughout their lives.

MAKE IT YOUR OWN

➤ Checklist for telling children about your divorce:

❑ Both parents told the children together.

❑ The situation was presented fairly and charitably.

❑ The reasons for the breakup were presented in ways the children could understand.

❑ Your love for the children was emphasized.

❑ The children were told specifically how their lives would be affected.

❑ The children were assured that they were not the cause of the divorce.

❑ The children were prepared for the fact that their parents probably would not get back together.

➤ If you have not yet talked thoroughly with your children about the breakup, use this space to practice what you'll say. _____

_____

_____

_____

_____

_____

➤ When and where will you talk with them about this? _____

_____

_____

RESTRUCTURING YOUR FAMILY

"My whole world was turned upside down when my parents broke up. My mom took my brother and me away from our home in order to live with our grandparents for a few months. After that, we moved into this lousy apartment with no furniture. I had to attend a school I used to make fun of. They were our rivals in sports, and the kids all seemed like druggies. Now I'm in this school, trying to make friends. It's like my worst nightmare come true.

Your children know more about your divorce than you think.

"My parents are always arguing about stupid stuff, mostly money and when my brother and I are coming over to see Dad. I get tired of being in the middle of it. My mom tells me to ask Dad for the support check when I see him. Then my dad starts yelling at me about how he'd send the check if 'your mother would let me see you guys when she's supposed to.'

KIDS IN THE MIDDLE **229**

"I hate it when my parents talk to each other because they always fight. But when they're not talking, I end up having to send messages back and forth" (a sixteen-year-old boy).

Restructuring a home and family is always difficult and stressful. When you add the grief and trauma of a divorce, you have the makings of an explosive situation. The purpose of this section is to provide guidelines for how to make those changes with the least turmoil and emotional harm to the participants. Granted, we can never eliminate all the negative consequences or even our own mistakes. However, there is much that you as a parent can do to smooth the transition.

Here are some of the more prevalent problem areas in the transition from married life to single parenting.

Custody and Visitation

Other than money issues, I'm sure there is no other issue more troublesome or emotionally charged than the custody and visitation rights of each parent. In this book, we won't discuss the different types of arrangements and which one would work best in your situation because too many variables are involved. For information on your options, talk with a lawyer or divorce mediation specialist. Each state has its own laws as well as trends, which vary according to the views of the judges who oversee such cases. You need to be advised by someone who is familiar with the system and the way it works in your specific area.

However, there's much I can say about the emotional side of the custody and visitation issue. Most of all, *don't make it a battle*. Remember, the more you can resolve amicably between yourselves, the more you will save in money, time, wear and tear on your nerves, and damaging effects on your children. I can't tell you how many times I've heard stories like this: "My husband and I fought over who would get the children for almost five years. It started out bad but only got worse with each new round of hearings. By the time we were done, we had used every possible devious tactic and called each other every name in the book. Of course, the children heard it all, and the only winners were the lawyers. Our legal fees were more than $40,000, which was more than we had tried to split between us some five years earlier."

Whenever I have a divorcing parent tell me that he or she wants to fight the other parent in order to "come out on top," I feel compelled to say that *there are no winners in a divorce*. If you think you're going to fight your particular case until you finally "win," please rethink what you're doing. You are not going to win. You will merely run out of resources and energy, at which point you'll probably compromise to a position you could have obtained much earlier and at half the expense.

Now that I've made an absolute statement, let me give you the exception. In cases of abuse or extreme misconduct on the part of the other parent, you need to fight for the rights of your children. I encourage all parents to stand up for their own rights, but they're not worth battling the other parent for unless you or your children are in some type of physical or emotional danger. (Fortunately, that's the exception rather than the rule.)

Since you're not the most objective person to judge whether your case falls into the extreme category, I encourage you to seek third-party objectivity from a counselor or spiritual adviser. Recognize that your friends and relatives are usually biased in your favor, and your lawyer may tend to advocate an adversarial position for obvious reasons.

Here are some other guidelines in regard to custody and visitation rights:

• Set up a good, workable visitation arrangement as soon as the separation occurs. That will help the children adjust to a new routine while assuring continuity with both parents. It also paves the way for a smoother settlement of the official agreement. Keep the visitation consistent so that children know what to expect and when they will see the other parent. When unscheduled changes occur, let your children know as soon as possible.

• With teenagers, flexibility is needed because of their busy schedules and outside activities. Both parents should respect the teens' wishes, but not at the expense of the relationship with the other parent. For example, if your teen is planning to work on weekends, it must be decided and arranged in consultation with both parents, since it tends to greatly affect the relationship with the noncustodial parent.

• Holidays need to be planned well in advance and then explained to the children. Don't wait until the week before Christmas to make arrangements with the other parent. That creates undue stress for the parents and children at a time when you need it the least. Older children and teens may be consulted about their wishes for the holidays, but once again, the final decision must be the parents'.

• Unless your children are preschoolers, you should consult with them about the visitation arrangement. This is particularly true of teenagers. Even though you ask them their opinion, however, make sure they understand that the final decision is up to the parents. Keep in mind your children's tendency to tell you what they think you want to hear. Therefore, expect that they will say one thing to you and something else to the other parent. Don't embarrass them or punish them for this. They desperately want the love and loyalty of both parents. Use their wishes as input into your final decision.

• If a court case becomes inevitable, try to keep the children out of it. If their testimony is crucial, see if it can be handled in the judge's chambers, through a court-appointed psychologist, or via videotape. Don't force a courtroom confrontation that will compel the children to testify for or against one of the parents.

• Keep the communication lines open between you and the other parent. Keep all discussions of changes in the arrangements and any money issues between the two of you. Don't pass messages through the children. Try to have those discussions over the phone when the kids are not around. That way, if they become unavoidably heated, your children won't be subjected to the disagreement. Don't wait until the other parent comes to pick up or drop off the children to say, "Oh, by the way . . ." As you know, that leads to disagreements the children can't help but witness. (If you have a particularly amicable relationship, however, you may have no problem with last-minute changes.)

• When the children are back with you, encourage them to talk about their time with the other parent unless you find you cannot listen without reacting. Don't pump them for specific information such as dating relationships or how "their mother" is spending her money. You know the motiva-

tion behind those questions, and you also know what that does to you. Ask, "Did you guys have fun with your father this weekend?" and then be prepared to bite your tongue when they talk about how much fun it was or even how nice his new girlfriend is. This is extremely difficult, but for the sake of your children, encourage their honest expression of that significant part of their lives.

If you find you cannot listen without reacting, be honest enough with your children to say, "It hurts me to hear this right now. I want you to have fun with your dad, and maybe someday we'll be able to talk all about it, but for right now maybe we shouldn't." Then find ways to work on your own adjustment so that you can later encourage your children to share all areas of their lives, especially their relationship with the other parent, and perhaps a stepparent.

• Both parents should set aside time alone with each child. That gives them opportunity to create special bonds and to talk on a deeper level than is possible when all children are constantly together. Such times have proved to be important in the building of a strong sense of security and a healthy self-image.

• Avoid being a "Disneyland Daddy" or a "Magic Mountain Mommy." Parents who don't normally live with the children tend to avoid the normal patterns of a realistic home environment. They want to make sure the children have a good time when they come to visit, so they may eat out frequently, do special things every visit, and fudge on the rules regarding bedtime, homework, and so on. To decrease the instability and competition between the parents, they should strive to provide the same stable and consistent discipline that is expected of the custodial parent. Although special events are nice, the majority of the time should be part of a daily routine, similar to what they do in the other home. Avoid presents or treats that seem like relationship bribes. Focus on building the relationship with your children through open communication and time spent doing everyday tasks.

• Each child needs to feel the continued love of both parents. The children should also feel they aren't betraying one parent by enjoying the company of the other. Ready access to the departed parent, by phone and in person, is necessary. You will benefit if you help your child accept and love the other parent, even when the other parent doesn't do the same.

Your Child and School

Mrs. Graham didn't want the school to find out her husband had left. She had her two children, Martha and Michael, in a private Christian school. She was afraid the school's conservative philosophy would prejudice the teachers and administrators against her children. If the teachers knew, they might watch her children too closely and almost look for trouble in her kids.

The problem with Mrs. Graham's cautious attitude is that her fears are unfounded and may be depriving the children of significant help. Teachers get harder on children when they start falling behind or missing assignments with no apparent reason. But they tend to be sensitive and compassionate when they became aware of students' struggles. In the case of divorce, teachers would make allowances for the children's distractibility, academic regression, emotional withdrawal, or hostility.

Teachers have a variety of resources available for helping children. Books, tapes, videos, and counselors are usually at the disposal of your children as long as the school is aware of your need. The school might be holding support groups for children of divorce or at least know where they're being held in your community. The bottom line is that you won't know this unless you inform the school of what's going on at home.

If you have a teenage child, he or she probably has a variety of teachers and likely would not appreciate your contacting all of them. In that case, a call to the guidance counselor or adviser may be most helpful. If it's a large school, there is little the counselor will probably do unless the school has a special program or unless your child comes in for help. Older children are more influenced by their peer group and therefore will tend to talk with friends far more than they will with teachers or a counselor. Encourage the peer interaction, especially with other children who have been through the same thing. They can become a tremendous help to one another. (This is a major premise of the "Kids in the Middle" programs we conduct: kids helping other kids.) However, you may need to correct distorted peer feedback from time to time, especially if your child's friends are immature or hostile. Try to be aware of the kinds of support your child is receiving from other kids.

MAKE IT YOUR OWN

➤ On a scale of 1 to 10 (1 being most peaceful), how much like a battle is your divorce? _____

➤ How does that affect your kids, positively or negatively? _____

_____

_____

➤ If your situation is rather heated, how could you make peace with your ex-spouse, at least as far as arrangements with the kids are concerned?

_____

_____

➤ Which of the following statements accurately present your feelings about custody arrangements? Check all that apply.

❑ I don't trust my ex-spouse with the kids.

❑ I'm afraid my kids will like my ex-spouse more than me.

❑ All the old feelings of love and anger come out when the kids tell me about visiting my ex.

❑ I don't get to see my kids as much as I'd like.

❑ I think my kids have a healthy love and respect for both parents.

❑ I like to give gifts to my kids to make up for the pain I've caused them.

❑ I think my ex-spouse is a pretty good parent.

❑ I wish I could talk more honestly with my kids about my feelings and theirs.

❑ Other:_____

_____

_____

➤ Outside of your home, where can your children find support? Are there resources at school or in the community that could help them? Are there other kids in similar situations who could help them? _____

_____

_____

_____

CHANGES AT HOME

"When my family got a divorce, my whole world changed forever. We moved to a new home, a new school district, a new church, and all new friends. I don't know what hurt the most, missing my dad or missing my friends from my old neighborhood and school."

That statement from an eleven-year-old girl illustrates children's need for stability amid the turmoil. There will always be changes to face. Some of them may even be good, especially over the long term. Yet when separation or divorce first occurs, it's helpful if you can keep the changes to a minimum. If you have to move, try to stay in the same school district or the same social group. Your friendships will evolve toward more single people and fewer married couples, but try to make this transition gradual and smooth.

As parents get together in singles groups and social clubs, the children will inevitably socialize as well. The result can be positive new relationships with other kids who have been through similar changes. This reinforces the thought that *I am not alone* and gives children the opportunity to talk to other kids about their concerns. Nevertheless, as a parent, you can't push those new friendships too quickly. Encourage children to continue their long-term friendships while allowing new ones to develop naturally.

Keep the household schedule, responsibilities, and discipline as consistent as possible. If you did not work before and now have to, your schedule will obviously change. Sit down with your children, explain the need for the changes, and let them know what they can expect for the future. Your children need to know that you want to be with them and care for them, but that the changes force everyone to take on more responsibilities. You might say, for example, "I have to go back to work to help pay the bills. That means I won't be here when you get home from school. I would love to be here for you, fix your snack, and hear all about your day. But unfortunately, you'll have to wait until I get home at 5:30. That means you'll have to fix your own snack, and you may even need to help set the table before I get home. What's important is that we work together and make our relationship even stronger than it was before."

Here are a few additional guidelines that should help you handle the changes at home:

• Although increased responsibilities are inevitable, don't allow your kids to become hyper-responsible, taking on burdens and chores they shouldn't shoulder. Let them remain children. No matter how maturely they act, don't fool yourself into believing they can take on adult responsibilities. Boys are particularly susceptible to thinking, *Now that I'm the man of the house, I need to be here for Mom.* One boy told me how he could not go away to college in the fall because his mom was going through a difficult time and would need a man around the house.

• Avoid confiding in your children as you would in other adults. Moms often talk to their daughters about "what a tough life it is out there." Dads tell their sons all about the women they're dating. Let your children remain children.

You want a close relationship with your kids, but there must be some boundaries in that relationship. If you have a problem with setting limits or grew up in a home where boundaries were confused, you may be unconsciously passing that on to your children. If that's the case, I encourage you to seek counseling for your own issues so you can create a healthier balance for your children.

• Don't force your children to make choices that will create loyalty conflicts for them. For example, don't ask your children, "Who do you want to spend your birthday with, your mom or your dad?" That creates a no-win situation for them. If they pick you, they hurt the other parent. And how can they tell you that they'd rather be with the other parent? It would be best to get their input by asking a neutral question like, "How would you like to spend the holiday?" If they neglect the other parent, you may want to suggest a compromise that includes both parents. This approach demonstrates you're sincere when you say you want your kids to have a good relationship with the other parent. It also discourages the children's tendency to tell you what they think you want to hear.

• Encourage your children to keep their fond memories of the other parent. Many times, upon separation, parents do a clean sweep of the house, throwing away all pictures or mementos that remind them of the other parent. While I understand the sentiment, try to save a photo album or two for your children that will remind them of good times together. A special picture or memento beside their beds or in their wallets should also be suggested. Remember your suggesting it gives children permission to love the other parent. If you don't suggest it, your kids may assume that "Mom would hit the roof if she saw a picture of *him* around."

MAKE IT YOUR OWN

➤ What things have changed in your children's lives since your divorce?

_____

_____

➤ What things have stayed the same? _____

_____

_____

➤ In what ways have you been able to keep changes at a minimum? In what ways could you do so?_____

_____

_____

➤ On a scale of 1 (not at all) to 5 (a great deal), to what extent do your children do each of the following?

a. Take on too much responsibility

not at all   1   2   3   4   5   a great deal

b. Act as your personal counselors

not at all   1   2   3   4   5   a great deal

c. Have to deal with conflicting loyalty

not at all   1   2   3   4   5   a great deal

d. Feel pressure not to keep mementos of your ex-spouse

not at all   1   2   3   4   5   a great deal

NEW RELATIONSHIPS

When you're trying to restructure the family, adding a new "friend" or a stepparent to the system is like throwing a monkey wrench into the works. Such additions generally cause a whole new set of adjustments that takes years to work through. If the change happens while children are still adjusting to the trauma of divorce, generally within the first two years, all the emotions can be intensified, and acceptance can be much farther away. Therefore, many therapists recommend that newly divorced people not get involved in intimate relationships for at least two years following their divorce. That not only helps you to make your adjustment to the divorce, but it also helps your children.

This doesn't mean you should avoid new friendships or even relationships with the opposite sex. On the contrary, those friendships, assuming they're healthy, are vital to your recovery. What you need to avoid is *committed* relationships with the opposite sex and emotional entanglements that complicate the recovery process for you and your children. Rebound relationships rarely last, and most often they lead to more pain for everybody involved. The statistics on remarriage show that when people remarry within two years of their divorce, they have a greater than 80 percent chance of going through another divorce. Do you or your children need that? For those who wait the two years, however, the odds of "making it" increase to about 50 percent, which is the same percentage as for first-time marriages.

Having read that advice, your reaction may be, "That's fine for me, but try telling that to the other parent. He's already involved with someone else, and we're not even divorced yet!" Unfortunately, reality suggests your divorce was probably exacerbated by the involvement of another party in the life of at least one parent, and perhaps both. So now what do you do?

Many parents will use the existence of an illicit affair as an excuse to keep the children away from the other parent. While I don't condone such relationships, and I certainly understand the depth of your resentment and jealousy, once again I must defer to the greater good of your children. As one "kid in the middle" put it: "My dad left my mom to live with his girlfriend.

When Dad asked if he could pick us up for a visit, my mom refused to let us go over because she didn't agree with his lifestyle.

> **Your children need your permission to love the other parent. That may be difficult for you to give, but it's essential for them.**

"We knew that what my dad had done was wrong, and in many ways we were really ticked at him. But he was still our father, and we still loved him. Mom not letting us go only created a bunch of mudslinging between my parents. I think I would have respected my mom a lot more if she had told us how she felt and then allowed us to see him. Now my dad is married to his girlfriend, and our relationship is still strained. I don't want to do it, but sometimes I blame my mom for the fact that I don't really have a relationship with my dad."

Unfortunately, dating relationships have a way of becoming an additional battleground in the postdivorce experience. Those and other pitfalls await your children as you move toward that "special relationship." Here are a few additional guidelines as you seek to include opposite-sex relationships in your restructured family:

• As the noncustodial parent, it would be best if you curtailed your dating on weekends when you have the children. Parenting needs to be your first priority. Particularly in the first few years of your restructured family, you need to give your children as much of your time as possible. Your dates will generally be viewed as an intrusion into your relationship with your kids. As one particular person becomes important, you'll want to introduce that person into your children's lives in a very gradual, nonthreatening way.

It's usually much harder for the custodial parent to have a social life. Some potential dates may be scared off by your children, and then there's the problem of the time and energy it takes to maintain a social life. When the opportunity arises, however, you should not feel guilty about getting a babysitter and enjoying a night out. A balance is needed between your right to privacy and your need to be honest with the kids. Your children don't need to meet and approve of everyone you go out with, but you shouldn't hide the fact that you're dating. Your children's trust is built when you're honest with them, even though they may not like your going out without them. Expect some acting out and jealousy of your time and attention.

• Don't encourage your casual dates to get close to your children. A positive male role model is *not* a series of men you happen to date. That only confuses your children and reinforces the idea that relationships are not permanent, adding to their insecurity. While teens are more understanding of temporary relationships, they, too, are not helped by your pushing your new "friends" on them. Integrate your opposite-sex friends into your children's lives only as they become an important part of yours. Allow a relationship to develop at its own pace, never pushing your children into an artificial acceptance.

• Avoid the temptation to ask your children about the other parent's new friends. Such probing puts your children in the position of a spy and creates additional loyalty conflicts. If they volunteer the information, try to show little reaction. Encourage your children to treat your friends and your ex-spouse's friends with respect. Don't allow the dating relationship to become a source of conflict.

• If your children ask you questions about your dating relationships, give them honest answers without personal details. For example, "Do you love Mr. So-and-So?" should be answered as honestly as you can without giving information about the depth of your relationship or your plans for the future. That should wait until you're ready to take definite steps.

If your child asks, "Do you and Mr. So-and-So kiss?" you should answer honestly without making a big deal out of it. Give no further details, however, about your physical relationship.

Once such a relationship progresses to a point where it looks as if a remarriage is imminent, you need to have a discussion with your children similar to the one suggested in an earlier section, when you were contemplating separation or divorce. Out of courtesy to your former mate, you may want to forewarn him or her before you tell the kids. That way your ex-spouse can prepare emotionally. Let's face it, remarriage of either spouse is a difficult transition for both the children and the parents.

Psychologically, it's an especially big hurdle for the children. It (1) ends the fantasy that their parents might get back together, (2) triggers the fear that the new spouse will take away the parent's love for them, and (3) creates anxiety about whether they will get along with this intruder in their family. For the parent getting married, it finally closes one chapter in his or her life and opens the door of new challenges and opportunities. For the parent remaining single, there's the feeling of being left behind and the anxiety of wondering, *Will I ever be able to move on like that?*

As everyone makes the necessary adjustments, the anxiety that increasingly grips your children is the feeling, *Now that Dad has a new life, he will have even less love and less time for me.* The feeling can be especially threatening when the new marriage includes children. The blending of families is filled with so many complexities that it needs to be the subject of another book. For our purposes, a general overview is in order.

Research statistics say that one-third of all children in the United States spend at least some time with a stepparent before their eighteenth birthday. It's estimated that in the next decade, the blended family will be the most common type of family in this country. Yet researchers estimate that it takes an average of five years to successfully blend a family. For most of those who get remarried, the children will be out of the house before the necessary transitions are made.

I have two close friends who both had teenagers at home and were both in long-term relationships that were moving toward marriage. Rather than go through the difficulties of blending a family, both couples decided to wait until the children were out of the house before they got remarried. I'm not saying you should do the same; I merely want to point out that the blending process is more difficult than most people realize. One of my friends explained the decision this way:

"I know of over twenty remarried couples, all with teenagers in their blended families. I can't name one family who hasn't had major difficulties with their children after the marriage. I just decided that I didn't want to do that to my kids, so I've postponed my remarriage for another two years. By then my youngest will leave for college."

A mother of a blended family described the following interaction between her teenage son and her new husband: "Before I married Jim, he and my son, Paul, were like best friends. I was so excited because I thought that now, after thirteen years of being by ourselves, Paul was going to have a father figure. The strangest thing happened, though. As soon as we got back from the honeymoon, I noticed my son acting a little strange around Jim. Within a few weeks they were barely speaking, and now, after three years of marriage, Paul and Jim can't even look at each other without getting in a fight. I don't know what happened when Jim and I married, but something obviously clicked off for my son."

That example is typical of many stories I've heard from stepparents who are horrified by what happens when they try to blend a family. It never seems to be easy, and the way everyone gets along before the wedding does not seem to be a very good indication of what to expect after. In fact, it's not unusual for the children to push you toward marrying Mr. So-and-So, and then to create havoc after the wedding, saying they never really liked him.

How can you increase your chances of blending families successfully? Here are a few guidelines:

- The potential stepparent needs to be introduced to the children in a gradual and natural way. In the beginning, fun outings are best since they reduce the tension of "making conversation." Once the initial transitions are over, however, natural family activities are best.

- Don't expect instant rapport between your children and the new stepparent. Those relationships take time, usually many years. If the relationship seems to go well from the beginning, expect a strained transition later.

- Younger children usually adjust more quickly to a stepparent than do older children and teenagers.

- The stepparent should try to observe the family customs and traditions, including giving the children gifts on special occasions. Be careful to not overdo the gift giving, however, since children will tend to view it as a bribe.

- Don't push your children to participate in your wedding. They may feel intense pressure to be loyal to the other parent. Let them know of your plans, and tell them you would like for them to take part, but that you will let them decide for themselves. Then give them several weeks, if possible, to make up their minds.

- If new stepparents don't have children, they need to educate themselves about childhood development and parenting. Don't assume it will come naturally. They are taking on a big commitment and need to prepare themselves.

- Don't expect your children to love or respect their stepparent as much as they do their biological parent. To do so is unrealistic and sets the stepparent up for tremendous disappointment.

- Don't force your children to call the new stepparent "Mom" or "Dad." Find out what they would prefer, and then try to compromise on a name or nickname that's acceptable to everyone, including your former spouse. (Yes, even after your remarriage, the lines of communication need to stay open.)

- Continue to spend individual time with each of your children, and constantly remind them of your undiminished love for them. Keep in mind their fear that with each new person or child in your life, you will have less love for them. The feeling is particularly strong if there is a stepchild about the same age as your own child, or if a new baby is born into the blended family.

- While your children need to respect and listen to your new spouse, you need to remain their primary disciplinarian. Younger children can take correction from their stepparent more easily than older children and teenagers. Therefore, it is unfair to the stepparent for you to expect him or her to take on the major disciplinary role.

• Children generally try to play one parent against the other, but the practice is particularly intense in a stepparent relationship. Try not to get sucked into this "divide and conquer" strategy. Avoid taking sides with your children or your spouse. Instead, discuss the matter privately with your spouse, and then come back and tell the children *your* decision. Remember, they will take it best if it comes from you, their natural parent.

• You and the stepparent need to keep in mind that intense feelings of anger and resentment are normal in the blended family, especially in teenagers. Try not to personalize the anger and respond in kind. You're probably bearing the brunt of years of perceived betrayal and disappointment. Be as patient and compassionate as you can, knowing this is a difficult transition for everyone—one that statistically will last five years.

If you are parenting as a single and your former spouse is remarrying, you also will have adjustments to make in your attitudes and with your children as they report their feelings toward the new "creature" in their lives. It's probably a no-win situation for you. If they love their new stepparent, you will feel "replaced"; if they don't like their new stepparent, you'll have to hear the weekly reports of how "she did this, and she did that."

Here are a few guidelines to help you and your children cope with these changes:

• If you can't be accepting of your former spouse's remarriage, at least try to stay as neutral and emotionally uninvolved as possible. If you're really struggling with the whole issue, you probably need to talk with a counselor or adviser about your feelings. Otherwise, they will affect your children's adjustment.

• Give your children permission to attend or participate in the wedding. Forbidding them will only hurt their relationship with *you* in the long run.

Remarriage of either spouse is a difficult transition for the children. It . . .

(1) ends the fantasy that their parents might get back together,

(2) triggers the fear that the new spouse will take away the love their parent has for them, and

(3) creates anxiety about whether they will get along with this intruder in their family.

As hard as it might be for you to accept, you need to have at least a casual relationship with your former mate's new spouse. You will probably need to talk with him or her on the phone occasionally, and it doesn't help the children if they see you snarling at each other every time you speak.

• Give your children permission to talk about the times at the other parent's house. Listen to their stories about the other partner and the other children, but try not to make any judgments or offer your opinion. Try to remain detached when they complain about or praise the stepparent. Stay out of what goes on in the other household unless you have good reason for significant concern, such as "They don't feed us over there." Then, don't assume it's true. Try to take it up calmly with your former spouse. Only involve the stepparent if you find you get along with him or her better than you do with your ex-spouse.

MAKE IT YOUR OWN

➤ Which of the following statements are true? Check all that apply.

❑ 1. I am rushing into another romantic relationship.

❑ 2. I'm getting involved in another romantic relationship, but it's no rush. We're all ready for it.

❑ 3. I have avoided romantic relationships, largely because of the children.

❑ 4. I've been seeking a romantic relationship, primarily because my children need another parent.

❑ 5. My children have been encouraging me to find a new romance.

❑ 6. My children seem quietly resentful about the dates I have.

❑ 7. My children have expressed open hostility toward my dates.

❑ 8. My children seem too interested in the details of my romantic relationships.

❑ 9. My ex-spouse is trying to find out about my romantic relationships through the kids.

❑ 10. I am trying to find out about my ex-spouse's romantic relationships through the kids.

❑ 11. My children are still hoping my ex and I will get back together.

❑ 12. My ex-spouse has remarried. (If not, skip to #18.)

❑ 13. My ex-spouse's remarriage hit me harder than I expected.

❑ 14. My children were involved in my ex-spouse's wedding.

❑ 15. My kids get along fine with my ex's new spouse.

❑ 16. I get along fine with my ex's new spouse.

❑ 17. I'm secretly worried that my ex's remarriage will make him or her a better parent than I am.

❑ 18. I have remarried or will soon remarry. (If not, skip to #30.)

❑ 19. My new spouse gets along great with my kids.

❑ 20. I have encouraged my kids to call my new spouse "Mom" or "Dad."

❑ 21. My new spouse is strongly involved in disciplining my children.

❑ 22. My new spouse doesn't know much about raising children.

❑ 23. It's taking time for my new spouse to learn how our family does things.

❑ 24. The children are harboring resentment against my new spouse.

❑ 25. The children sometimes try to create disagreements between my spouse and me.

❑ 26. My new spouse has children of his or her own. (If not, skip to #30.)

❑ 27. Our families are blending very nicely.

❑ 28. The children seem to be competing with each other for our love.

❑ 29. Our two families have conflicting traditions.

❑ 30. I have communicated love and acceptance to my children throughout this whole process.

➤ Comments:

❑ 1. Obviously, not healthy.

❑ 2. Fine, if you are not carrying emotional baggage from the past. Check the chapter on reentry.

❏   3. You need to avoid romance because it is best for you. Therefore, it is also best for your children.

❏   4. Bad move. Watch out for it.

❏   5. Common, but beware. Kids are not your counselors.

❏   6. Common. Don't worry, but *communicate.*

❏   7. Also common. Communicate with your kids, but be sure to express *your* needs.

❏   8. Common. Don't divulge too much. Keep it private.

❏   9. Common. Not much you can do.

❏ 10. Don't do this. It makes the kids spies.

❏ 11. Common. Gently wean them away from this hope.

❏ 13. Common. All sorts of emotions rise to the surface.

❏ 14. This can hurt, especially if you feel rejected and left out.

❏ 15. This is good. You are bound to feel jealous, but don't give in to your feeling.

❏ 16. This is good—uncommon, but good. For the kids' sake, at least, you need to be on good terms.

❏ 17. Common, but relax. Focus on being the best parent you can be.

❏ 19. Wonderful! But expect ups and downs.

❏ 20. Not necessarily a good idea. You don't want to displace their other parent. Find a suitable new term.

❏ 21. Not necessarily a good idea. At first, *you* should remain the primary disciplinarian (especially with older kids).

❏ 22. These issues should be explored before marriage. However, if you are now married, you must invest extra effort in developing parental skills.

❏ 23. Each family has its traditions. It takes time to learn them and to make up new ones.

❏ 24. Common. But talk it through.

❑ 25. Common. Don't let it work. Present a united front to the kids.

❑ 27. If so, be thankful.

❑ 28. Common. Keep spreading the love around.

❑ 29. See #23.

❑ 30. This is the key. You will need to keep affirming your love for your children over and over.

Summary

In this chapter we have looked at some common areas of contention for single parents and then presented practical guidelines for helping your children over some of the difficult hurdles. The following is a brief summary:

Increases Negative Effect of Divorce	*Lessens Negative Effect of Divorce*
1. Children are involved in visitation and custody squabbles.	1. Parents work out custody and visitation arrangements cooperatively.
2. Children are asked to choose between the parents.	2. Parents help children avoid loyalty conflicts by encouraging the relationship with the other parent.
3. Parents use the children to send messages.	3. Parents keep lines of communication open.
4. Parents become too busy or distracted from their children.	4. Parents spend quality time with each child.
5. Parents use the children and money as leverage to get what they want.	5. Parents keep money issues separate and away from the children.
6. Parents isolate themselves and their children.	6. Parents seek resources and support from a variety of settings, including church, school, family.
7. Parents expect the children to take the place of the missing parent.	7. The child remains a child, even though increased responsibilities may be necessary.
8. Parents deny feelings and do not facilitate discussion with children.	8. Parents allow children to grieve.
9. Parents push children into relationships with a series of dating partners.	9. Parents provide stable adult relationships with relatives and family friends.

10. A remarriage occurs before the children have had time to adjust to the divorce.	10. Give your children at least two years of adjustment before bringing a potential stepparent into their lives.
11. Parents maintain angry, bitter feelings.	11. Parents recover and move on in a healthy, new lifestyle.
12. Parents speak negatively about the other parent in front of the children.	12. Parents show respect for each other.
13. Absent parent loses contact with the children.	13. Absent parent maintains consistent contact with the children.

Action Point: In the summary, which areas are still a problem for you? Set a goal, or perhaps several, for the areas you still need to work on. Write those goals here and on page 282 (Appendix A) for future reference.

_____

_____

_____

_____

_____

_____

_____

Chapter 11

YOU'LL NEVER WALK ALONE
SUPPORT GROUPS FOR THE SEPARATED AND THE DIVORCED

I received Ken's call late in the afternoon. "Things have gotten so bad that my wife tells me she wants a divorce," he explained. "I don't know what to do. Is there anybody at the church I can talk to?"

Ken had been exploring the claims of Jesus Christ for a number of months. But in the midst of his spiritual journey, the problems in his family life went from bad to worse.

It would have been easy for me to set up a time to talk with Ken. Yet I sensed that he needed more than a one-hour conversation. He needed some friends who understood his circumstances and would walk with him through the painful days ahead. So, I put him in touch with one of the Fresh Start alumni in our church. I didn't realize it, but Ken's telephone call was the beginning of a twelve-step support group for the separated and the divorced.

Looking back, I'm surprised that such a group didn't develop sooner. This church had been presenting the Fresh Start Divorce Recovery Seminar since 1985, even spinning off a Sunday morning community for the separated and the divorced called Genesis. This community sponsors socials, monthly "talk it overs," and Bible studies for its members and visitors. Since we offered the Fresh Start Seminar twice a year, we had a continual flow of new people facing the realities of marital separation.

Genesis was a great chance for people to share their concerns and get to know one another, but Ken needed something else, something deeper. Our church had several other support groups for people dealing with various crises and personal problems. Why not a support group for the separated and the divorced?

Five people attended the first meeting of this group. Next there were ten. Now between twenty and thirty-five people meet weekly. Why the sudden popularity of this group? A few distinguishing characteristics stand out.

POWERLESSNESS

The new people who come to the support group have a feeling of futility. They don't know anything else they can do, and yet they feel they must do something. As they share their woes and hear the experiences of others, they begin to see the benefit in admitting that they are, in fact, powerless to control the outcome of their circumstances.

For years it has been recognized that this is the initial hurdle toward personal recovery: admitting you are powerless. It's the first of the famous twelve steps of Alcoholics Anonymous and other recovery groups, but it has been overlooked in most of the divorce recovery literature.

For the person who has been abandoned by a spouse, this admission is crucial. You cannot be responsible for the decisions and actions of your estranged mate; you can be responsible only for yourself. By recognizing this, you can begin to move out of the initial grieving process and move toward wholeness.

HONEST SHARING WITH OPEN PEOPLE

A support group also provides a chance for struggling people to talk honestly with other strugglers.

As I wrote this last sentence the phone rang.

"My wife left me two weeks ago," Lonny told me. "I'm getting pretty lonely." Even over the phone, I could sense the courage he needed to admit that.

"I know a group where you can find some friends, Lonny. And they're meeting tonight."

When a man or woman enters the process of separation and divorce, it is often hidden from friends, family, and others as long as possible. When the facts do "go public," the confusion and grief of the experience are often compounded by embarrassment. Where can you go to share your pain without getting stares or sermons from people who mean well but just don't understand? You need to be with people, but you're afraid! Who can you trust?

In a support group, people find a safe haven for encouragement, coping, and growth. They find others who understand. They no longer feel alone. They're not the only ones who've lost their dreams and seen their most important relationships destroyed. In this environment, they begin to trust, face the facts, face the future and, most important, face themselves.

TRUSTED SERVANTS

Our support group also has a corps of trusted servants who faithfully attend the meetings and facilitate the process. No, they're not leaders, merely helpers. They must be committed Christians with at least six months of faithful involvement in a support group.

The job description of a trusted servant is simple: to participate regularly in the support group, occasionally to be the monthly chairperson for the group, and to serve as a speaker for the meetings as needed.

MEETING FORMAT

Another reason for success in the support group is the simplicity of its meeting format. Gathering on Tuesday evenings from 7:00 to 8:00 P.M., the group begins with a few opening comments on its purpose made by the chairperson. Using information adapted from numerous sources,[1] a handout is provided that includes portions to be read out loud by the participants.

The meeting begins with a unison praying of the Serenity Prayer. This is followed by the entire group reading the following proclamation from the Rapha *Right Step Facilitator Training Manual:*

THE SIGNIFICANCE

The first step was taken one day by the Savior Jesus Christ when He stepped down from heaven to demonstrate God's love for mankind. The step led to the cross, the grave, and ended in resurrected power. The Right Step is now up to you. He said if you will turn toward the cross and follow Him, He will give you the strength necessary for restoration and you will be set free.

THE PERSPECTIVE

We acknowledge that we are living in a war zone . . . that the mind is a battlefield. The good news is that the war has already been won by Christ. Defeat comes only when deception is believed; victory comes when truth is substituted for deception. Absolute truth and authority is found in God's Word, the rock and the foundation of our restoration.

THE CHALLENGE

The challenge is to break the devastating cycle of deception by restoring our relationship to God and to one another.

THE PROVISION

Having taken the right step, I have been set free. I know God has provided His unconditional love for me. Regardless of the past, and no matter what the future brings, this fact can never change![2]

After this proclamation there are two other readings shared in the group: the twelve steps of Alcoholics Anonymous (adapted to a Christian format) and the group guidelines. Group members usually take turns reading the steps and guidelines.

Our group guidelines, familiar to many who participate in twelve-step studies, are designed to allow safe sharing without fear of interruption.

GUIDELINES

1. Confidentiality may not be breached by any member or visitor of this group, for any reason, at any time.

2. Trust is the basis for the success or failure of this group.

3. Any person has the right to pass at any time when asked to share. No explanation is necessary; simply decline your privilege by stating, "I pass."

4. Speak one person at a time. No side conversations. Listen attentively to the person speaking.

5. Speak only from your own personal experience. Avoid generalizing by using the responsible "I" rather than "we."

6. Do not sermonize, moralize, or give advice. It is your responsibility to be compassionate, supportive, and understanding of each other.

7. Again, confidentiality may not be breached at any time. It is all right to say you were here; it is not all right to say you saw someone else here.

All of this reading might seem a little too much if you have never participated in a group like the one I am describing. However, a weekly repetition of the prayer, proclamation, twelve steps, and guidelines reinforces the basic tenets of the support group: our commitment to Christ-centered, spiritual recovery and our commitment to maintaining a safe, supportive environment.

Following these readings, the chairperson asks all who feel comfortable doing so to briefly introduce themselves and share why they've come. Because of the low self-esteem experienced by many newcomers, assurances are given that people should not feel obligated to talk unless they feel safe and secure in the group. After this comes an opportunity for those who would like to make a donation to the ministry. Again, newcomers are encouraged not to contribute unless they feel comfortable in doing so.

Finally, the chairperson introduces the speaker. This speaker is a member of the group and is usually prepared to spend approximately five minutes sharing about one of the twelve steps or a related experience in the process of recovery.

However, before the speaker begins, he or she always asks: "Does anyone need to talk about or share something?" This offer may very well change the entire format for the evening. However, since the agenda is focused on support rather than on the presentation of content, such changes are viewed as an opportunity rather than a problem.

After this sharing time, the group breaks into two or more subgroups of six to eight persons. Ideally, this group breakout divides between the separated and the divorced when attendance is adequate to support such a division. In these subgroups (each facilitated by a trusted servant), every person is given the opportunity to share his or her experience, strength, and hope in the midst of marital disruption.

(The idea of breaking into distinct sharing groups for the separated and the divorced developed over a period of time. In the early days of the group, both the separated and the divorced met and shared together. Although that was beneficial to all, there were unique needs that concerned some of the separated participants. A primary concern was their desire to talk about the struggles of working on reconciliation with the spouse. In order to encourage one another during the separation/reconciliation struggle, a number of these participants requested a distinct sharing opportunity. The group had a special meeting to consider this request and agreed to it. The result has been an even more supportive and significant sharing experience for both groups.)

After the time of sharing, everyone gathers back together. Any announcements pertaining to the group activities are made. Then, everyone rises and recites the Lord's Prayer. That last sentence of encouragement is repeated: "Keep coming back. It works if you work it."

SUPPORTIVE CHURCH PROGRAM

One distinct advantage of our support group is that it's nestled in a broader church ministry program that's committed to recovery. This begins with the church leadership, which believes in meeting the real needs of people. This commitment has led the church to direct primary church resources into support ministries.

The church also works closely with couples seeking reconciliation of their separated marriages. The church believes that marital disruption falls into the context of broken relationships described by Jesus in Matthew 18:15–17 (NKJV). In that passage Jesus taught that there is a time when relational disruption is so bad that one must "tell it to the church." In response, the church must do what it can to bring about reconciliation. This has meant providing couples with counseling and group therapy, assigning elders to the couples for shepherding, and employing church discipline in a caring way.

For the separated and the divorced, this commitment also includes a growing singles ministry. The singles ministry is divided into three communities that reflect various age and life-experience levels. As I mentioned earlier, one of these communities, called Genesis, exists specifically for the separated and the divorced.

As noted at the beginning of this chapter, the Genesis community sponsors a Fresh Start Divorce Recovery Seminar every six months. This seminar is designed to meet the needs of both the churched and the unchurched. Therefore, it provides a primary rallying point for church members and outreach to those in the community.

This program has been expanded to include a Kids' Hope Seminar for children of divorce. Growing out of this program is a support group for children of divorcing homes (meeting at the same time as the adult group).

The Genesis class, which meets on Sunday mornings, is developed around a six-month follow-up curriculum to Fresh Start. The Genesis community also sponsors a full range of ministry activities for the benefit of its members.

Therefore, the separated and divorced support group does not exist in a vacuum. It is one component of a varied ministry menu available for those experiencing the trauma of a broken or disrupted marriage.

At the same time, the divorced and separated group fits into the broader support group ministry context. The church sponsors groups that focus on many issues, including groups for adult children, codependency, substance addiction, and survivors of rape. We have found that many who are going through separation and divorce are facing what are commonly called cross addictions. That is, the circumstances that precipitate the marriage breakup often involve issues of one's past or matters of personal life control. We strongly encourage those who come to the divorced and separated group to consider attending one or more of these other groups, as appropriate. Many of our trusted servants come to two or more groups a week! These other groups provide a supportive context where participants can face issues related to both personal and family dysfunctions. Many have come to grips with the deeper implications of their marital problems by becoming involved in mutual support groups.

GROUP LIMITATIONS

As I interact with regular participants and trusted servants of the separated and divorced support group, I have discovered two primary limitations to the group.

The first is that the group meets only once a week. Participants in our group who are experienced in recovery share that a daily meeting would be most conducive for personal recovery. In this way a hurting person could always know that a meeting was available. While the once-a-week format is consistent, it does not provide the immediate encouragement many feel necessary.

Although we do not currently have the resource base to run daily separated and divorced support group meetings, we attempt to meet this need for daily opportunities by strongly encouraging participants to share names and telephone numbers. Again and again in the group one hears, "Can I call you?" or "You can call me if you need to talk." Group members make themselves available because they know the need!

A second group limitation is our need for a better sponsorship system in the support group. Sponsorship takes place when an experienced member of the group commits to some level of personalized support for another member.

We promote sponsorship in our entire support group system. And we work with our trusted servants in the encouragement of developing sponsors. Where sponsorship occurs, it has worked quite well. However, there is a shortage of experienced, recovering participants.

CHANGED LIVES

In the beginning of this chapter I shared about Ken, whose telephone call began the process that eventually led to our support group for the separated and the divorced. Ken has been involved with our group since it started. I sat down with him over lunch and asked him what difference it has made in his life.

"The support group does two things for me," he said. "First, it gives me a chance to listen to other people. When they share, I can pick up on their feelings and what is happening to them. This helps me with my recovery. I grow by hearing their points of view. I relate to their experiences. And I learn to identify my feelings by listening to them share.

"At the same time, I get to share my experience with people who will listen, understand, and not criticize me. This sharing is real important to me. When I first started coming to the group, I only told the facts. But this didn't get to the core of my problems. But as I have listened, learned, and developed trust, I have gotten in touch with my feelings.

"Before I got involved with the support group, I never had been in touch with my feelings. I still struggle to understand them because it is all so new to me. All my life I have either stuffed my feelings or reacted to them. I was never in touch with them, never able to share them, and certainly never capable of responding to them in a healthy way.

"Another thing I have learned from the group is that I've got to work one moment at a time. If I start projecting into the future, that's when I crash and burn. If I can keep in focus today, then I am all right."

"Ken," I asked, "what has it meant for you to have a group to support you?"

He responded, "I couldn't imagine how I would be able to deal with the situations I've had to face without this support system. I just couldn't handle it. I probably would have tried to commit suicide or done something really crazy. I might be in a padded cell due to the amount of stress that I have had with the divorce and the added hassles at work.

"Where I have been spiritually is a key too," he continued. "Since I've been separated, I've accepted Jesus Christ. I've been learning how to turn things over to him. That is another aspect of the group that's been important to me. Because this is a Christ-centered support group, I haven't been held back in sharing my beliefs. It's been a tremendous encouragement to my spiritual development and growth."

Ken is one of many who have found the friendship and encouragement they needed to grow through the experience of separation and divorce. I believe what Ken has discovered is a basic truth for healthy divorce recovery;

you can't do it alone. However, with the encouragement of recovering friends, one can do more than survive. As a man in the support group put it: "I wouldn't wish my divorce experience on my worst enemy. But I wouldn't give up the personal growth I have experienced because of it. I hate divorce, but I'm a better person because of my recovery from it."

MAKE IT YOUR OWN

➤ This chapter describes a serious recovery support group, highly structured and extremely effective in treating the deep needs of its participants. This is great if you have the personnel and resources to do it. We recognize that many churches and organizations would like to do some Fresh Start follow-up, but can't handle such a serious recovery group.

You can be more casual about it if you like, gathering a group of separated and/or divorced people together on a regular basis for sharing, Bible study, prayer, or perhaps even working through this book. That becomes more of a community and less of a support group (though the members will offer support to one another). Without experienced leadership or strict guidelines (such as the confidentiality code), you may not be able to dig into some of the deeper personal issues of the group, but you can still offer friendship and encouragement as you share your common experiences.

➤ Where could you find or start a divorce recovery group?

❑ Your church

❑ A group within your church

❑ Your community

❑ A network of churches

❑ Some other organization

❑ Among a handful of friends

❑ Other: _____

_____

➤ What sort of group do you envision?

❑ A twelve-step-style support group

❏ A Bible study group that deals with the biblical aspects of your situation

❏ A community where people can share their concerns and needs

❏ A group that works through a book like this one

❏ A group that just does fun stuff together

❏ Other: _____

_____

➤ How often would the group meet?

❏ Twice a week

❏ Weekly

❏ Every two weeks

❏ Monthly

❏ Other: _____

_____

➤ What needs do you have that a group like this could meet?

_____

_____

➤ How would you go about starting (or even finding) a group like this?

_____

_____

SUGGESTED QUESTIONS
FOR GROUP MEETINGS

The Stages of Grieving

1. Share the process of your separation and/or divorce in terms of the stages of recovery (denial, anger, bargaining, depression, acceptance, forgiveness).

2. Which stage do you think is most difficult to deal with?

3. Where do you see yourself right now on the slippery slope of these stages?

4. Are there significant persons who have supported you? Who are they? How have they supported you?

Separation/Reconciliation (for groups of separated people)

1. Which way are you leaning? Back toward the marriage or away from it? What do you want to happen? What do you expect to happen?

2. What are you learning about yourself in this time of separation?

3. What's the hardest thing about being separated, as opposed to being divorced?

Biblical Insights on Divorce

1. How do you feel about the biblical teaching on marriage, divorce, and remarriage? How does this relate to your circumstances?

2. What help or support would you like to receive from other Christians as you go through this process of recovery?

3. How do you react to the idea that

- marriage for the wrong reasons is wrong?
- marriage should not be used as an escape from single life?
- you are ready for remarriage when you don't need to remarry?

The Legal Issues

1. What do you see as the advantages and disadvantages of mediation, as opposed to the normal legal process?

2. What positive or negative experiences have you had in the legal/mediation process?

Reentry into the Single Life

1. What are one or two adjustments you have faced in reentering the single life?

2. Share some ways you have sought to take responsibility for your future.

3. How do you respond to the encouragement to go slow and seek friendships rather than romance?

Finances

1. What is your biggest financial concern right now?

2. In what ways have you cut expenses or increased your income? (Perhaps others could learn from you.)

3. How could we as a group help each other financially?

Communication

   1. What communication skills do you have? Which do you lack?

   2. How has your style of communication helped or hurt your relationships? Give examples.

   3. What can someone do to improve communication skills?

Sexuality

   1. How do you deal with sexual temptation?

   2. Do you think it's harder to remain celibate after you've been married than when you've never married?

   3. In your own words, why do you think a Christian should abstain from sex outside marriage?

Working Through Bitterness: Learning to Forgive

   1. Share some of the bitterness you might be struggling with right now. Why is it so difficult to forgive?

   2. What do you think would be the impact of forgiveness on

   • your separation?
   • your ex-spouse?
   • your children?
   • your new relationships?
   • you?

   3. How would you respond to the following comment? "I can't forgive him. That would be like saying what he did was okay!"

Children

   1. How have your children reacted to the breakup of your marriage?

   2. What's the best thing you can do for your kids in this situation?

   3. How can others in the group help you with your children?

Support Groups

   1. How has this group helped you?

   2. What could we do to support one another more?

   3. How can we reach out to others who need this support too?

DEVELOPING A POSITIVE SELF-IMAGE

by Tom Whiteman

Without question, one of the consequences of a divorce is a damaged self-image. We all go through the self-doubts, the second-guessing, and perhaps even self-abasement. And there's good reason for us to feel the way we do. One of the most important things in life was our marriage and family. When that has fallen apart, of course we will feel like a failure. And even for couples who have been fairly hospitable to each other, toward the end of the relationship, the name-calling and accusations get pretty ugly.

So now one of your divorce recovery tasks is to rebuild your self-image. That may become one of the first things you work on since it's critical for every other relationship you'll develop. As mentioned in several chapters in this workbook, your self-image will affect the way and speed at which you recover from your divorce. Examining and improving your self-image as quickly as possible are vital.

Prior to my divorce, there was a period when I was growing in confidence and comfort with myself and other people. I had grown up somewhat withdrawn and feeling as if everyone else was better than I was, but after marriage, a few good relationships, and a fulfilling job, I really began to like myself. That gave me the confidence to reach out and take some risks I never had the courage to take before.

Then I was hit by the trauma of divorce. Suddenly, I was that awkward junior high school kid again, shying away from people and filled with insecurities. Divorce has a way of setting us back emotionally and undoing most, if not all, the progress we've made on our self-image over the past several years.

Why do we have such a hard time maintaining a proper self-image, and how can we rebuild it once it's been shattered?

ORIGINS OF A POOR SELF-IMAGE

The origins of our struggle with self-image certainly precede our separation or divorce. Those incidents merely undo much of the work we have done to improve our view of self. In some cases, self-image may be at an all-time low. Why is this such a struggle? Let me outline some basic reasons.

- *We're in a spiritual battle.* I believe wholeheartedly that one of the major reasons we struggle so much—and many times lose the battle for our mind—is that we're not battling flesh and blood or anything else we can get our hands on; we are battling a spiritual warfare or, as some would call it, "a battle against the evil one."

I don't intend to sound mystical or as if I believe there are demons lurking around trying to "get us." I'm merely referring to the fact that Satan loves to defeat us and keep us there. What better way to do that than to ruin our marriages and then have us believe we're no longer any good or useful to anyone?

God wants us to believe in him, love him, and then love others *as we love ourselves.* He says that's his most important commandment (Matt. 22:35–40). How can we love God and other people when we don't believe in ourselves and instead believe we are defeated and useless? God does not send us those messages. They come straight from the pit of hell. So the next time you start to think, *I'm no good, I'm not lovable,* or that God can't use you anymore, acknowledge to yourself immediately where those kinds of thoughts originate. *Then fight back.*

- *Our fallen state.* We can't always blame Satan for our having bad thoughts. (The devil doesn't make us do it.) We must recognize our sinful nature, which basically means that left to ourselves, we are quite capable of making poor choices and thinking wrong thoughts. The Bible states that this is all part of being human. That's why I believe that if we don't *work* on our self-image, we will naturally gravitate toward a negative one—a self-centered one that focuses on me, me, me.

After all, aren't we all naturally selfish? And isn't our poor self-image a reflection of this preoccupation with self? We focus on how *we* feel, on how *we've* been hurt, and on how *we* come across. This "me" attitude is what I refer to as the "dance floor syndrome."

Are you self-conscious about dancing in front of other people? If you're like me and never really learned how to dance, it can be fairly traumatic to have to dance in public. Why is that?

You're probably convinced that everyone in the place is looking at you and laughing inside over your gyrations out on the floor. But the truth is that all the others are concerned only about how *they* look and are therefore too preoccupied with themselves to even notice what you're doing. So go out there and make a fool of yourself because no one else is watching.

So it is with our self-image and many of our insecurities. We're focused on ourselves and how we come across. This "me" preoccupation may lead us to shy away from people, from challenging new situations, and perhaps even from discussions if we believe we will make fools of ourselves. The truth is, no one is really paying that much attention to what we're doing or saying because they're primarily concerned about their own image. So speak up!

• *Our background and experiences.* Our background and family of origin have a large bearing on our personalities, which include self-image. And even if you were raised in the most loving of homes, you probably still struggle for a variety of reasons.

Researchers estimate that about 85 percent of your personality is developed by the age of six. And what is your image of self at age six? Just about everyone around you is taller than you, stronger than you, smarter than you; in fact, you're probably pretty dependent on other people for just about everything. Those experiences help to form our personalities. Is it any wonder we grow up to feel inferior in many situations?

Then add to those experiences the criticism of a parent, the inevitable teasing of peers, and the occasional failures we all face and you can see how our background and experiences can affect our self-image. And I need to point out that I have mentioned only *normal* childhood experiences. Your personality is affected even more if you've had to endure any type of emotional or physical abuse or other significant trauma.

HOW DO YOU EVALUATE YOURSELF?

We are constantly evaluating ourselves according to a variety of criteria. These are some of the more prevalent:

• *The ideal self:* We evaluate ourselves according to our own standards. These are standards we set for ourselves for who we think we should be or who we would like to be. The degree to which you expect a lot or only a little from yourself is largely a reflection of the standards you grew up with. Carried to an extreme degree, they can actually make you your own worst enemy. You can set up a list of "shoulds" and "ought to's" that no one could satisfy. That type of perfectionism can cause an unending cycle of never measuring up.

• *Feedback from significant others:* Another important ingredient in your evaluation of self-image is the feedback you get from the significant people in your life. As mentioned earlier, in your early years, that was mostly your parents. While parents continue to have a significant impact on your life well into your adult years, your peer group gradually becomes more influential to your view of self. Eventually, your spouse and maybe one or two close friends become the largest influences.

What happens when divorce enters your life? Obviously, you lose the affirmation of your spouse, and for many, even your best friends can grow cold and distant (which you probably interpret as another rejection).

• *Feedback from our society:* This last area of evaluation should not be underestimated. Our society has a large bearing on our self-image. How? By the subtle influences and hidden messages it sends us constantly about what's important and what is valued in life.

Our society affirms us in four major areas: beauty, brains, brawn, and bucks. We see those values in every TV show, every commercial, our schools, our neighborhoods and, unfortunately, even our churches. As soon as you start to socialize, you quickly learn that if you're a woman, beauty is critical. You're brought up to believe you need to look like a Barbie doll. (What a drag!) If you're a man, beauty is okay, but you can get away with not being good looking if you're strong. (Then you can beat up anyone who makes fun of you.)

If you're not the school athlete or the cheerleader type, you need to be smart—very smart, in fact, because now you have to go on to be a doctor, lawyer, or corporate executive in order to be valued.

The final category, bucks, is one that becomes more and more important as we get older. That's probably because the older we get, the more we lose of the other three. If you have money and lots of it, let's face it—you don't need to be good looking, strong, or smart. You get instant respect when people find out what you're worth; that even includes how you're treated by the church.

If you're like me, on a good day, you consider yourself to be average in the first three categories. But when it comes to money, I'm still waiting. The problem is, though, that we face a losing battle because we all know we're gradually losing what we have in the physical areas, and the money problem isn't getting any better. Those temporal measures of self-image are a no-win proposition because even if you're beautiful, strong, smart, or rich, what you eventually find out is that there will always be others who are more beautiful, stronger, smarter, and richer.

So how can our self-image remain stable? It can't be based on our own view because we've seen that that fluctuates according to our moods. It can't be based on what others think of us. We've learned the hard way that other people can turn on us, which devastates our self-image. And society's values are a never-ending cycle of trying to measure up but never quite making it.

How should we value ourselves? Our self-image needs to be based on something constant and unconditional, and that's why it must be based on God and his love toward us. This is so important, yet I meet so few people who have a clear understanding of how the truth can revolutionize our self-image. My self-image was devastated when I went through divorce, but as I rebuilt it, I tried to focus on God's love for me and who I was in him. I knew enough theology to know that as a Christian, I was considered part of God's family. And with him as my Father, I could be assured of his constant love and care. That understanding helped me to build a healthier self-image.

The Bible states that God *delights* in his children and that we have obtained his inheritance (Eph. 1). Think about that. If you hear you've just received an inheritance, how do you react? Think about God delighting in *you* in the same way. That makes you feel pretty good, doesn't it? You've probably never had anyone who felt that way about you consistently. But that's what we need if we're going to learn to love ourselves and view ourselves the way God views us.

Please note, however, that this knowledge does not solve our problem because it's an abstract concept, and we don't have a tangible Christ to hold on to and whisper in our ear when the world begins to beat us down. That's why we need to be reminded every day about who we are in Christ and to work on our self-image. It's like a fish swimming upstream. We need constantly to be swimming against the current. The current is what the world tells us about who we are and what we tend to tell ourselves, or what Satan wants us to think. As soon as we stop swimming, we automatically will go with the current.

Here are some steps we need to take:

1. View ourselves as God views us.

As outlined earlier, the way God views us is vastly different from the way society views us. In 1 Samuel, God reminds us that "man looks at the outward appearance, but the LORD looks at the heart" (16:7 NKJV). When the men of Israel were looking for their king, they looked for someone who was tall, rugged, and mature. Yet after looking at all of David's older brothers, God drew Samuel to a small, scrawny kid named David whom God knew to be of good character.

Let's reject the standards of our world and not be so consumed with the pursuit of beauty, brains, brawn, or bucks. Instead, let's focus on developing godlike character. By seeking God's guidance and allowing his love to flow through us, we can become very attractive to others.

As children of God, we know our worth to him and, therefore, need to begin viewing ourselves as he views us. If we could do that, we would believe we really are unique individuals, created in God's image and extremely valuable.

2. Renew our minds.

As we view ourselves in a more godly way, and as we try to develop more Christlike character, we must also transform our minds (Rom. 12:2). We must stop the constant thoughts that invade our minds about how we don't measure up or how we really aren't very valuable, and we must force ourselves to think as God thinks. I suggest memorizing some passages like Psalm 139:14, which tells us we're "fearfully and wonderfully made" (NKJV). Second Corinthians 5:17 tells us that in Christ, we're "a new creation" (NKJV). Repeat these thoughts at least a dozen times a day.

Every time you look in the mirror, instead of thinking, *Ugh! What am I going to do with this?!* think, *I'm a unique individual, created in God's image, and I'm going to make the most of this day.* This is not the same as "the power of positive thinking"; it's merely retraining ourselves to think the way God would want us to think rather than dwelling on the garbage we have picked up from society.

3. Associate with healthy people who can help to build us up.

Let's face it, we all have some friends who build us up and some who don't do a whole lot to help us. Someone who feeds into our "victim mentality" or encourages our feeling down and out is not the type of friend we should be developing. You've heard that misery loves company, and if you're going through a divorce, there's an abundance of people and groups who will feed your misery.

Instead, we need to find some healthy friends—those who have perhaps been through a similar change but have moved on with their lives in a healthy way. They should have a good self-image, a mature view of God and his healing power, and the ability to reach out to us without expecting anything in return. (Mostly that's because we probably can't reciprocate for a while.) Eventually, as we begin to heal and develop a better self-image, this friendship can become more of a two-way street, or we can become instruments of healing for others.

4. Set some short-term goals that we know we can accomplish in order to experience success.

This point is important for those of us who need some real concrete evidence that we're worthwhile, just to get us off to a good start. As we work on our self-image, it would be wonderful if we immediately got a big raise and promotion or had a book published with our names on the cover, but that *rarely* happens. Many times, though, good things don't happen to us because we're not taking any chances. We're too timid or insecure, so we play it safe for a while. There's nothing wrong with that. It's certainly natural. But as we seek to move on with our lives, we need to start taking some chances.

At first these need to be small steps, and perhaps something we *know* we can accomplish. Why bother trying something we know we can do? As we start out, it's vital that we succeed in the beginning because that motivates us to try again. We know we'll fail at something sooner or later, but if we have a string of successes under our belts, the failure is much less likely to set us back significantly.

If your goal is to write a book and have it published, for example, the way to go about it is to first pick something you know you can do. (If you just start sending out manuscripts, I can assure you that you'll experience a lot of rejection.) You can enroll in night school and take a course in writing. You can also start journaling some of your thoughts and ideas for a while. Once you've succeeded at those goals, perhaps a contact with a small local newspaper or a newsletter publisher would be in order. And you build from there.

What if you meet with failure? Anywhere along the way, you can back up and try again, or perhaps you'll want to rethink or fine-tune your goals a bit.

5. Pray for God's help and strength.

Although this is listed last, it certainly is not least. The process of developing a positive self-image is not easy or natural, and it is best accomplished with God's help. Therefore, part of our thinking must include an attitude of constant prayer to God.

"Lord, I need your help. I want to move on with my life, and I know I need to work on my self-image. Help me to see myself as you do. Give me the strength and the courage to move out in new directions. Guide my path, Lord, so that I can begin to experience success and see quickly the things I do well. Then help me to do those things to your honor and glory.

"Protect me from the decisions that would set me back or perhaps even destroy my self-image. I need your help in making wise decisions. Help me to change my thought life, Lord, from one that accepts the world's standards to one that focuses on you, your love, and your mercy. Thank you, Lord!"

HANDLING THE HOLIDAYS

by Tom Whiteman

While the holidays are joyously anticipated by the typical household, for the newly separated or divorced, they can be some of the most difficult times of the year. All the expectations, stresses, and financial concerns that accompany most people's holiday season are greatly compounded for those experiencing a family disruption.

I remember my own first few Thanksgivings, Christmases, and Independence Day celebrations (if you could call them celebrations). To say they just weren't the same anymore would be a gross understatement. For me, they were dreaded. The familiar traditions became sources of pain; the stored decorations, a reminder of how much I had lost; and the family gatherings, a glaring indication that someone was missing.

I remember that for the first two Christmases following my divorce, I didn't put up a single decoration. Then, for my third Christmas, I set up a small tree. It wasn't much, but it was an indication I was beginning to heal.

If you have children, you probably go through the motions during the holidays, trying to keep things as consistent as possible, just for their sakes. You want their childhood memories to be nice, but the truth is that the holidays can be all the more difficult when children are involved.

If you've been married any length of time, you've developed your own traditions and celebration styles that the children will obviously miss once one parent is gone. So how can you handle the major holidays? Here are some guidelines you might want to consider:

• It's important (although hard) for you to talk with your ex-spouse well before the holiday in order to arrange a visitation schedule. Working through this difficult and emotional subject will do much to make the special days more enjoyable for you and your children. Once you've decided on a schedule, sit down with your children and tell them what they can expect. But once again, try to do this months before the actual holiday.

Be upbeat and supportive about the arrangements, and encourage their questions. Remember, they may not ask you questions in advance, but you can be sure they will be thinking about it regularly. And the more important the holiday, the more they'll think about it. So ease their fears, and tell them months in advance about what they can expect on that special day.

• If you don't have children or if the children are not going to be with you on the actual holiday, make sure you plan to be with family or friends.

You don't want to stay home alone with the memories of how it used to be. And don't wait until someone invites you over. Make your calls well in advance because as the holiday approaches, you may find you don't have the energy to make last-minute arrangements.

If your children can't be with you, plan a separate holiday for them around the time of the actual day. Over time, this can become a much-cherished tradition as the children look forward to their "celebration after the celebration." One eight-year-old recently told me that the best part of being from a divorced family was having two birthdays and two Christmases!

• If you do have the children for the holiday, don't try to replicate all the old traditions. That will only remind your children that the other parent is no longer around. Part of the acceptance phase involves being able to move on to new traditions and family interactions. The sooner you begin new traditions, the earlier your children can begin healing and moving on to a new lifestyle. Be consistent and traditional, but include some new, special events that will grow into new traditions.

• Watch your expectation level. Many people expect a joyous time and therefore have a greater chance of disappointment and postholiday depression. On the other hand, don't go into the holiday expecting everything to be horrible. That will only contribute to the problem by making your attitude unnecessarily negative. Approach each event with a little anticipation, but be realistic about the difficulties you must face.

• Many newly divorced people take a break from sending out Christmas cards and baking cookies, or they may find they have to make drastic cuts in the amount of money they spend on gifts. That's perfectly understandable, so don't feel guilty for those setbacks. You hope to work through this drought quickly. But in the meantime, it's probably best to explain to your close friends, family, and children that things will need to be different for a while.

This can actually be a good time to refocus on the true meaning of the holidays, the values of friends, family—and where God is in the whole process. The difficult times are typically a period of soul-searching and reevaluation of priorities. As painful as it might be, we can emerge from this as stronger, healthier individuals and families.

THERE'S NO SUCH THING AS AN EX-GRANDPARENT

by Tom Whiteman

The following article is designed for you to share with your parents or in-laws. Please feel free to make a few copies and pass them along.

"Mom, tell Dad to pick up the other extension, I've got something I've got to tell you."

All over America, people are hearing those words. Unfortunately, many times the call is to inform you of the disturbing news that your son or daughter is getting a divorce.

Immediately, you're gripped with a flood of thoughts and feelings. *What will we tell our friends and relatives? Will I still be Mom or Dad to my son- or daughter-in-law? What will become of my grandchildren?*

When most people think about divorce, they usually conjure up images of the embittered parents, the emotionally torn children, or maybe even the crafty legal posturing of the lawyers. Yet another drama also unfolds that we typically hear little about. It's the plight of the *parents* of the divorcing couple.

It's fairly surprising that we don't hear more about how divorce affects the previous generation. After all, there's hardly a mature family that hasn't been affected. Just think about it statistically; about 50 percent of all marriages end in divorce, and the typical family has just over two children. It stands to reason that sooner or later, most of us will be touched by this family tragedy.

So what can you expect when it does happen to you? First, realize that it's normal to go through an intense grieving reaction. You might be surprised by how much you actually hurt.

You might reason, *This is ridiculous. After all, it's not* my *marriage that's falling apart. Why am I getting so upset?*

The news that part of your family is breaking up is very much like hearing of the death of a loved one. For many, the end result will be the death of a relationship. Perhaps we will lose our son- or daughter-in-law, the grandchildren, or the other set of grandparents. In all cases, we know the family will never be the same.

This is very difficult to hear and much harder to experience, especially since the emotional healing takes at least two years to complete.

Let's review some of the emotional stages of grieving as they relate to divorce so you can be better prepared for the emotional onslaught and be better able to help your family through the crisis.

THE INITIAL SHOCK OF DENIAL

As a parent, you probably feel a great sense of pride when your whole family gets together for a special holiday or reunion. You imagine others as thinking, *My! What a beautiful family*. After all, that's what you think. When this Walton-like scene is marred by the dissolution of a marriage, most parents go into emotional shock.

Sure, you knew your kids were having problems. But you always assumed they'd work out their differences. Now, when you hear the news, you tell yourself, *They've just had a fight. I'm sure they'll get back together*. This denial is understandable. Your kids have probably kept the worst of the problems to themselves, not wanting to hurt or worry you. How can you be expected to absorb in a few days what it has taken your children months, if not years, to conclude?

The denial stage allows you to think life will go on as usual. It's a natural and necessary reaction when the news is too painful to bear. You want to pretend it really isn't going to happen or that life will remain unchanged. *I'll still see the grandchildren on the weekends. I'll still go fishing with my son-in-law.*

You move beyond this initial stage when your son or daughter begins to come by without the spouse. The more your child talks, the more you realize things really are different. This reality moves you on to the next stage in the grieving process, one that is much more emotionally charged.

SECONDARY EMOTIONAL RESPONSES

You enter this next phase with a flood of emotions, including anger, guilt, and depression. This phase is distinguished by your realization that the true ramifications of your child's divorce will be much more serious than you expected. It's typical to think, *This really does affect me. I knew our son had a temper, but I never dreamed he could go that far. My child really does have a drug problem. I don't think I will ever be able to forgive my daughter-in-law for what she has done.*

The circumstances surrounding divorce can tear you up inside. Yet you're powerless to bring about any changes. Perhaps you lie in bed at night thinking about your responsibility in the mess. Or you pace in anger over what you'd like to tell "that no good . . ." The range of emotions varies between anger, guilt, intense worry, and depression. Many vacillate between all these emotions over a period of many months, sometimes years.

You must move beyond those intense emotions to be helpful in the situation. Once again, it's certainly normal to have all the feelings, but in spite of your mental anguish, you must realize there's really nothing you can say or do that will change your child's decision. There is, however, much you can do to help. In fact, this crisis probably presents one time when your child needs you the most. But if you're to have a *positive* influence on the situation, you must first reach a point of acceptance in your healing.

Acceptance

Acceptance is not the same thing as resignation. Resignation is giving up in utter frustration. That's more of a depressed response than one of acceptance. When you accept the situation as it is, you face the fact that *for better or for worse, this is my family, and now we just have to make the best of it.* You see, acceptance really depends on your attitude about what has happened. It doesn't help to blame yourself or someone else. Nor does worrying or depression improve anything. Your ability to rise above your emotions determines how helpful you'll be to your children and grandchildren.

Gaining objectivity in the crisis is a sign of acceptance. Certainly in most cases, your major loyalty will remain with your own flesh and blood. But loyalty doesn't mean you need to feed into the hatred or name-calling, particularly when it comes to your grandchildren. Never put yourself in the position of bad-mouthing the other parent in front of the kids. He or she will always be their parent in spite of any wrongs that may have been done. If your grandchildren and your own child express criticism of the ex, it's fine for you to listen and be supportive, but that doesn't include fueling the fire.

For example, it's fine to say, "Yeah, I know what you mean," when the family member is critical of the absent parent. But it's not helpful to take the next step: "Yeah, I know what you mean. You know what he did to me one day. Your father . . ." That kind of venting might help you when you're in the anger stage, but you need to find a neutral friend or counselor to vent to, not your child or grandchildren.

Acceptance also means accepting changes. If your child is now a single parent, he or she will be much busier and less attentive to your needs. You need to accept those changes and try to help wherever you can. The holidays will also be different, but different does not have to mean worse. Try to help your child plan holidays and special events well in advance. You need to be as understanding as you can of the time constraints. After all, there's now a whole new person who must share the holidays with the kids—the ex. That's why you need to be as objective as possible and not become just one more source of stress for your son or daughter.

How Can I Help?

Perhaps more than ever before, your children and grandchildren need your stability, your objectivity, and your wisdom. Here are a few suggestions on how you can provide those:

- If you can continue to love both your child and the ex without betraying your child, it can be one of the healthiest postdivorce arrangements. Just because your son- or daughter-in-law did not work out as a spouse doesn't necessarily mean he or she is a bad person, parent, or child. By having a good relationship with both parties, you can be a positive influence on the whole situation.

- If a relationship with both parties is not possible, try to be gracious toward the former spouse, particularly in front of the grandchildren.

- Encourage your child and grandchildren to talk with you about how they're feeling. Listen without condemning them. If you find you can't do this objectively, admit your struggle and suggest they talk to someone more neutral.

- If you disagree with their decisions or lifestyle, it's all right to let them know how you feel. Tell them, but then let it go. If they ask for your opinion, let them know. Otherwise, try not to nag them or hold your will for their lives over their heads (as in "we'll support you if you do what we tell you").

- If your child asks for support, either financial or emotional, give what you can without allowing a dependency to develop. Set limits on what you can do. For example, "I can help you get settled in a new place, but I can only support you financially for the first few months," or, "I can help you by watching the children, but only until the summer is over." You want your child to get back on his or her feet, but you also need to encourage independence and self-reliance. Dependence on you will only prolong feelings of despair, worthlessness, and hopelessness.

- Don't allow yourself to be shut out of the lives of your child and grandchildren. Other than their actual parents, grandparents are children's most important relationships. If need be, speak up and request that your visitation rights be included in any custody arrangement.

- If you have a specific issue with your former son- or daughter-in-law, take it up directly with him or her. Don't put your child or the grandchildren in the middle by telling them, "Your father was supposed to bring you by last weekend and never did. Tell him that we said . . ."

- If your child or grandchildren seem to need additional help, encourage them to seek counseling, a support group, or other self-help materials. You might even want to provide the resources for them to get started in this direction.

Remember the grieving process can take up to two years to work through. So be patient with yourself and your child. The sooner you can find yourself emotionally healed, the quicker and more effective you will be at supporting your child and grandchildren. They certainly need your help now more than when they were an intact family.

DIVORCE AND THE CHURCH

by Bob Burns

Noah was loading the animals into his ark two by two. Imagine how it might have felt being an unpaired animal in line. There you would have been, alone and rejected, while the other animals entered the craft. You would have been left off the ark.

The Christian who is single again through divorce often feels left off the ark of God's church, where marriage is the socially acceptable status, even if the marriage is in shambles. When the single who has been married enters the church, he or she often feels like the odd one out.

When the Bible addresses the issue of divorce, it approaches the topic from two mutually dependent perspectives. The first is that of doctrine. This is extremely important, for doctrine must always form one's foundation for living.

In our day, it's crucial for the church to grapple with its theological convictions regarding divorce. The believer in the pew is looking for clear understanding and direction in the matter. With a national average of close to 50 percent of all marriages failing in the 1990s, each denomination and each local congregation must clearly explain its position on this nationwide epidemic. Such a clarification before God's people will solidify their conviction before a personal, congregational, or denominational crisis occurs. It will also fortify their ability to deal with problems when they take place.

At the same time, another biblical perspective coordinates with the doctrinal imperative. It is the relational side of divorce. By highlighting the relational concerns of divorce, I do not wish to create an implied barrier between doctrine and life. But it's far too easy to examine the theology of divorce while remaining isolated from persons involved in it. That, too, can create an artificial separation of doctrine from life.

The relational concerns of divorce don't refer simply to the way a couple handle their differences. They also refer to the way believers in Christ are called by the Scriptures to care for those who are going through or have gone through the wrenching death of a relationship.

The prophet Malachi said that God hates divorce (Mal. 2:16). But does God call his people to treat those shattered by such a covenant breaking with the same hatred? My thesis is that both Old and New Testaments mandate God's people to give themselves in compassionate ministry to the separated and the divorced. Because of that mandate, the church must take specific restorative action to maintain corporate health and an effective witness in the world.

THE OLD TESTAMENT MANDATE

In the Old Testament, divorce is neither encouraged nor condoned. Rather, it is viewed as the shattering of a commitment that was meant to be forever.

It was not a simple matter. The impact it would have upon the individuals involved and the community as a whole was taken seriously. A number of passages, including Genesis 3, Leviticus 18, Deuteronomy 24, Jeremiah 3, and Malachi 2, are usually cited with reference to the Old Testament perspective on divorce. Indeed, those texts must be considered in formulating a doctrinal position on marital separation. They state the moral context of divorce, describing it as the breaking of a marriage covenant, and also provide the legal context of divorce, with the steps of litigation necessary for proper regulation and protection of each party described in detail.

However, those passages do not provide us with the full understanding of the care and concern God required his people to give to those who were being divorced. Such a perspective can be clarified when we study the contextual use of the Hebrew word for widow, *almanah*. The word refers to a woman who has been divested of her male protector, usually—though not always—through death. But the *Assyrian Dictionary of the University of Chicago Oriental Institute* states that *almanah* does not simply refer to a woman whose husband is dead. It also applies to a woman who enjoys no financial support from a male member of her family. Such a woman is in need of legal protection. She is also able to exercise freedom by starting a profession or entering into a second marriage. Thus, the word can be used in the sense of bereavement (such as loss of a spouse) or for one who has been discarded or forsaken (such as a divorced person).

This interpretation of *almanah* as the widowed or abandoned fits several Old Testament passages. For example, when God forsook his people and their land, they were characterized as *almanah* (Isa. 47:8), and their situation as *almanuth* (Isa. 54:4). But Israel's "husband" had not passed away! Rather, he had written her a certificate of divorce (Jer. 3:8). Similarly, when King David returned to Jerusalem after Absalom's revolt, "the king took the ten women [with whom Absalom had committed adultery] . . . and put them in seclusion and supported them, but did not go in to them. So they were shut up to the day of their death, *living in widowhood*" (2 Sam. 20:3 NKJV, emphasis added). Technically, they were in widowhood while their husband was still alive. All this is to say that the Old Testament taught that the forsaken spouse was considered in the same category as the widow.

The implications of this connection between the forsaken and the widow are powerful indeed because the Old Testament is full of God's concerns and commands for the widow. God declared that he would execute justice for the widow (Deut. 10:18; Prov. 15:25), and he required his people to do so as well (Isa. 1:17; Jer. 7:5–6; 22:3; Zech. 7:10). He would punish those who refused to do so (Isa. 1:23–25; Mal. 3:5). His people were to provide for the physical needs of the widow (Deut. 14:28–29; 24:19–22). God was clearly on the side of the widow (Pss. 68:4; 146:9), and he expected his people to be as well.

The Old Testament also addressed the member of the marriage covenant who was initiating the abandonment. While it described the proper legal procedure those individuals were to take to obtain a divorce, it also provided for legal discipline within the community directed toward them.

It is beyond the scope of this article to explicate the detailed instructions in the Law given for specific offenses. It must suffice to say that God took a firm stand for justice toward the oppressed, and God expected his people to administer justice in a meaningful way. With regard to divorce, others have shown that legal stipulations encouraged a lengthy and systematic procedure that sought to ensure both justice for the forsaken spouse and public responsibility for the one taking action.

THE NEW TESTAMENT MANDATE

The New Testament carried on the tradition of the Old regarding the treatment of divorced persons. But it went farther, clarifying how God's people were to deal with all parties in the divorce.

First, let's consider Jesus' attitude toward the divorced as seen in the story of the woman at the well (John 4). Here we observe our Lord initiating a conversation with a woman who had been married five times and was currently living in an adulterous relationship with yet another man.

We find a balance in Jesus' ministry with this woman. On the one hand, we notice that he understood her circumstances and feelings. He knew of her previous marriages and her present adultery. But he didn't use those against her. Rather, Jesus' honest and open handling of her situation broke through her emotional and religious smoke screens of resistance, preparing her to hear the word of truth.

Further, Jesus demonstrated an honest concern for this woman by breaking significant cultural taboos in order to communicate with her. He spoke in the open with a woman whose husband was not present (a questionable act in the Middle East to this day). She was also a "despised Samaritan." And to make matters worse, she was a flagrant sinner! But Jesus did not allow those social matters to keep him from sharing with her the good news.

On the other hand, Jesus never condoned the woman's sin. He brought up the topic of her loose morality. Perhaps he delved into more of her past than we read in the narrative, for she later reported he "told me all things that I ever did" (John 4:29 NKJV). Our Lord refused to carry on a superficial conversation when both he and the woman knew her circumstances.

According to John 1:14, Jesus ministered with grace and truth. Revealing his understanding of the woman's condition, he spoke with candor and truth.

Yet truth was couched in the grace of his power to cleanse and restore wholeness. This combination of caring acceptance and honest confrontation prepared her for the life change of conversion.

The response of this woman was phenomenal. She confessed her sin by returning to the town and owning up to her past. In addition, she urged everyone to come and see this man. It's obvious that significant healing had taken place in her life. Past failure and weakness provided the basis of ministry to others.

This entire scene took place because our Savior extended himself to one who had been divorced. He initiated the conversation. He disclosed the truth of her circumstances. He led her to an understanding of lifelong fulfillment beyond the disappointment of a broken marriage or a new sexual liaison.

Following our Lord's example, a similar pattern of ministry to the rejected took place in the early church. In 1 Corinthians 6, Paul explained that some of the new believers had come out of a variety of backgrounds, including sexual immorality, adultery, thievery, and other sordid lifestyles. (He did not include divorce in that list, but his obvious concern with their circumstances in the next chapter must mean that many in this situation were within the fellowship.) Like the woman at the well, those people who knew they were sinners grasped for the gospel of grace with eagerness.

An examination of other New Testament writers highlights the same theme: spiritual rebirth extends hope to the rejected, healing to the brokenhearted, and opportunities for meaningful service to those who once thought their lives had little significance.

While the New Testament described the gospel as a source of renewal, it also provided for a specific framework for parties involved in divorce. It addressed the problem of mixed marriages between believer and nonbeliever (1 Cor. 7). It explicated the restorative role that church discipline should take in the life of God's people (Matt. 18:15–20; 1 Cor. 5:1–5; 2 Cor. 2:5–11). It required the appointment of church leaders who were expected to provide a supportive context where difficult issues would be handled before God with objectivity and compassion (Matt. 18:15–20; Acts 20:28; 1 Cor. 6:1–6; Heb. 13:17; 1 Peter 5:2–4).

We have observed that the New Testament developed the expectation of the Old. God's people were to extend themselves to those in the agony of divorce. Although the church was never to tolerate sin, it was to provide a context where the conditions preceding (and following) divorce would be handled. At the same time, the church was responsible to follow the lead of the Lord Jesus, who actively sought out and ministered to divorced persons.

THE MANDATE IN OUR DAY

Both Old and New Testaments affirm the church's need to actively involve itself in the divorce recovery process. To fulfill this role, the church must evaluate and implement change in three areas: attitudes, discipline, and program ministries.

Over the last few years, some marked attitudinal changes have occurred in the church. Some believers have developed a tolerance of divorce for any reason. This "do your own thing" mentality does not square with faithfulness to Christ's lordship. Such "liberation" is not the attitudinal change needed among believers today. Neither is there a need for hardened insensitivity that writes off all persons going through divorce as sinners who no longer hold an equal position in the church.

Rather, the mind-set necessary toward the divorced individual is one of practical grace, the humility of recognizing that every believer stands before God in need of mercy. No one person is better than another at the foot of the cross.

While most Christians would affirm that concept of grace in theory, the practical side means applying the truth of godly acceptance toward our relationships with others. Developing an attitude of practical grace means we must beware lest we take on the attitude of the boasting Pharisee in Luke 18:10–14 who said, "God, I thank You that I am not like other men" (v. 11 NKJV). It also requires that we treat the divorced person in the same way Jesus Christ has treated us: redeeming us from our past failures, forgiving us for our present sin, and challenging us to live and relate on the basis of the truth revealed in his Word.

Acceptance can never be based on anything less than our mutual submission to Jesus Christ. When that's the standard, a caring attitude toward the divorced should follow. Where divorced persons experience rejection simply on the basis of their single-again status, the church should examine itself regarding its understanding of justification in practical terms.

A partner of attitudinal change must be restorative discipline, which is the church's corporate responsibility to maintain the standard of God's Word as its lifestyle pattern. It's unfortunate that God's people tend to view discipline as either a method of punishment or a theoretical idea rarely put into practice. The scriptural imperative for church discipline is restoration: to bring a fallen member back to the full status of an active participant in the fellowship. Only with this restorative purpose in view can discipline be used as an effective tool in the reconciliation of marriages and in the care of those shattered by divorce.

Restorative discipline takes hard work. It is one of the most taxing responsibilities of the church. The process is outlined in Matthew 18:15–20. It begins with reconciliation on a one-to-one basis. If that attempt fails, one or two believers are to be called in as objective arbitrators. If that's also unsuccessful, the final step is to bring the matter before the church (which requires the involvement of the leadership).

This process demands cooperation from the entire body of believers. When a member seeks the aid of a fellow believer to intercede in a divided relationship, the one requested must be willing to participate. It's one thing to express concern. It's quite another to diminish one's personal comfort through involvement with another!

If the situation continues to deteriorate, the church leaders must take action. Extended time and effort will be demanded if they're to properly understand, negotiate, and exercise authority. Such an oversight role is often much more than a typical board member expected when he agreed to serve. Yet this is vital care for those who turn to their church for help in a crisis.

If the problem comes before the entire congregation, each member needs to clearly understand and consistently follow through on the decision of the fellowship. And of course, with all these dynamics, there is the added requirement of keeping restoration, not vindication, as the purpose of the procedure.

• If discipline is so difficult, why is it necessary? First, it's necessary because it is God's provision for maintaining a healthy lifestyle in the church. If the body of believers is to take seriously its faithfulness to God's Word, it must deal biblically with circumstances that flagrantly violate scriptural responsibilities. Without that, all admonitions to faithfulness take the form of empty words with no moral authority to substantiate the exhortation.

• A second reason for discipline is to provide a supportive context for the ones involved in the marital dissension. Where will the battered wife turn when she desires to remain faithful, yet fears for her life? Where will the believing husband receive counsel when he is struggling with a decision to contest his divorce? Where will the separated Christian turn when faced with the desire to date after the failure of his marriage seems a foregone conclusion? Conscientious Christians in these types of circumstances welcome the network of support and counsel offered by God's people when it is available. The painful fact, however, is that thousands of Christians who honestly desire such objective guidance and encouragement from the church receive the answer that other believers don't want to get involved.

In separation and divorce, there is rarely, if ever, a case where one party is beyond reproach and the other should receive total blame for the failure. Marriage is a shared responsibility, and those involved in church discipline must labor to maintain joint accountability as the issues are handled. At the same time, in most divorce cases only one partner seeks the aid of the church. For that person, the discipline should not create deeper guilt but should provide a healthy context for restoration so that the person can maintain the status of a fully functioning member of Christ's church in the process.

In the meantime, what is the purpose of discipline toward the one who lacks any desire for the church's involvement? It is to win the brother or sister back through a prolonged, concerned call for accountability to the lifestyle promises he or she acknowledged in church membership and in marital vows.

Jesus declared that he came to give abundant life. He expected his people to be part of this life-giving and life-restoring process. Restorative discipline means the use of the authority of the church for the purpose of bringing persons back to such a state of wholeness. It's difficult. It's exhausting. It demands a long-term commitment. But it is an imperative if the church is to fulfill its ministry to the divorced.

• A third change for the church to explore is in the area of program ministries. Distinct from the need for attitudinal change and restorative discipline, program ministries deal with the ongoing expression of the church in the form of its activities and schedule.

What is happening in the church regularly for the divorced and separated in the congregation? Planned activities can communicate to those people that the congregation cares for them and is ready to invest the effort necessary to meet their needs. Such programs validate the full role the congregation feels these persons have in the fellowship. Weekly Bible studies, single-parent support groups, classes for singles in the Sunday school curriculum, and divorce recovery seminars are examples of some useful programs. Some churches with multistaff capabilities are even beginning to hire full-time professionals to serve in the area of single adult ministries.

The church must also assume responsibilities to establish programs of outreach to the separated and divorced of the community. It has been observed that the divorce experience is a complex process during which further personality growth can take place. Old lifestyle patterns and goals that were once assumed are challenged during this time of transition. Such reevaluation provides an exceptional context for thoughtful consideration of the gospel if the church is prepared to contact such persons at their point of need. Creative programs must be explored on this point.

The form that any particular church would decide to use in a ministry to single-again persons is not at issue here. Rather, the concern is for the divorced and separated people in the congregation and the surrounding community to sense that a redemptive fellowship is prepared to take action on their behalf. When this concern is present and expressed, the details of specific programs will work themselves out according to the various situations.

Appendix A

ACTION POINTS

Throughout this workbook, you have been recording action points or things you need to work on over the next few months and perhaps years. You have also recorded them on this page "for future reference." Well, the future is now. You should have a list of goals on this page that you can refer to at a glance. If you haven't got anything out of this workbook other than this list of goals, it has been worth the price of the workbook. I say that because if you went to a counselor, the first session would probably be spent identifying areas you need to work on. That session would certainly cost much more than the price of this book. May God bless and strengthen you as you work through these issues.

_____

_____

_____

_____

_____

_____

_____

_____

_____

_____

_____

_____

_____

_____

Appendix B

TEST-RETEST ADJECTIVE CHECKLIST

You should have taken this test in Chapter 1. Fill this out again when you're finished working through the workbook.

Place a check next to all the adjectives that describe how you feel right now. Read through the list by reading across the columns from left to right.

❑ angry	❑ annoyed	❑ ambivalent	❑ amused	❑ attractive
❑ anxious	❑ bored	❑ apathetic	❑ brave	❑ bright
❑ ashamed	❑ cheated	❑ collected	❑ calm	❑ confident
❑ bitter	❑ confused	❑ hesitant	❑ contented	❑ delighted
❑ defeated	❑ dejected	❑ disinterested	❑ engaged	❑ excited
❑ depressed	❑ detached	❑ different	❑ funny	❑ fulfilled
❑ disgusted	❑ discouraged	❑ glib	❑ grateful	❑ glad
❑ foolish	❑ empty	❑ interested	❑ helpful	❑ happy
❑ guilty	❑ exhausted	❑ hopeful	❑ interested	❑ inspired
❑ hateful	❑ helpless	❑ impatient	❑ involved	❑ independent
❑ inferior	❑ hurt	❑ indifferent	❑ joyful	❑ jubilant
❑ insecure	❑ irritated	❑ judged	❑ loyal	❑ loved
❑ lonely	❑ jealous	❑ at peace	❑ optimistic	❑ overjoyed
❑ miserable	❑ misunderstood	❑ misguided	❑ neglected	❑ needy
❑ overwhelmed	❑ nervous	❑ neutral	❑ pleased	❑ powerful
❑ pessimistic	❑ phony	❑ preoccupied	❑ relieved	❑ resilient
❑ rejected	❑ puzzled	❑ quiet	❑ respectful	❑ satisfied
❑ resentful	❑ restless	❑ reluctant	❑ romantic	❑ secure
❑ sadistic	❑ sad	❑ sexual	❑ sexy	❑ smart
❑ stupid	❑ sorry	❑ shy	❑ supported	❑ strong
❑ suicidal	❑ selfish	❑ silly	❑ thankful	❑ touched
❑ terrible	❑ tense	❑ surprised	❑ tough	❑ trusting
❑ ugly	❑ unappreciated	❑ unsure	❑ useful	❑ whole
❑ unhappy	❑ upset	❑ weary	❑ welcome	❑ well
❑ violent	❑ worried	❑ questioning	❑ willing	❑ wise

To score:

1. Add all of the checks in column 1, and then multiply that number by (−4).

_____ x −4 = (−___).

2. Add all of the checks in column 2, and then multiply that number by (−2).

        ____ x −2 = (−____).

3. Add all of the checks in column 3, and then multiply that number by zero (getting zero).

        ____ x 0 = 0.

4. Add all of the checks in column 4, and then multiply by 2.

        ____ x 2 = ____.

5. Add all of the checks in column 5, and then multiply by 4.

        ____ x 4 = ____.

Total your score from the five columns to see if your overall feelings are overwhelmingly negative (indicated by a high negative score), basically neutral, or overwhelmingly positive. This score may not reflect anything more than how you were feeling when you took the test. But it's helpful to compare this score to the one you got earlier.

Enter your total score here: _____

What was your total score the first time you took the test? _____

Did you make any progress? _____

Why or why not?_____

_____

Would you be willing to share your results? Please drop us a line at the Fresh Start office, 2971 Flowers Road South, Suite 220, Atlanta, GA 30341, or call us at 1-888-373-7478.

Appendix C

MARRIAGE AND DIVORCE
POSITION PAPER—FRESH START SEMINARS, INC.

I. WHAT THE BIBLE SAYS ABOUT MARRIAGE

A. Marriage is a DIVINE INSTITUTION.

Contrary to some contemporary opinion, marriage is not a human institution that has evolved over the millennia to meet the needs of society. If it were no more than that, then conceivably it could be discarded when it is deemed no longer to be meeting those needs. Rather, marriage was God's idea, and human history begins with the Lord himself presiding over the first wedding (Gen. 2:18–25).

B. Marriage is to be regulated by DIVINE INSTRUCTIONS.

Since God made marriage, it stands to reason that it must be regulated by his commands. In marriage, both husband and wife stand beneath the authority of the Lord. "Unless the LORD builds the house, / They labor in vain who build it" (Ps. 127:1 NKJV).

C. Marriage is a DIVINE ILLUSTRATION.

In both Old and New Testaments, marriage is used as the supreme illustration of the love relationship that God established with his people. Israel is spoken of as the wife of Jehovah (Isa. 54:5; Jer. 3:8; Hos. 2:19—20). The church is called the bride of Christ (Eph. 5:22–32). The Christian marriage is sort of a "pageant" in which the husband takes the part of the Lord Jesus, loving and leading his wife as Christ does the church, and the wife plays the role of the believer, loving and submitting to her husband as the Christian does to the Lord. Thus, Christian marriage should be an object lesson in which others can see something of the divine-human relationship reflected.

D. Marriage is a COVENANT.

From the earliest chapters of the Bible, the idea of covenant is the framework by which man's relationship to God is to be understood, and it also regulates the lives of God's people. A covenant is an agreement between two parties based upon mutual promises and solemnly binding obligations. It is like a contract, with the additional idea that it establishes personal relationships. God's covenant with Abraham and his descendants is summarized in the statement "I will be your God, and you shall be my people." Marriage is called a covenant (Mal. 2:14), the most intimate of all human covenants. The key ingredient in a covenant is faithfulness, being committed irreversibly to the fulfillment of the covenant obligations. The most important factor in the marriage covenant is not romance; it is faithfulness to the covenant vows, even if the romance flickers.

E. Marriage is a WHOLE-PERSON COMMITMENT.

God meant marriage to be the total commitment of a man and a woman to each other. It is not two solo performances, but a duet. In marriage, two people give themselves unreservedly to each other (Gen. 2:25; 1 Cor. 7:3–4).

F. "What God has joined together, let not man separate," declared our Lord (Matt. 19:6 NKJV). "Till death do us part" is not a carryover from old-fashioned romanticism but a sober reflection of God's intention regarding marriage (Rom. 7:2–3; 1 Cor. 7:39).

II. WHAT THE BIBLE TEACHES ABOUT DIVORCE

A. Divorce is abhorrent to God (Mal. 2:15–16).

B. Divorce is always the result of sin.

God's basic intention for marriage never included divorce; but when sin entered human experience, God's intention was distorted and marred. Under perfect conditions, there was no provision for divorce, but God allowed divorce to become a reality because of man's sinfulness (Deut. 24:1–4; Matt. 19:7–8). To say that divorce is always the result of sin is not to say, however, that all divorce is itself a sin. It may be the only way to deal with the sinfulness of the other party that has disrupted the marriage relationship.

C. There are two conditions under which divorce is biblically permissible.

Since divorce is a sinful distortion of God's intention for marriage, it is an alternative of last recourse, to be avoided whenever possible. However, Scripture does teach that there are two circumstances in which divorce is permitted (though never required):
   1. In the case of sexual unfaithfulness (Matt. 19:9).
   2. In the case of desertion of a believing partner by an unbelieving spouse (1 Cor. 7:15–16).

D. Divorce carries with it consequences and complications.

Divorce, because it is a violation of God's plan, carries with it painful consequences and complications. God has made perfect provisions for the complete forgiveness of all our sin through the death of Christ, even the sins of sexual infidelity and unjustified divorce (1 Peter 2:24; Col. 2:13).

Forgiveness, however, does not remove the temporal consequences of our sins or the pain and grief involved in the death of a relationship. Divorced singles, single-parent families, remarriage, and the problems of "blended" families are part of the consequences of God's intention being thwarted. The church is to minister to individuals and families suffering these consequences, and to seek to help them respond with maturity to their problems.

E. Reconciliation is to be preferred to divorce.

While divorce is permitted, it is never commanded. Forgiveness and reconciliation are always to be preferred (1 Cor. 7:10–11).

III. WHAT THE BIBLE TEACHES ABOUT REMARRIAGE

A. Remarriage is permitted when the former spouse is deceased (Rom. 7:2; 1 Cor. 7:39).

B. Where a divorce occurred prior to conversion, remarriage may be permitted.

"If anyone is in Christ, he is a new creation; old things have passed away; behold, all things have become new" (2 Cor. 5:17 NKJV). When one becomes a Christian, all sin is forgiven, and all condemnation is removed (Rom. 8:1). Thus, preconversion conditions do not necessarily preclude remarriage to a Christian mate.

If the former marriage partner has also become a Christian, remarriage to that partner should be sought. Where the former partner has not been converted and attempts to share the gospel with him or her are rejected, however, remarriage to that person would be disobedient to Scripture (2 Cor. 6:14).

Even though remarriage is allowable biblically, there may be consequences from past sins that continue or destructive patterns from the old life that can carry into new relationships. Thus, a new marriage should be entered into with due thoughtfulness and with the counsel of mature Christians.

C. Where a divorce has occurred on scriptural grounds, the offended party is free to remarry.

A person who has been divorced because of infidelity of a marriage partner or desertion by an unbelieving partner is free to remarry (1 Cor. 7:15).

D. What about desertion by a "Christian" spouse?

First Corinthians 7 deals specifically with the case of a nonbeliever who refuses to live with the believing spouse. The question then arises about the remarriage of a believer who was divorced by a partner who also professed to be a Christian. Such a situation ideally should involve the church in the steps of disciplinary action outlined in Matthew 18. A Christian who decides to walk out of a marriage without biblical cause is in violation of Scripture. Such a person who refuses the counsel and admonition of the elders and persists in following the course of disobedience ultimately is to be dealt with as though he or she is an unbeliever (Matt. 18:17). The deserted spouse would then be in a position of having been deserted by one whose sinful behavior and unresponsiveness to spiritual admonition give evidence of an unregenerate heart, and thus he or she falls under the provision of 1 Corinthians 7:15.

E. Where a former spouse has remarried, remarriage is permitted for the other person.

Regardless of the reasons for the divorce itself, if one of the partners has remarried, the union is permanently broken and reconciliation is impossible, and thus the remaining partner is free to remarry.

F. Scripture does not absolutely forbid remarriage of a person who has caused a nonbiblical divorce.

Where there has been conversion (in the case of a person who was not a Christian when the divorce occurred) or the demonstration of genuine and heartfelt repentance (in the case of one who was a Christian at the time of the divorce), remarriage may be permitted for the offending party if (1) the former spouse has remarried or (2) the former partner refuses reconciliation (1 Cor. 7:15).

G. Scripture recognizes the possibility of separation that does not lead to divorce.

Because of humankind's sinful nature, couples can, at times, be involved in a marital relationship that is destructive, either physically or emotionally, to the two marriage partners and/or their children. It is possible that separation might become necessary because of the destructive nature of the relationship or the potential danger to one or more of the family members. Such a situation does not provide grounds for dissolution of the marriage and the establishment of a new marriage. Where no biblical ground for remarriage exists, a Christian is bound to seek reconciliation as long as there is a possibility of such reconciliation taking place (1 Cor. 7:11).

IV. ANSWERS TO SOME RELATED QUESTIONS

A. Is there ever a totally innocent party in marital discord or divorce?

No one is ever free from sinful conduct or attitudes, so in this sense there is no "innocent party." However, there are some sins that nullify the marriage covenant and some that, though they may be serious, do not. In any case of marital discord, both partners should be encouraged to try to understand how they contributed to the conflict.

B. Will divorced persons be allowed to participate in service opportunities in the church?

Spiritual, psychological, and relational maturity are primary qualifications for service opportunities. Divorce would be considered only one part of a much broader evaluation of a person's suitability for service. Divorce would not necessarily preclude serving. A primary consideration must be the reputation the individual has in the body of Christ and the community (1 Tim. 3:2, 7; Titus 1:6).

C. What if there has been no sexual unfaithfulness in a Christian marriage, but two Christians decide to dissolve their marriage because they are incompatible?

The Bible does not recognize incompatibility as grounds for divorce. Reconciliation must be achieved, and every means possible should be considered, including individual and/or marriage counseling. If Christ is on the throne of two human hearts, conflict will cease. He does not fight with himself.

D. A frequent reason given for seeking a divorce is that the original marriage was a mistake. The couple believe they got married for the wrong reasons and are asking why they should perpetuate a mistake.

God's promise is that he is able to cause all things to work together for good, even our human mistakes (Rom. 8:28). The Bible does not recognize a "mistake" as grounds for divorce. A deliberate, knowledgeable violation of God's revealed will for marriage is never an appropriate response to a mistake made earlier in life. Two wrongs do not make a right.

E. What if a couple are separated or divorced, and both desire to have sexual intimacy with each other?

Sexual intimacy is the privilege of a marriage relationship. If the couple are already divorced, such intimacy would be classed as fornication. If the couple are not actually divorced, sexual intimacy might be appropriate (1 Cor. 7:4–7). However, serious consideration should be given by both partners to their personal motivation in the relationship. One of the considerations a couple must have is their reputation with their children and friends.

V. SUGGESTED BOOKS ON MARRIAGE, DIVORCE, AND REMARRIAGE IN THE BIBLE

Adams, Jay E. *Marriage, Divorce, and Remarriage in the Bible*. Grand Rapids: Zondervan, 1980.

Duty, Guy. *Divorce & Remarriage*. Minneapolis: Bethany Fellowship, 1967.

House, H. Wayne, ed. *Divorce and Remarriage: Four Christian Views*. Downers Grove, IL: InterVarsity, 1990.

Murray, John. *Divorce*. Phillipsburg, NJ: Presbyterian and Reformed Publishing Co., 1978.

NOTES

Chapter 2
1. This book is available from Fresh Start. To order a copy, call 1-888-373-7478.
2. James Dobson, *What Wives Wish Their Husbands Knew About Women* (Wheaton, IL: Tyndale, 1975), 78–79, 82–84.
3. Bob Burns, *Recovery from Divorce*, 96–97.

Chapter 3
1. This chapter provides a general understanding of this topic and is not meant to be a technical study. For a more detailed review of the topic, see Appendix C: The Fresh Start Position Paper on Marriage and Divorce. The appendix also includes titles of numerous books of a technical nature.
2. Tom Jones, *The Single Again Handbook* (Nashville: Thomas Nelson, 1993), 248.
3. Ad Interim Committee on Marriage, Divorce, and Remarriage to the Twentieth General Assembly, *PCA Digest Position Papers*, 1993, 228–30.
4. Tapes from the Second Wind Seminar are available from Fresh Start, 1-888-373-7478.

Chapter 4
1. Our great thanks go to attorney Robert H. Klima for his substantial contribution to the section "Finding a Lawyer."
2. Our great thanks go to counselor/mediator Virginia Cadle for her substantial contribution to the section "Mediation."

Chapter 6
1. Our great thanks go to financial adviser Don Nicholson Sr. for his ideas and input into this chapter.

Chapter 8
1. This chapter was written primarily by Tom Jones, vice president of Fresh Start.

Chapter 9
1. This chapter has been supplemented with material adapted from *The Adult Child of Divorce* by Bob Burns and Michael J. Brissett (Nashville: Thomas Nelson, 1991).

Chapter 11
1. These materials include the Rapha Right Step materials (*Right Step Facilitator Training Manual* [Houston: Rapha Publishing, 1990], *Rapha's 12-Step Program for Overcoming Codependency,* by Pat Springle [Houston and Dallas: Rapha Publishing/Word, Inc., 1990], Claire W's *God Help Me, I'm Still Hurting* [San Diego: Books West, 1988], *The Twelve Steps for Christians* [San Diego: Recovery Publications, 1988], and *The Twelve Steps: A Spiritual Journey* [San Diego: Recovery Publications, 1988]).
2. *Right Step Facilitator Training Manual* (Houston: Rapha Publishing, 1990), 30.

ABOUT THE AUTHORS

Bob Burns is the founder of Fresh Start Seminars, Inc., a support group for persons going through divorce. He holds a D.Min. focusing on marriage and divorce issues from Westminster Theological Seminary. He is pastor of adult ministries at Perimeter Church in Norcross, Georgia, and is the author of *The Adult Child of Divorce* and *Recovery from Divorce*.

Tom Whiteman, the mid-Atlantic codirector of Fresh Start Seminars, Inc., is the founder and director of Life Counseling Services of Pennsylvania. A licensed psychologist, Whiteman earned a master's degree in counseling from West Chester University and a Ph.D. in psychology and human development from Bryn Mawr College. He is the author of many books, including *Innocent Victims: Helping Children Cope with the Trauma of Divorce* and *Men Who Love Too Little.*